The Films of Katharine Hepburn

W9-CTS-690

Alexander Brook's
famous painting, 1938

THE FILMS OF

Katharine Hepburn

By HOMER DICKENS

THE CITADEL PRESS   SECAUCUS, NEW JERSEY

Third paperbound printing, 1974
Copyright © 1971 by Homer Dickens
All rights reserved
Published by Citadel Press
A division of Lyle Stuart, Inc.
120 Enterprise Avenue, Secaucus, N.J. 07094
In Canada: George J. McLeod Limited
73 Bathurst St., Toronto, Ontario
Manufactured in the United States of America
Designed by A. Christopher Simon
ISBN 0-8065-0361-0

FOR KATHARINE
some Shoffner, some Hepburn, all
VAUGHAN
with love

Acknowledgments

My indebtedness to the expertise of friends exceeds any acknowledgment possible, but gratitude is nonetheless real for being briefly indicated:

CARLOS CLARENS, RICHARD M. HUDSON, LLOYD IBERT, ALIX JEFFRY, AL KILGORE, CLIFF McCARTY, DOUG McCLELLAND, DION McGREGOR, NORMAN MILLER, MARY ALICE MORRIS, MARK RICCI, GENE RINGGOLD, MICHAEL SPARKS, ERIK SPILKER, ROMANO TOZZI, LOU VALENTINO, JAMES WATTERS, DOUGLAS WHITNEY

and the entire staff of the Theatre and Film Collection of the New York Public Library; the Van Damn Studio; Friedman-Abeles, Inc.; The American Shakespeare Theatre, Inc.; and United Press International (L.A. and N.Y.C.)

Contents

The Films of Katharine Hepburn

Rebellious Lady

A BIOGRAPHICAL CAPSULE

In its years of churning out movies, Hollywood has had its share of *rebels* and, upon occasion, has even been known to employ the services of a few *ladies,* in the true aristocratic sense of the word. Yet, in 1932, the Hollywood community was hardly prepared for—or ready to accept—the strong-minded, extremely promising, and much too frank Katharine Hepburn, a *rebellious lady* par excellence.

Perhaps more than any other profession, the motion picture industry has required its practitioners to expose their private lives to the gaze of an overly inquisitive public. The studios' reasons for this policy, not at all groundless, were primarily to cultivate the continued interest of the attending public. Stars were to be generous to the public at large in such matters as granting interviews, signing autographs, and so on. This conduct was, in other words, the name of the game in Hollywood society.

Miss Hepburn, who swiftly became a celebrity, fought in her inherently thoroughbred style to distinguish between her private and her professional life, declaiming, "My privacy is my own and I am the one to decide when it shall be invaded." She was tremendously eager to make good as an actress and, even though innately shy, she possessed enough good New England horse sense, dauntless enthusiasm, boundless energy, and brash bravado to give her plenty of speed.

Her angular looks, high-bred Connecticut "accent" (which was likened by some to a buzz saw), and complete candor increased her detractors ten to one in those early years. In her general unwillingness to adhere to the rules of the game, Kate hired a Rolls Royce to take her about

As Tracy Lord in Philip Barry's *The Philadelphia Story*— her greatest stage success

Kate at four

Kate, right, with her
older brother Tom

the film capital, dressed casually in slacks and sandals, wore little or no make-up, refused to coo in the established starlet manner, avoided nosy fan-magazine writers, and paraded around with her pet gibbon monkey while her contemporaries were accompanied by sleek and sassy Russian wolfhounds.

Despite all this—and perhaps a little because of it—Katharine Hepburn brought a distinguished touch of class to her movies and projected a magic all her own. Although more of a unique personality than a versatile actress, she never gave a bad account of herself in any of her performances. Even when, on frequent occasions, the material was less than stimulating, she more often than not inspired others to give more of themselves for a total effect. Any general unevenness in her performances seems merely to give rise to differences in the estimation and evaluation of her work.

Katharine Houghton Hepburn was born in Hartford, Connecticut, on November 8, 1907, the second of six children of Dr. Thomas Norval Hepburn, a noted urologist and surgeon, and Katharine Martha Houghton. Her red-haired father, a crack athlete as an undergraduate at Virginia's Randolph-Macon College, in 1900, was studying medicine at Johns Hopkins when he met the headstrong and vibrant Miss Houghton. They married during his last year there and after his graduation settled in Hartford, because of the excellent Hartford Hospital.

The couple rented half of a small house across from the doctors' entrance, where their first child, Thomas Jr., was born. Soon after Kate's birth, three years later, the Hepburns moved to 133 Hawthorne Street—a charming home with trees and shrubs. By the time Katharine was a young lady, the Hepburn home was a spacious brick house on Bloomfield Avenue in fashionable West Hartford.

Dr. Hepburn, who became head urologist of Hartford Hospital and consultant to many others, was frequently ostracized for his advanced medical beliefs and active campaign to bring the facts about venereal disease into the open. Despite some opposition, he and Harvard's Dr. Charles Eliot founded the Connecticut Social Hygiene Association. At some later date, he happened upon Mrs. George Bernard Shaw's English translation of Eugene Brieux' *Damaged Goods*, a play whose central theme argued that society was foolish not to face the problem of syphilis. Dr. Hepburn had, of course, long supported this theory, and shortly got Shaw's permission to distribute the play through the Association.

Mrs. Hepburn was a Boston Houghton and a cousin of an American Ambassador to the Court of St. James's, Alanson Bigelow Houghton. Her deep pride in her heritage is illustrated by the fact that she gave each of her children the same middle name (Houghton). Prior to her marriage, she graduated from Bryn Mawr, in 1898, and earned a Master's Degree in Art at Radcliffe. Like her husband, Mrs. Hepburn was a campaigner; she was a true suffragette and a crusader for birth control. Long before such a practice became commonplace, she was one of the group which picketed the White House when President Woodrow Wilson was undecided on woman suffrage. Mrs. Emmeline Pankhurst, the British suffragist leader and her American counterparts, Charlotte Perkins Gilman and Emma Goldman, were frequent visitors at the Hepburn home.

The Hepburns reared their children (Tom, Kate, Dick, Bob, Marion, and Peggy) in their own unorthodox manner—which meant in an atmosphere of complete freedom. This technique usually, but not always, worked to their mutual satisfaction, and the unusual and highly independent couple soon grew indifferent to Hartford's mild ostracism.

Dr. Hepburn's tremendous enthusiasm for physical culture was a direct influence on Kate's life and career. With the credo "Exercise is the surest road to health," he made an all-round athlete of her. As a child, Kate became an expert wrestler, tumbler, and trapeze performer. Later, her physical drive continued and she expanded her fields of endeavor to include figure skating, swimming, and diving.

Due to her mother's activities, Kate's first public appearance was made in a Votes-for-Women Crusade when she

As Pandora, at Bryn Mawr, in pastoral *The Woman in the Moone*

was only eight. Dressed as a young Hollander, she appeared on a float furnished by Dutch Cleanser. Said Hepburn later: "I remember as a child going round with 'Votes for Women' balloons. I learned early what it is to be snubbed for a good cause. Snobbery has never worried me since." When she approached her teens, Kate was often found passing out handbills on the sidewalk at 5:00 P.M. to men leaving the factories.

Like many children of her years, her movie-going was restricted to Westerns and, reportedly, her first screen idol was William S. Hart. At home, she contented herself with the operation of two puppet theatres. Her first, dubbed The Little Red Ridinghood Theatre, later gave way to the ornate Aladdin Theatre, complete with cardboard characters. Kate improvised the dialogue and spoke for her actors, as well as providing the scripts.

Kate and her older brother Tom spent Easter weekend in New York with a family friend in the spring of her twelfth year. The children were taken to see a matinee of *A Connecticut Yankee in King Arthur's Court* and were both fascinated by a noose trick, in which a man tightened the muscles of his neck so that he could not be choked. Later that same day, young Tom was "teased" during a party game.

When Tom didn't appear for breakfast the following morning, Kate discovered his body hanging in the attic. She was later told by an ambulance doctor that Tom had been

Kate at fourteen

3

Her arrival at Pasadena, California, ready to embark on a screen career

dead for five hours, which would have set the time of death at approximately 3:00 A.M. It was never established that the popular and cheerful boy had taken his own life purposely. His feet were touching the floor, which indicated that he might have been practicing the trick with the noose. This tragedy left Kate moody and totally on the defensive for months afterward.

During that summer, Kate plunged herself into theatricals at the family's summer home at Fenwick, Connecticut. With a stock company of actors, she presented *Bluebeard*, which proved to be something of a local hit. After the appearance of Bishop Howden of the Episcopal diocese of New Mexico, who preached at Fenwick about the deprivations suffered by Navajo Indians in his state, the Hepburn Players gave benefit performances—with a 50-cent top—to buy a phonograph and records to be sent to Indian children. The trio of plays were *Bluebeard, Beauty and the Beast* and *Marley's Ghost.*

Kate was educated largely by private tutors until she attended the West Middle School (where she once recited "The Wreck of the Hesperus") and then Oxford School for Girls in Hartford. She entered Pennsylvania's famous Bryn Mawr, her mother's alma mater, in 1924. As a freshman, she found the high scholastic demands rough going, and nearly flunked out. In order to qualify to act in college plays, she had to get higher grades and thus applied herself. As a freshman, she appeared in the chorus of one of the big productions. She also was suspended—briefly—when caught smoking her first cigarette.

Her marks continued to improve and, in her junior and senior years (although her major was history), she played the part of a young man in Milne's *The Truth About Blayds* and appeared as Teresa in *The Cradle Song.* Kate became seriously interested in dramatics, at last, when the noted Shakespearean scholar Horace Howard Furness chose her for the role of Pandora in the Elizabethan pastoral called *The Woman in the Moone.*

Shortly before her romp as Pandora, Kate met Robert McKnight, a graduate of Yale Art School, at a Yale prom. He was later to win the Prix de Rome for sculpture and his bust of Kate was once exhibited at the Carnegie Institute in Pittsburgh. It now commands a place of honor in her New York brownstone. McKnight was intrigued with this lass with a tight bun of reddish hair atop her head and wanted to marry her. Kate had other thoughts.

In the spring of her senior year at Bryn Mawr (1928), Kate went to Baltimore, using money loaned to her by McKnight, to seek out Edwin H. Knopf (the brother of the book publisher and later an MGM producer), who had a stock company there. She carried a letter of introduction from Knopf's friend John S. Clarke. Knopf's first reaction toward this frecklefaced, bony, spindly girl with shocking red hair was typical of the first reactions this opinionated and brittle-voiced novice would continue to command. "She was tremendously sincere, but awkward, green, freaky-looking. I wanted no part of her," he later commented. "But," he added, "it wasn't so easy to get rid of Hepburn."

No sooner had she graduated in June (on a Friday) than she arrived in Baltimore (on Saturday) and reported to Mr. Knopf, who was right in the middle of rehearsals of *The Czarina*. Rather than endure her persistence, he gave the eager young tyro a small role as a lady-in-waiting to Mary Boland in the Melchior Lengyel-Lajos Biro play, which Edward Sheldon had adapted in 1922 for Doris Keane.

Knopf's players included such seasoned performers as Alison Skipworth, Violet Heming, and Dudley Digges. During the third day of rehearsals of *The Czarina*, Mary Boland railed at Knopf: "I can't stand it, Eddie! That Hepburn girl's on stage only five minutes, and the rest of the time she sits in the wings staring at me. I feel her every minute." Hepburn learned much from her backstage vigils and by opening night Mary Boland was helping Kate dress and make up.

She looked and acted well enough on her first appearance to win a few kind words from a Baltimore reviewer. During the week that *The Czarina* ran, Kate rehearsed the next week's offering, in which she played a flapper. The play was Mary Boland's 1925 stage hit *The Cradle Snatchers*. Kate was having trouble with her movement and difficulties with her voice drove her to the point of distraction. The company stage manager, Kenneth McKenna (a well-known actor in his own right and later chief of MGM's Story Department), advised her to leave the company and study voice under Frances Robinson-Duff. Students of this noted coach have included such actors and actresses as Cornelia Otis Skinner, Helen Hayes, Ruth Chatterton, Ina Claire, Osgood Perkins, Miriam Hopkins, and Clark Gable.

Hepburn took his advice and left for New York City after the closing of *The Cradle Snatchers*. It took the Hepburn family some time getting used to the fact that their eldest daughter had decided on an acting career. "It's not much better than that of a circus performer" was the general family comment, but Dr. Hepburn soon came around and subsidized his daughter's lean years of struggle. Later on, he helped her manage her business affairs.

With undying determination to become a great actress, Kate pursued her goal in the theatre with an intensity and conviction which fascinated agents and producers alike and brought instant resentment from many other actors. In addition to her vocal work with Miss Robinson-Duff, Hepburn studied movement and dance with Michael Mordkin for almost three years (Kate had seen her teacher perform—using only the name Mordkin—with the great Pavlova when she was just a teenager). This important training with a strict coach proved invaluable in her physical control and heightened the superb sense of timing that would later serve her so well.

After only a few weeks in New York City, Kate learned that Knopf had given up his Baltimore stock company and

With her gibbon monkey, Amos

had decided to produce a new play in New York in association with William P. Farnsworth, with Kenneth McKenna in the lead. The play, by George Middleton and A. E. Thomas, was entitled *The Big Pond*. Kate was offered the small part of the secretary, as well as the opportunity of understudying the leading lady.

After ten days of rehearsal, Knopf, displeased with his leading lady, replaced her with Kate. She now had the leading role of Barbara opposite McKenna's Pierre De Mirande. Hepburn worked hard with Miss Robinson-Duff who had managed, in a short time, to remove much of the gawkiness and refine the cockiness in the girl's nature.

The initial opening was approaching when Hepburn had her first bout with a newspaperman asking for an interview. She refused to grant one, on the theory that advance publicity would make her ridiculous if she failed. Great Neck, Long Island, a suburb of New York City, was selected as the first tryout town.

Kate became very nervous with thoughts of the opening and arrived at the theatre just fifteen minutes before curtain time. Everyone rushed to get her ready and at first everything seemed to be going along just fine until she imitated McKenna, who played a Frenchman. Her imitation was so deft that the audience applauded wildly, thus unsettling her for the rest of the performance. She began speaking her lines faster and faster until no one could understand a word she said.

Needless to say, she was fired after just the one performance. All was not lost, however, for both Arthur Hopkins and A. H. Woods, the producers, had been in that particular audience. Hopkins, known for his keen eye for talent, was not swayed by Hepburn's hysteria on stage and offered her a small part in Katharine Clugston's *These Days*. After the usual rehearsal time and pre-Broadway tryouts, Katharine Hepburn—as Veronica Sims—finally reached Broadway at the Cort Theatre on November 12, 1928.

The critics were anything but overjoyed with Miss Clugston's play, but Richard Lockridge noted in his review in the *New York Sun*: "Again, the action could have been compressed to advantage into a fifth the time, but the pleasing antics of Miss Mary Hall and Miss Katharine Hepburn, among others, passed the wasted minutes pleasantly enough." *These Days* closed after eight performances.

Producer Hopkins then installed Hepburn as understudy to socialite star Hope Williams in Philip Barry's *Holiday*, which was then enjoying its out-of-town tryout in New Haven. After two weeks of this, Kate announced she was going to marry Ludlow Ogden Smith, a Philadelphia socialite and graduate of the University of Grenoble. *Holiday* opened at New York's Plymouth Theatre on November 26, 1928, and was an instant hit.

Mr. and Mrs. Smith were married on December 12, 1928, and the pair honeymooned in Bermuda. Her grandfather Hepburn, then the oldest Episcopal minister in Virginia, read the service at the family home in West Hartford.

Kate couldn't see herself as "Mrs. Smith," and convinced her husband to have his name changed, which he did, to Ogden Ludlow. When their brief honeymoon was over, Kate couldn't see herself living on Philadelphia's Main Line, so the couple moved to Manhattan. After a short while, Kate couldn't see herself playing housewife in their three-story walk-up apartment on East 39th Street and, three weeks (to the day) later, she returned to Hopkins, who gave her the understudy job back.

Holiday ran until June 1929, but Hope Williams never missed a performance. After it closed, Kate went to Europe with her husband for a short vacation. At her return, *Holiday*'s road company was testing at the uptown Riviera Theatre, at 97th Street and Broadway, before a projected cross-country tour when Miss Williams fell ill one evening. Hopkins luckily got hold of Kate, who finally went on as Linda Seton—a role she would later perform so beautifully on the screen. "So," she said later, "I played it just once."

The Theatre Guild then offered her the ingenue's role in S. N. Behrman's *Meteor* with Alfred Lunt and Lynn Fontanne at $225 per week; she promptly accepted. However, at the same time, she was given the chance to play a *lead* in another play, and Hepburn opted for the larger role. The Guild wasn't too pleased by this decision since *Meteor* was about to open, and tried to hogtie the young actress. But they didn't know Miss Hepburn well enough at that time, and finally relented.

The *other play* was the fantasy-drama *Death Takes a Holiday* by Alberto Casella, which Walter Ferris had adapted from the Italian. Philip Merivale played the shadowy Prince Sirki and Hepburn was the lovely Grazia. Throughout the rehearsal period and for the five weeks of pre-Broadway performances, Hepburn battled almost continually with director Lawrence Marston and also collected too many "mixed" reviews. A few days before the Broadway opening, producer Lee Shubert sent word asking for her resignation. "Resign, hell!" Kate shouted. "If he wants me out of the cast, he can kick me out!" He did. *Death Takes a Holiday* opened at the Ethel Barrymore Theatre on December 26, 1929, with Rose Hobart as Grazia, and ran for 180 performances.

In March 1930 the Theatre Guild hired Kate to understudy Eunice Stoddard—in the role of Viera Aleksandrovna—in Ivan Turgenev's comedy *A Month in the Country*. The play starred Alla Nazimova in a sumptuous production staged (and adapted) by Rouben Mamoulian at the Guild Theatre. Her salary was $35 per week, a far cry from her previous Guild offer for *Meteor*. After a short time, Hortense Alden, who played the maid Katia, left the company; Hepburn replaced her and kept up her understudy duties with no increase in salary. It is interesting to note that the same Hortense Alden appeared in the off-Broadway production of Tennessee Williams' short play *Suddenly, Last Summer* years later as Mrs. Violet Venable—the role that Hepburn was to essay on the screen.

Miss Robinson-Duff then arranged for Kate and another student, Laura Harding, to do a summer of stock at the Berkshire Playhouse in Stockbridge, Massachusetts. Instead of providing the experience she needed, the venture proved disastrous. The Hepburn confidence had quickly given way to arrogance. After mediocre parts in three plays (including Sir James M. Barrie's *The Admirable Crichton* with George Coulouris and the lead in G. Martinez Sierra's *A Romantic Young Lady*), she quit.

Pro-Hepburn and anti-Hepburn factions, which were to dot her lengthy career, sprang into existence during rehearsals of her next play. Producers Kenneth MacGowan and Joseph Verner Reed presented Jane Cowl in a repertory of alternating plays at the Maxine Elliott Theatre: William Shakespeare's *Twelfth Night* and Benn W. Levy's *Art and Mrs. Bottle*. Kate got the role of Miss Cowl's daughter Judy in the latter.

Miss Cowl was enthusiastic about Kate, but British playwright Levy disliked her from the first. He soon fired her. "She looks a fright, her manner is objectionable and she has no talent," he shrieked. However, after unsuccessful experiments with fourteen other actresses, Kate was rehired at a higher salary. Miss Cowl, it seems, persuaded him to rehire her and, as Judy Bottle, Kate won praise from a number of critics. Said Howard Barnes in the *New York Herald Tribune*: "Katharine Hepburn, whose acting has, unfortunately, not been noticed, particularly by this reviewer in the past, is splendid as Mrs. Bottle's daughter. . . . She is agreeable to look at, assured and altogether a proficient actress."

Jane Cowl later told a reporter: "I was never close to her as much as I wanted to be. But I was for her all the way along. I've never seen any newcomer in the theater who was more thrilled, anyone who loved the theater more. Her absorption in her work, her dedication to the stage, her promise of power—all these made her an experience to know."

During the summer of 1931, Kate joined the Ivoryton Players at Ivoryton, Connecticut, for a season of stock. Joining Henry Hull in his pre-*Tobacco Road* days, Kate appeared in *Just Married*, *The Man Who Came Back*, and *The Cat and the Canary*.

Having benefited considerably from her strenuous summer schedule, Kate landed the plum role of Daisy Sage in Philip Barry's comedy *The Animal Kingdom*. Gilbert Miller was producing the play in association with its star, Leslie Howard. Barry was fascinated with what Hepburn was doing with the character he had created and began adding bits of dialogue here and a scene or two there until the Pittsburgh

With her husband Ludlow Ogden Smith

Diving from the board—
an early RKO publicity shot

Bust by Robert McKnight

opening, when it became all too apparent that the play was overlong and that Howard wasn't particularly pleased with Barry's additions—and, besides, Miss Hepburn was too tall (5 feet 7 inches).

As co-producer, Howard issued immediate orders that the play would have to be cut and, since he and William Gargan had become fast friends by this time, the part to get the scissor treatment was Kate's. Before the Boston opening, Hepburn received a registered letter terminating her contract from Mr. Miller. Frances Fuller replaced her as Daisy and the play—and Mr. Howard—were hits when it opened on Broadway January 12, 1932.

Meanwhile, the Hepburn trend of being hired, fired, and rehired plagued her next venture. Julien Thompson's farce *The Warrior's Husband,* based loosely on Aristophanes' *Lysistrata,* offered her a marvelous role. Her earlier training as a gymnast and all-round athlete, plus her natural fire and dash, made her a prodigious lady warrior in the early sequences and a highly competent love slave in the latter ones. As Antiope, an Amazon queen, Kate romped around the stage, wrestling with co-star Colin Keith-Johnston in a short tunic which displayed her shapely legs to advantage. At last, her technique caught up with her personality.

The Warrior's Husband opened at the Morosco Theatre on March 11, 1932, and ran for 83 performances. The critics liked this new star more than they liked the play. Said *Time* magazine: "What manner of men these strange Greeks be is soon discovered by the Amazons when Theseus (Colin Keith-Johnston) runs away with Antiope (a blond thin-cheeked girl named Katharine Hepburn). Praise goes to wet-lipped Romney Brent for an effeminate impersonation which is notable in that it amuses and does not repel. Praise, too, for Miss Hepburn as the volatile but vulnerable warrior and for Mr. Johnston is indicated."

Mrs. Kermet Roosevelt saw Kate and immediately telegramed Merian C. Cooper, executive producer of RKO Radio Pictures, about her. Soon their head of production, David O. Selznick, was offering her a contract, but Hepburn muttered, "They didn't like me until I got into a leg show." Her first movie offer came from Paramount Pictures but she flatly turned them down.

Although Kate was only making about $100 a week in the play, she didn't really want to go to Hollywood, so she demanded a ridiculous salary of $1,500 per week. She knew the studio would never accept that figure for a relative newcomer. However, RKO did convince her to make a screen test for them in New York. She did a brief scene from *Holiday* which was rushed to the coast.

No one was more surprised than Kate when her agent Leland Hayward informed her that RKO had met her price. While he began to make arrangements for her departure to the coast, she fulfilled a previously committed engagement with a stock company in Ossining, New York, playing Psyche Marbury in Will Cotton's *The Bride the Sun Shines On,* which Dorothy Gish had done on Broadway.

8

The hottest property on Selznick's schedule at that time (mid-1932) was Clemence Dane's *A Bill of Divorcement*, which had made a star of another Katharine (Cornell) on the stage a decade earlier. Selznick had assigned the directorial chores to George Cukor, who had just finished his first picture for RKO, called *What Price Hollywood*, receiving rave notices for himself and star Constance Bennett.

Everyone, it seems, wanted to play the pivotal role of Sydney, especially since the father would be played by John Barrymore. Even MGM's Norma Shearer, who had already had considerable success appearing with one Barrymore (Lionel) wanted to be loaned to RKO to appear with the other. RKO's own Irene Dunne also was being considered, as were Anita Louise, and Jill Esmond, and many others, until director Cukor happened to see Hepburn's test. That did it! Cukor detected a spark of nobility in her when, at one point, she put down a glass. That was all, but that was enough.

Katharine Hepburn arrived at Pasadena on July 4, 1932, accompanied by her friend Laura Harding; she was met by Hayward and his partner Myron Selznick. As Fate would have it, Kate had just gotten a piece of steel filing in her eye, which was almost swollen shut, and was wearing what she thought to be an "arty" dress. This sight caused Selznick to quip, "*This* is what they're paying $1,500 for?"

Hepburn and Hollywood clashed from the start. She went out of her way to insult everyone in sight, lighting hardest on newspapermen, studio publicists, and autograph hounds. They became her targets; she became theirs. RKO executives were beginning to wonder if this "typhoon Tillie" was worth putting up with—especially at the high price. However, Cukor intervened and the results paid off.

It was probably due to this initial run-in with newsmen and publicists that stories of Hepburn and Barrymore began to circulate with alarming regularity. The first story reported that Barrymore tried to seduce Hepburn in his spacious, penthouse-like dressingroom on the first day's shooting. Another story which won wide acceptance—and was later used by Gene Fowler in his biography of Mr. Barrymore *Good Night, Sweet Prince*—had Hepburn allegedly screaming to Barrymore, "I'll never play another scene with you," to which he calmly replied, "But, my dear, you never have."

Filming of *A Bill of Divorcement* began on July 9, 1932, and from the start Cukor knew he had been right. He had chosen a fine, raw talent and, during many ten-hour days, he maneuvered with skill and patience to evoke it. For a film debut, her performance is near perfect. Barrymore, too, surprised everyone—even his staunch detractors—by giving a low-key and moving performance as a man governed by insanity. His portrayal of Hillary Fairfield must rank as his finest screen impersonation.

When the picture was sneaked, the preview audiences laughed at two serious scenes, which were quickly reshot. Hepburn and her husband then sailed for Europe. When it was released in September 1932, *A Bill of Divorcement* was an unexpected hit and—in true Hollywood fashion—a star was born.

After returning from Europe, Kate shared an isolated house with Laura Harding while her husband remained in the East. She seldom did the "Hollywood scene" but, through friends of Laura's, she had met Mary Pickford. A few mornings later she chided Cukor, saying, "I hope you're satisfied, I had dinner at Pickfair last night." Cukor, taking in the full view of Kate in pants and sweater, said, "I assume you ate in the kitchen. Certainly they'd never let you in the front door."

Cukor and Hepburn became great friends. Sundays at Cukor's home were informal social events, with guests who included Tallulah Bankhead, whom he had directed in *Tarnished Lady*, Hugh Walpole, Mary Garden, and Tilly Losch. Garbo came one Sunday and met Kate. Later, she reportedly visited Kate and Laura's hideaway. Said Garbo: "God, what a dreary place! But then, I always loved dreary places."

Joel McCrea, whose popularity had soared since he had appeared in Dolores Del Rio's *Bird of Paradise*, was to be Kate's co-star in *Three Came Unarmed*, an adaptation of the British novel by E. Arnot Robertson, with Gregory La Cava directing. Publicity had already begun on it when top studio brass decided to star Hepburn in her second movie because of the tremendous critical reception her first picture received.

With Joel McCrea in 1933

9

In front of her New York brownstone in 1934

At preview of *The Merry Widow* with
Ernst Lubitsch, Rudolf Sieber,
Dorothy Arzner (in white suit) and Marlene Dietrich

Her second film now became *Christopher Strong*, which had been intended for Ann Harding and Leslie Howard because of their successful version of *The Animal Kingdom*. Her co-star was Colin Clive and Dorothy Arzner, one of the few wome▮ ▮rectors in films, directed with verve from a scenario ▮▮▮ ▮kins. The film did not do well at the box office ▮▮ ▮▮y critics were indifferent to what was referred to as "over-acting."

While she was making *Christopher Strong*, Broadway producer Jed Harris, who had just secured the American rights to the British stage hit *The Lake*, sent Kate the script. She liked it, but had to make three more films before she would be free to do it.

Hepburn's third film, *Morning Glory*, provided her with a role she could easily identify with and there was much of Hepburn in the role of Eva Lovelace. Her compelling portrayal won her her first Academy Award; she was the sixth actress to win the Academy's "Oscar."

A far better picture and a far better Hepburn performance followed. RKO, under Selznick's guidance, was planning a new film version of Louisa May Alcott's classic *Little Women*, with Dorothy Wilson as Jo and Helen Mack as Beth, when director Cukor expressed great interest in directing it as a major production. Selznick assigned the best RKO craftsman to the project and Cukor carefully assembled a first-rate cast for Sarah Y. Mason and Victor Heerman's brilliant adaptation of the book. What emerged not only became a fantastic box-office hit, but also one of the all-time great motion pictures. Cukor's attention to atmospheric details and total respect for the period made this version the best ever filmed.

Hepburn's subsequent career as an actress has been marked, almost rhythmically, by the alternation of success and failure. The success-failure pattern is probably due to the fact that her training has never had chance to catch up with her genius.

Jesse L. Lasky filmed *The Warrior's Husband* at Fox that same year, with Elissa Landi in the role Hepburn created on the stage. Lasky wanted to borrow Hepburn for his projected filming of the life of ballerina Anna Pavlova, entitled *The Flight of the Swan*, but RKO wouldn't let their hottest property go for any amount.

Kate was still interested in doing *The Lake* on Broadway, even though RKO had several projects lined up for her. These included: Edith Wharton's *Age of Innocence;* a film based on the life of Sarah Bernhardt; one on Nell Gwyn; *Without Sin*, an original screenplay by Melville Baker and Jack Kirkland; Ainsworth Morgan's scenario about Queen Elizabeth (from age fifteen to old womanhood) which had two tentative titles—*Lady of Tudor* and *The Tudor Wench*.

With her vocal coach Frances Robinson-Duff

In watercolor by Ginger Rogers

About this time, one of her detractors quipped, "If she were cast as Little Red Riding Hood she'd end up by eating the wolf."

RKO executives finally agreed to let Kate off to do the play, if she would first agree to make *Trigger* for director John Cromwell. Later retitled *Spitfire*, this backwoods melodrama provided her with the opportunity to be a real hillbilly tomboy. The script wasn't particularly exciting, but she would have agreed to anything to get the chance to return to Broadway. There were the usual delays during its filming and by the time RKO discovered that Hepburn's contract had lapsed—with the conclusion of *Spitfire* yet to be filmed—she charged them $10,000 for her overtime. And got it.

The Lake, written by Dorothy Massingham and Murray MacDonald, opened for one week in Washington, D.C., after a brief rehearsal period. Said the critic for the *Washington Post:* "There were moments last evening, perhaps, when Miss Hepburn seemed a trifle too staccato for best effect, and, now and again, her timing of speeches lacked something of perfect rhythm, but there was never an instant when she failed to command attention, hold the audience's undivided interest and win its unstinted acclaim."

In New York City, the story was a bit different. Her movie fame had caused an unheard-of advance sale of $40,000

and the first night (December 26, 1933) at the Martin Beck Theatre remains one of the historic catastrophes of the theatre. Those attending the glamorous opening included Kay Francis, Nancy Carroll, Dr. and Mrs. Hepburn, Judith Anderson, Laura Harding, George S. Kaufman, Leland Hayward, Frances Robinson-Duff, and Amelia Earhart.

In essence, *The Lake* was not a bad play, but its star was not ready for the responsibility required of a performer to maintain a three-act play. Dorothy Parker was the star wisecracker of the evening, uttering the immortal line, "She ran the gamut of emotions from A to B." Hepburn, years later, commented on Parker's remark: "It was extremely accurate and funny."

The Lake closed on February 10, 1934, after 55 performances. Actually, the play was still doing good business, but Kate wanted *out* and offered to pay. Since she and producer Harris had no written contract—only a verbal agreement—she said, "How much do you want?" He replied, "How much have you got?" Jed Harris got $15,461.67 for closing *The Lake*.

Kate had good reasons for wanting out; she had just won the Academy Award for *Morning Glory* and the Cannes Film Festival award for *Little Women*. After a brief jaunt to Europe, Kate went to Mérida, Yucatán, and there obtained a divorce from Ogden Ludlow (May 9, 1934).

11

Meeting Howard Hughes on the runway, 1937

RKO was trying to entice Hepburn back to Hollywood with promises of various pictures, such as a film based on the life of George Sand, the role of Joan of Arc in Shaw's *Saint Joan* and an essay of John Galsworthy's monumental novel *The Forsyte Saga*. Meanwhile, she was considering Helen Jerome's dramatization of Jane Austen's *Pride and Prejudice* for producer Arthur Hopkins for the following Broadway season.

She almost returned to the stage at the Ivoryton Summer Theatre for producer Milton Steifel in a preview engagement of a new play entitled *Dark Victory* with Stanley Ridges. Unfortunately, the production had to be cancelled at the last minute when Ridges withdrew from the cast due to an illness in his family. Steifel wanted Kate to return later, promising to reschedule *Holiday*, but she returned to Hollywood and signed a new contract with RKO, which called for $300,000 for six films in two years.

Upon her return, it was more than casually noticed that there was a marked change in Hepburn's attitude. Not only had her last film (*Spitfire*) been unsuccessful, but her stage venture had also failed. She approached her next screen role with renewed vigor and complete abandon. James M. Barrie's *The Little Minister* for director Richard Wallace proved what an actress of depth and variety she was—but to audiences it was no *Little Women*. In a change-of-pace decision, RKO next put her into a turgid melodrama called *Break of Hearts* opposite Charles Boyer. She looked ravishing in a modern wardrobe, but couldn't surmount the banalities of the script. This was the lowest point in her 1930s films.

Since Hepburn's biggest hits to date had been costume pieces, she suggested Booth Tarkington's *Seventeen* as her next vehicle and William Wyler as director. Wyler was under contract to Samuel Goldwyn, so RKO did Hepburn one better. They prepared Tarkington's 1921 Pulitzer Prize novel *Alice Adams*. George Stevens, a minor director of various short-subject series and a few dreary Wheeler and Woolsey slapstick features, met his big break with tremendous opposition from the reigning queen of the RKO lot. But, after the *expected* initial head-on collision between star and director, Stevens and Hepburn got along famously. In fact, he extracted one of her all-time great performances.

As with *Little Women*, this production was given the full attention of RKO's finest technicians and craftsmen, who created a charming atmosphere with their sets and costumes. The cast included Fred Stone, in his first major film, and the script afforded Hattie McDaniel some delicious comic moments as the Adamses' maid. Young Fred MacMurray was not the perfect choice for Alice's suitor. Hepburn won her second Academy Award nomination.

George Cukor then got involved in a fascinating script from a Compton MacKenzie novel, which he thought ideal for Kate. Together with Cary Grant, Brian Aherne, and Edmund Gwenn, they made *Sylvia Scarlett*, a moody, highly sensitive escapade in which Kate spends most of her time masquerading as a boy. Cukor, Grant, and Kate each thought this was a fine film effort and attended the sneak preview with great anticipation. They were shocked at the reactions of the audience. It wasn't released to the general public until early 1936. At that time Grant was acclaimed for his portrayal of a cockney crook, but the film was a dismal box-office failure. In retrospect, *Sylvia Scarlett* stands today as a film much ahead of its time—a highly personal film of its director and cast.

Max Reinhardt offered Kate the role of Viola in his summer production of *Twelfth Night* at the Hollywood Bowl, but her movie schedule wouldn't permit it. RKO producer Pandro S. Berman announced to the press that he had purchased the Hungarian play *Marie Bashkirtseff* for Hepburn and that Anthony Veiller was adapting it for the screen, and MGM wanted her for *The Gorgeous Hussy*.

Despite that announcement, Kate next appeared under John Ford's direction in his film version of Maxwell Anderson's celebrated play *Mary of Scotland*. Fredric March was her co-star and his wife Florence Eldridge headed an enormous cast. Dudley Nichols, in his screen adaptation, replaced Anderson's poetic blank verse with contemporary speech. Even this change did not save this from being a beautifully mounted, well-acted, but static, historical drama.

Another period piece followed on its heels. Netta Syrett's novel *Portrait of a Rebel* traced an outspoken young lady in Victorian England. Kate gave a well-modulated performance in another well-made picture. Herbert Marshall was her co-star and the cast included two young players Kate had seen in Ina Claire's *End of Summer* and had asked RKO to hire: Doris Dudley and Van Heflin. It was released to the public as *A Woman Rebels*, but the public couldn't have cared less—they stayed away.

Once again shooting in the dark for another box-office bonanza like *Little Women*, RKO executives offered her Barrie's *Quality Street*. George Stevens did an all-round capable job of direction and all production values were perfect in every last detail. RKO had even borrowed Franchot Tone from MGM for Kate's co-star, but it was not a popular film. Kate was delightful as Phoebe Throssel, but to no avail.

Meanwhile, with her six-film deal over, Hepburn accepted The Theatre Guild's offer to return to the stage in Helen Jerome's adaptation of Charlotte Brontë's *Jane Eyre*. They offered her $1,000 per week but Hepburn, remembering the trouble she had had over release from *Meteor* and the salary dispute in *A Month in the Country*, demanded $1,500 and got it. The play opened its pre-Broadway tour in New Haven on December 26, 1936, to a lukewarm reception and, through the early months of 1937, she toured with it in hopes that the script would improve somehow. It didn't.

However, Hepburn's tour did land-office business, due to another factor. Her hide-and-seek romance with billionaire pilot Howard Hughes made the front pages during the entire 14-week engagement. He followed Kate in his private plane everywhere she played and both were constantly besieged by reporters at every turn. Hughes had formerly been linked romantically with Billie Dove, June Lang, and Ginger Rogers, and Kate, who had been rumored engaged to Leland Hayward, had just lost him to Margaret Sullavan, so marriage rumors were in the air.

Because of her earlier experience with *The Lake*, Kate decided to end this highly successful tour in Baltimore on April 3, 1937, after a record $340,000 gross for the 14-week period.

Hepburn's beautiful brownstone on East 49th Street, in Manhattan's Turtle Bay Section, became hers outright in 1937 when she paid it off. She had moved there in 1934.

A four-picture deal for an undisclosed amount was RKO's next offering. Although she was considering Max Gordon's plans to revive *Peter Pan*, Kate returned to RKO. Her first film under the new deal was to have been a script originally intended for Irene Dunne, called *The Mad Miss Manton*. That script later went to Barbara Stanwyck and Henry Fonda. Instead, she began work on the screen version of Edna Ferber and George S. Kaufman's *Stage Door*, which was in the capable hands of Gregory La Cava, fresh from his comedy triumph *My Man Godfrey* at Universal.

La Cava, who almost directed Hepburn in *Three Came Unarmed* in 1932, seldom worked directly from a script. He used it as an outline or guideline for his actors. His theory was based purely on improvisation, which is—or certainly was at that time—unusual for a film director to employ. After long improvisational sessions with his actors, La Cava knew exactly what each member of the cast could do and which action to highlight.

The play had been totally revamped to make Kate a spoiled rich girl. The surprise came when Ginger Rogers proved what a first-rate comedienne she was. *Stage Door* cost $900,000 to make and grossed RKO over 2 million. The play-within-a-play sequence resembled a scene from *The Lake* and Hepburn's rendition of the line "The calla lilies are in bloom again" became a tag line for her for years. George S. Kaufman, upon seeing La Cava's version, remarked, "Why didn't he call it 'Screen Door'?"

Next came a publicity release saying that Hepburn's next film would either be something called *Bridge in the Sky* or *Violette*. However, at this point, studio officials were so excited by the response to her work in *Stage Door* that she was cast, opposite Cary Grant, in Howard Hawk's *Bringing Up Baby*. This was her first taste of true screwball comedy and Kate went in for the full ride. The result was a tremendously funny comedy—full of zany touches—which proved how well she could handle light and funny situations.

Immediately after *Bringing Up Baby*, Hepburn was labeled *Box Office Poison* by exhibitor Harry Brandt, then president of the powerful Independent Theatre Owners of America. Also under attack were Greta Garbo, Marlene Dietrich, Mae West, Joan Crawford, Kay Francis, Edward Arnold, and Fred Astaire. In typical Hepburn fashion she snickered, "They say I'm a has-been. If I weren't laughing so hard, I might cry."

RKO then offered its "poisonous" star a B film called *Mother Carey's Chickens*, but rather than commit professional suicide Kate bought her contract for $200,000 plus $20,000 overtime pay she had insisted on getting when *Bringing Up Baby* had run behind schedule, and reported to work for Columbia, where George Cukor and Donald Ogden Stewart were ready to begin a remake of Barry's *Holiday*. Finally, she got to play Linda Seton and act again with Cary Grant.

This is still one of the best-acted comedies in cinema annals. The supporting cast, headed by Edward Everett Horton (in the role Donald Ogden Stewart performed on stage), Lew Ayres, and Jean Dixon, couldn't have been bettered. Doris Nolan played well the role of Kate's younger sister, a role for which Columbia's starlet Rita Hayworth had been tested.

Columbia spent much to give this production its necessary gloss and Kate's characterization is one of the finest of her entire career. Pauline Kael, of *The New Yorker*, was to comment years later, "At her best—in the archetypal Hepburn role as the tomboy Linda in *Holiday*, in 1938—her wit and nonconformity made ordinary heroines seem mushy, and her angular beauty made the round-faced ingenues look piggy and stupid. She was hard when they were soft—in both head and body."

When Hepburn returned to her Connecticut home in May 1938 she vowed she would not return to Hollywood until "I can come in a good picture."

Soon afterward, Hepburn told the *New York Herald Tribune's* Eighth Forum on Current Problems, "Motion Pictures *could* be one of our greatest mediums of education today. However, let a movie try to depict situations in which we are all involved now; let a movie try to wake people up to their own plight. . . let a movie try to present a moral, economic or political problem of today honestly and simply, and they are advised to hear nothing, say nothing, do nothing."

Broadway offers started pouring in almost imediately. She was sent George Corey and Rachel Maddux's play *Turnip's Blood* and Paul Vincent Carroll's *The White Steed*, and her friend Howard Hughes offered to produce a film based on the life of Amelia Earhart with Kate in the lead. But Kate's thoughts were on the prize of prizes: Scarlett O'Hara in David O. Selznick's production of Margaret Mitchell's *Gone With the Wind*. The following item actually had appeared in the *New York Times* (October 13, 1938): "Katharine Hepburn will arrive at Selznick-International next week to be tested for the lead in *Gone With the Wind*. Selznick is negotiating with Samuel Goldwyn for the loan of Andrea Leeds to play Melanie in the same picture."

Nearly every actress in Hollywood and New York had tested for the coveted part and it must be remembered that George Cukor was the first (of three) directors of that classic film. Kate had Cukor on her side, but Selznick was not an easy man to convince. As reports go, Hepburn was quoted as having said: "The part was practically written for me. I *am* Scarlett O'Hara!" Selznick supposedly retorted, "I just can't imagine Clark Gable chasing you for ten years."

Whether or not that exchange of dialogue ever did take place matters little now. Kate's being on the "Box-Office Poison" list probably was closer to the core of the problem. However, it soon became apparent to both Selznick and Cukor that what was needed was a totally *new* face—a face the public didn't know at all. During one of Cukor's Sunday afternoon gatherings, he told Vivien Leigh that the prize role was hers, although she herself had thought that Kate would be given it.

Hepburn remained inactive and in total seclusion for weeks, during which time the studios offered her contracts. MGM's offer was $5,000 a week, 40 weeks a year for two years, but didn't contain script approval, which meant that, again, she would have to do anything put before her. Hepburn had had enough of that routine at RKO and was determined to get a *script approval* clause in any future contract she would sign.

When all might have seemed lost, a voice from the past beckoned. One person on whom Kate had left an indelible impression over the years was playwright Philip Barry. They first met during his initial Broadway production of *Holiday* when Kate was understudying Hope Williams. Their paths crossed again in late 1931 when she played his divine mistress Daisy Sage in *The Animal Kingdom* (only to be fired after the Pittsburgh opening) and still later, in 1938, when she appeared as Linda in the second film version of *Holiday*.

Hepburn was now at Fenwick, the Hepburn summer house on Long Island Sound near Old Saybrook, Connecticut, inspecting the damage caused by a terrific hurricane which had swept away much of the charming cottage. Barry visited Kate and showed her an outline of his new play. After hearing Barry's verbal description of its heroine, Tracy Lord, Hepburn had already decided this was the play for her. She liked this Tracy Lord.

After further meetings with Barry at his home in Maine, Kate agreed to invest one-fourth of the cost, as well as star in it. She waived salary and agreed to take 10 percent of the gross profits from the New York run and 12½ percent from the road company. In a burst of shrewd foresight, Hepburn also bought up the movie rights. The play was, of course, *The Philadelphia Story*.

A great deal depended upon the success of this play, not only for its star (whose last six films had produced only *two* box-office hits), but for its author (Barry's last three plays

With Carl Sandburg
and Secretary of the Interior
Harold L. Ickes
at a political dinner

With Bill Grady and
Louis B. Mayer at
Cinematographers' Party
at the Cocoanut Grove

Going over a radio script
with Spencer Tracy for a Screen
Guild of the Air broadcast

15

With President Franklin D. Roosevelt
at Hyde Park, 1940

With Spencer Tracy, Eddie Rickenbacker
(being given a tour of M-G-M),
Lana Turner and Clarence Brown

With Clark Gable at a party
at the Hotel Georges V in Paris

had failed) and the producing company, The Theatre Guild, Inc. (whose last four productions had been flops). Each had put up one-fourth of the cost required to get *The Philadelphia Story* on the boards. The "silent" fourth belonged to Howard Hughes.

Through the long rehearsals and tryouts of *The Philadelphia Story,* Barry watched every move, gesture, and—yes—"mannerism" of his star. He wrote around those he didn't feel suited Kate and punctuated those which she had injected through her naturalness of playing. Day by day, the play became more a part of her and soon every thing she did was perfection itself. And there was a certain *mannered* quality in her performance—how could there not be?—but appositely, so that those who saw her Tracy Lord felt they were really watching the real Katharine Hepburn. The Guild acquired a top cast which included Joseph Cotten, Van Heflin, Shirley Booth, Nicholas Joy, and teenage Anne Baxter (who was later replaced by eleven-year-old Lenore Lonergan).

When *The Philadelphia Story* finally arrived at the Shubert Theatre on Broadway on March 28, 1939, there was no doubt in anyone's mind that Hepburn had reached histrionic maturity. This was also the perfect example of the right play at the right time.

Said Richard Watts, Jr., in the *New York Herald Tribune:* "As an ardent admirer of Miss Katharine Hepburn, I find something particularly pleasant about the triumph she has made in Philip Barry's new comedy. Few actresses have been so relentlessly assailed by critics, wits, columnists, magazine editors and other professional assailers over so long a period of time and, even if you confess that some of the abuse had a certain justice to it, you must admit she faced it gamely and unflinchingly and fought back with courage and gallantry."

By June 1939, RKO wanted Kate back and offered her the sister role opposite Carole Lombard in George Stevens' *Vigil in the Night.* Kate was not only too busy with the hit play, but was also overseeing reconstruction of the Fenwick cottage, which became a sumptuous brick residence, complete with tennis court.

The Philadelphia Story closed its New York run after 415 performances to gross $961,310.37. Hepburn got 10 percent in salary plus 25 percent of the net in return for her quarter interest. Next, she toured the country, playing 254 performances with the road company, which grossed $753,538.50. She got 12½ percent as salary plus a quarter of the net.

Hepburn then sold the screen rights to Metro-Goldwyn-Mayer, along with her services on this one-picture deal, for $250,000. The old "box-office poison girl" had left Hollywood in May 1938 after paying RKO $220,000 for her release; she returned in June 1940 with almost $500,000 profit from her stage venture.

Several top studios had made offers for the screen rights

—and one had actually surpassed MGM's price—but Louis B. Mayer, a shrewd businessman to be sure, had made several concessions Kate felt too important to pass up. *She* got the role of Tracy Lord; Cukor was to direct; her insistence that Cary Grant and James Stewart co-star was granted; and she was granted "reasonable" consultation on the script.

Cukor shot the film version in a record eight weeks, with virtually no retakes. Grant received top billing (the only way MGM could get him), making it the first time since *A Bill of Divorcement* Kate had not been billed first. But, then, she didn't care that much about billing, if the part was good enough. Donald Ogden Stewart—a close friend of Barry's since their Yale days—enhanced *The Philadelphia Story* considerably in his screen adaptation, as he had done with *Holiday.*

When the film opened in November 1940, it proved a great hit with critics and public alike. Kate won her third Academy Award nomination, but Ginger Rogers won the golden statuette for her portrayal of *Kitty Foyle.* Although Kate had won the New York Film Critics award it was felt that she had been deliberately slighted in the Oscar race.

Cue magazine referred to this development as "The Revenge of the Little People of Hollywood," citing the old motto that used to hang in a famous star's dressing room: "Be nice to the people you pass on the way up. They're the same people you'll be meeting on your way down." This was further in evidence by the fact that her second leading man, James Stewart, *won* an Academy Award for his performance opposite Kate in *The Philadelphia Story.*

At Hyde Park, on September 21, 1940, Hepburn joined Edna Ferber, Booth Tarkington, Robert E. Sherwood, and other writers, actors, and composers on the picnic grounds of Mrs. Roosevelt's Val Kill cottage as a prelude to a radio symposium in which these notables pledged their support of a third term for the chief executive. One reporter termed the gathering a "pro-Willkie literary group."

The Philadelphia Story broke all records at New York's cinema palace, Radio City Music Hall, with a six-week engagement grossing $594,000, more than half its total Broadway earnings. Harry Brandt got his comeuppance when lines of patrons at Radio City wound around the block and uttered, "Come on back, Katie, all is forgiven."

Meanwhile, the road company finally closed—in Philadelphia of all places—on February 15, 1941. Hepburn had continued in the part after completing the film version. After the closing, Hepburn considered following up this success with Dorothy Day Wendell's play *Bow to the Wittiest,* but nothing ever came of this venture.

Eleanor Roosevelt, then assistant director of the Office of Civilian Defense, secured Kate's voluntary services as narrator for an Office of War Information (OWI) documentary short subject entitled *Women in Defense,* which served the defense effort by helping to recruit volunteers for the nation in science and industry. This 11-minute short was released in December 1941, and was Hepburn's *only* released film for that year.

What happened after the closing of *The Philadelphia Story* changed the course of her career—and her life—considerably. Ring Lardner, Jr., brought a tentative outline for a screenplay to Garson Kanin's attention. Kanin had just been drafted and couldn't execute any of the ideas he imparted to young Lardner, so he introduced him to his younger brother Michael and the two turned out a first-rate scenario. They got in touch with Hepburn, upon Garson's advice, and she—looking for a strong follow-up script to *The Philadelphia Story*—sent the script to MGM.

Woman of the Year, as it was called, provided Kate with the second neat business coup in her dealings with Louis B. Mayer. She persuaded him to buy this "anonymous" story for $211,000 ($50,000 each for the unknown writers, $100,000 for herself, plus $11,000 commission and agents' fees). In addition, she wangled an MGM star contract and assurance that, naturally, she was to play the lead and have say in selection of director and co-star.

MGM bought the whole package. They hired director George Stevens who was Kate's choice, but couldn't supply her demands for Spencer Tracy to co-star, since he was on location in Florida with Marjorie Kinnan Rawlings' *The Yearling.* Hepburn admired Tracy as an actor, but they had never met. Oddly enough, they had actually been "teamed" together in the 1938 Walt Disney cartoon, *Mother Goose Goes Hollywood,* in which Hepburn became Little Bo Peep and Tracy, Freddie Bartholomew of *Captains Courageous* and Charles Laughton of *Mutiny on the Bounty* became the captains of the nursery rhyme "Rub a Dub Dub."

As Fate would have it, *The Yearling* company returned from location—after many difficulties—and suspended production. (Gregory Peck later filmed this Pulitzer Prize–winning story after the war.) This left Tracy free, and just at the right time.

Their celebrated meeting contained dialogue that would set the standard for their films together. Said Hepburn, "I'm afraid I'm a little tall for you, Mr. Tracy." He replied, "Don't worry, Miss Hepburn, I'll cut you down to my size." Whether Hepburn or Tracy actually got those cracks off is of less importance than the fact they *might* have. At any rate, the Tracy-Hepburn formula was molded and, in most of their pictures together, Tracy would topple the haughty Kate from her pedestal and bring her down to his earthy level.

The pairing of these two distinct individual personalities, despite their different temperaments and backgrounds, worked amazingly well, for they complemented each other as artists. Tracy's innate shyness, under his bold exterior, came to the foreground, adding new subtleties to his craft. Hepburn, on the other hand, although equally shy, became sexy for the first time on the screen. Who can forget the very first minute they meet on the screen, in the newspaper

With Charles Laughton, Spencer Tracy and Freddie Bartholomew in Walt Disney's 1938 Mickey Mouse cartoon *Mother Goose Goes Hollywood.* © *Walt Disney Productions.*

Rub-a-Dub Dub

publisher's office, and the exchange that generated between them?

Off screen, Hepburn and Tracy became fast friends and lasting ones, enjoying a close friendship of which little was known and less was told. That's the way they wanted it and that's the way it was.

Woman of the Year was finished in late 1941, but was not released until January 1942. It equaled the record *The Philadelphia Story* had set at Radio City Music Hall. Kate won her fourth Academy Award nomination and the screen established a new team that would serve it well.

On March 5, 1942, Hepburn opened at the McCarter Theatre in Princeton, New Jersey, with Elliott Nugent in Philip Barry's *Without Love*—which had also been written to serve her talents—and then proceeded to tour with it for three months. The New York opening was postponed, however, so that Barry could do some rewriting and Kate could make *Keeper of the Flame* on the coast.

Tracy and Hepburn were together again in Donald Ogden Stewart's fascinating and suspenseful screenplay based on I. A. R. Wylie's novel *Keeper of the Flame.* At the time, this seemed a strange choice for both stars to make, for the script was almost totally devoid of romantic interest. However, they met the challenge, proving they weren't just a lucky comedy team.

After completing her second film with Tracy, Hepburn opened on Broadway in The Theatre Guild's production of Barry's *Without Love* at the St. James Theatre on November 10, 1942. She was acclaimed, but the play received mixed notices. During her run in this play (113 perform-

ances), she appeared as herself in the film *Stage Door Canteen*—the all-star tribute produced in association with the American Theatre Wing. Like the other actors in this film, Kate's salary was contributed to the operation of canteens for servicemen in the larger cities of the United States.

In 1943 it was rumored that she would be filming Shaw's *The Millionairess,* but plans for this production never materialized. Also, Paramount had hopes of borrowing her from MGM for Daphne du Maurier's *Frenchman's Creek,* co-starring Ray Milland.

Hepburn's next film didn't change her type—for she was still a woman of great determination—but it did change her *race.* In the film version of Pearl S. Buck's popular novel *Dragon Seed,* she became Chinese for her portrayal of the peasant girl Jade. Although most critics slammed the white cast for "masquerading" as Chinese peasants—the Chinese actors were playing the Japanese—the acting was of a high caliber. The production was handsomely mounted and made money.

Harold S. Bucquet, who co-directed *Dragon Seed* with Jack Conway, was then assigned the directorial chores on Donald Ogden Stewart's screenplay of Barry's *Without Love.* Tracy was again teamed with Hepburn, a move which made this film far superior to its legitimate counterpart.

During the 1940s, Hepburn did a great deal of radio work. On July 20, 1942, she did *The Philadelphia Story* on Cecil B. DeMille's "Lux Radio Theatre" as a special Victory Show for the government. Her co-stars were also from the movie: Cary Grant, Lt. James Stewart, Ruth Hussey, and Virginia Weidler. (Grant and Kate did it again in 1947 for the "Screen Guild of the Air.") She then did *Little Women* twice for "The Theatre Guild of the Air," first with Elliott Reid doubling as narrator and Laurie, John Lodge repeating his role of Brooke, and Oscar Homolka as Professor Bhaer. The second broadcast was on December 21, 1947, with Paul Lukas repeating his movie role of Professor Bhaer. She and Tracy did *Woman of the Year* on CBS for the "Screen Guild of the Air" and on January 2, 1949, Kate was joined by Paul Henreid and Claude Rains in Romain Rolland's *The Game of Love and Death* for "The Theatre Guild of the Air."

MGM then put their biggest team—Tracy and Hepburn—into *The Sea of Grass*, which was based on the Conrad Richter novel. Elia Kazan directed as best he could and, although the scenario failed to capture the beauty and meaning of Richter's original, the breathtaking photography of Harry Stradling did.

Metro then announced that Hepburn would next be cast as Marianne in *Green Dolphin Street* (which later went to Lana Turner) and that it had purchased John van Druten's play *The Damask Cheek* for her. Unfortunately, these two properties would not be Hepburn vehicles. She did, how-

ever, consent to appear in *The American Creed*, an American Brotherhood Week Trailer, which David O. Selznick produced in 1946, with Robert Stevenson directing. With her appeared such stars as Ingrid Bergman, Eddie Cantor, Van Johnson, James Stewart, Shirley Temple, Jennifer Jones, Edward G. Robinson, and Walter Pidgeon.

Kate's next film, which was released *before The Sea of Grass*, marked the return of Robert Taylor to the screen after a three-year stint in the U.S. Navy. The studio publicity boys almost tagged it "Taylor's Back and Hepburn's Got Him," but thought better of it since that phrase had done nothing for the Clark Gable–Greer Garson *Adventure*.

Undercurrent didn't win any new laurels for Hepburn, although she gave a competent performance that ranged from naïve young girl to sophisticated woman caught up in a melodrama. It was directed by Vincente Minnelli, in his first encounter with melodrama, and was a great asset to the budding career of Robert Mitchum.

Her studio announced in March 1947 that Kate would star in the screen version of John B. Marquand's *B.F.'s Daughter* for producer Edwin H. Knopf, but that assignment ultimately went to Barbara Stanwyck. Later, MGM decided

At Ethel Barrymore's 70th birthday party. With (standing) Billie Burke, Judy Garland, Lucile Watson, Constance Collier, Laura Harding, and (seated) Lionel Barrymore, Miss Barrymore, Spencer Tracy and host George Cukor

As Rosalind in the successful
Theatre Guild production of
As You Like It

to do a glossy musical drama based on the lives of Robert and Clara Schumann, prompted by Columbia Studio's success with its quasi-biographical treatment of the life and music of Fredric Chopin (*A Song to Remember*). *Song of Love* starred Kate as Clara Schumann and Paul Henreid as her husband Robert, and MGM gave the production a lush mounting. The emphasis was on the music (of Liszt, Brahms, Strauss, and Schumann) and not the scenario. Clarence Brown directed the film, which was released in the fall of 1947.

Hepburn's career dipped slightly when she ran afoul of the Un-American Activities Committee. In May 1947 she had made a fiery speech of protest when candidate Henry Wallace was barred from using the Hollywood Bowl for a campaign address. Her outburst was a typical example of her instinct for the underdog—for she didn't even know Wallace. Her speech in his behalf was delivered at Gilmore Stadium, before an estimated audience of some 28,000, including Edward G. Robinson, Charles Chaplin, and Hedy Lamarr.

Kate, along with Helen Hayes (for whom it was originally written) and Margaret Sullavan, turned down *State of the Union* in 1945. Ruth Hussey got the part and the play enjoyed a two-year run. When Liberty Films purchased the movie rights to the Howard Lindsay–Russel Crouse Pulitzer Prize–winning play, the studio hoped that Gary Cooper and Claudette Colbert would play the leads. When MGM suddenly entered into the transaction, in association with Liberty, the play was designated as a vehicle for the Tracy-Hepburn combo. Director Frank Capra strengthened the play's attack on machine-ruled politics, pressure groups, and voter apathy, and directed a first-rate cast.

When that film was completed, MGM said plans were underway for Kate to make *Drivin' Woman* or *Woman of Distinction* for Capra but, as Hepburn later related, "Walter Huston and I wanted to revive *Desire Under the Elms*. It was just before he died. In the early forties George Cukor wanted me to play *Electra* with Garbo as Clytemnestra. Metro was horrified."

Next, the successful team of Ruth Gordon-Garson Kanin-George Cukor (who had produced at Universal Ronald Colman's award-winning *A Double Life*) appeared with a new comedy for Tracy and Hepburn. Called *Adam's Rib,* it was 1949's brightest and wittiest film, and it paved the way for Judy Holliday's screen stardom. Kate, the Kanins, and Cukor were all involved in a plot to get Judy Holliday the Billie Dawn role in the film version of Kanin's *Born Yesterday,* which she had done so beautifully on the stage. Columbia Pictures had purchased the property, with Rita Hayworth in mind, and Columbia czar Harry Cohn declared he could not see Holliday repeating her original role. Kate, joined by her cohorts, built up Holliday's part in *Adam's Rib* and even did publicity stints in her behalf. Finally, Cohn relented and Judy had the part—and an Oscar, as things turned out.

In late 1949, Kate was coached by Constance Collier for months to ready her for her first journey into Shakespeare. "Why do I want to do it?" she answered a reporter at the time. "The part of Rosalind is really a test of how good an actress you are, and I want to find out." On January 26, 1950, she opened at New York's Cort Theatre in The Theatre Guild's revival of *As You Like It*. The beautiful production proceeded to set a new record for this comedy: 145 consecutive performances. The extended run surpassed the record previously set by Henrietta Crosman in 1902. Hepburn's Rosalind dazzled the audiences—not only in New York, but on a cross-country tour. Whether she was the ideal conception of Rosalind is of less importance than the fact that the public was enchanted by her stage presence.

Said Sidney B. Whipple in the *New York World-Telegram*: "Miss Hepburn, herself captures every possibility in the part and seems, indeed, to take great joy in playing it—a joy that is communicated to the audience. She moves buoyantly and gracefully, living the part rather than acting it."

So popular was this Shakespearean endeavor that Kate was already thinking of mounting *The Taming of the Shrew* when she was approached by John Huston to appear in his production of C. S. Forester's 1935 novel *The African Queen*. Huston himself was working on the scenario with James Agee, and Humphrey Bogart was to star. The film wouldn't be easy to make, Huston explained from the first, for the shooting would be done on actual location in Africa. Kate, never one to ignore a good challenge—or role—quickly agreed. She also obtained a financial interest in the project.

Filming in Africa along the Ruki River, a tributary of the Lulaba River in the Congo, became extremely dangerous when the company's campsite was invaded by giant man-eating ants. They were forced to change their location. Then, several weeks later, Kate fell sick, along with most of the technical crew, and it was finally decided to return to London and complete filming there.

Bogie had this to say about his co-star: "She talks a blue streak. We listened for the first couple of days when she hit Africa and then began asking ourselves 'How affected can you be in the middle of Africa?' She used to say that everything was 'divine.' The Goddam stinking natives were 'divine.' 'Oh, what a *divine* native!' she'd say. 'Oh, what a *divine* pile of manure!' You had to ask yourself, 'Is this really the dame or is this something left over from *Woman of the Year?*'

"She does pretty much as she Goddam pleases. She came in lugging a full-length mirror and a flock of toothbrushes. She brushed her teeth all the time and she habitually takes four or five baths a day. She talks at you as though you were a microphone. I guess she was nervous, though, and scared of John and me. She lectured the hell out of us on temperance and the evils of drinking.

"She's actually kind of sweet and loveable, though, and she's absolutely honest and absolutely fair about her work.

Making her London stage debut as Shaw's heroine in *The Millionairess*

21

Arriving in London with
Lauren Bacall and Humphrey Bogart
after location-shooting
The African Queen

None of this late on the set or demanding closeups or any of that kind of thing. She doesn't give a damn how she looks. She doesn't have to be waited on, either. You never pull up a chair for Kate. You tell her 'Kate, pull me up a chair willya and while you're at it get one for yourself.' I don't think she tries to be a character. I think she is one."

The African Queen became one of the all-time great films, a true tour-de-force for Bogie and Kate—the more unkempt she became, the less uncouth he became. Quite naturally, it brought in Academy Award nominations for both the stars and director Huston. Bogie deservedly won the Best Actor award for a fine performance.

After her return to the States, the *Adam's Rib* team of Hepburn, Tracy, Gordon, Kanin, and Cukor assembled to start filming another of those original screenplays which had been written especially for Kate and Spencer. *Pat and Mike,* their seventh film together, gave her the opportunity to display her many athletic skills—golf, tennis, basketball, and so on.

Once shooting was completed, Kate left for London to star in the first professional production ever done of George Bernard Shaw's minor play *The Millionairess.* Shaw wrote the play in 1935 for Edith Evans, but it was never produced on a major scale. Her co-stars were Robert Helpmann and Cyril Ritchard. The director was Michael Benthall, who had performed similar chores for her production of *As You Like It.* This marked Kate's London debut and, opening at the same time as *The African Queen,* it caused quite a stir with British audiences.

W. A. Darlington, of the *London Daily Telegraph,* wrote for *The New York Times:* "Other actresses from America have had great triumphs, swept to success by some play which has hit the public taste. But nobody else that I can remember has appeared in a play for which hardly any critic has a good word and by sheer personal vitality has bludgeoned her way to success. Critical opinion has never been more unanimous."

Hepburn didn't believe *The Millionairess* would do well in America, but the producers nonetheless closed in London on September 20. It opened on Broadway October 10 for a 10-week limited engagement at the Shubert Theatre, where she had stayed so long as Tracy Lord. *The Millionairess* closed December 27, 1952.

While in London, Hepburn told a British reporter: "Movies are a cinch. I always said so, and still believe it. You have no deadline, you can always do it over again, and there are no people to throw rotten eggs at you. Now, you must get this clear. Movie-making is an honorable business. People work their guts out at it. I admire a lot of foreign movies, many of them are brilliant, but I'm not going to be made to say anything snobbish about American movies."

Her contract with MGM had terminated with *Pat and Mike,* and now Kate was free to do just those properties (stage and screen) which interested her most. Taking the time to do just as she pleased, Hepburn appeared neither on the stage nor the screen during 1953. However, in the summer of 1954 she went to Venice for director David Lean to make the film version of Arthur Laurents' play *The Time of the Cuckoo.*

The scenario, by David Lean and H. E. Bates, removed the severity of the play, glamorized the two principals, and was renamed *Summertime.* Jack Hildyard's superb color photography was one outstanding reason for the film's enormous popularity when it was released in the summer of 1955. Hepburn, who added her own special magic to the character of spinster Jane Hudson, was directly responsible for Rossano Brazzi's co-star billing.

By the time *Summertime* was being seen by world audiences, Kate and Robert Helpmann were touring Australia with the Old Vic Company in three Shakespearean offerings. She appeared as Katharina in *The Taming of the Shrew,* as Isabella in *Measure for Measure,* and as Portia in *The Merchant of Venice.*

Returning to England after the highly successful tour Down Under, the pair got involved with Bob Hope in Ben Hecht's "original" script *Not for Money,* which bore more than a slight resemblance to *Ninotchka.* According to legend, Hecht had written it with Hepburn in mind and Hope happened on a copy. He immediately expressed a desire

to play the A.A.F. officer, whose assignment it is to convert a Russian aviatrix from communism to the ways of the West. Hepburn thought the offbeat casting would be unique and was delighted at the prospect of working with Bob Hope. Filmed in VistaVision and Technicolor at the Pinewood Studios in London, it was produced by Betty E. Box and directed by Ralph Thomas.

Script problems arose almost from the start and, after the first of the "rushes," Hope's entourage of gag writers were omnipresent on the set, continually revamping his dialogue and bits of business. Hecht finally pulled out, insisting that his name be removed from the credits. By the time *The Iron Petticoat,* as it was now called, had been finally edited, a good deal of Kate's footage had disappeared and what began as "unique casting" turned into a unique disaster. It was first shown at the Berlin Film Festival in mid-1956, and released in England shortly thereafter. In the United States, it was released in December 1956 (on the West Coast) and in April 1957 (on the East Coast).

John Huston sought Kate for his projected film entitled *Miss Hargreaves,* based on a British novel about a seventy-year-old woman who scandalizes a cathedral town, but nothing ever came of it.

In June 1956, however, Kate was at Paramount, working on N. Richard Nash's *The Rainmaker* for producer Hal B.

With Alfred Drake at the American Shakespeare Festival Theatre, Stratford, Connecticut

Wallis. Her co-star was Burt Lancaster, and it was the first film for stage director Joseph Anthony. Kate offered a sensitive portrait of Lizzie Curry and, as the smooth-talking Starbuck, Burt Lancaster gave a fine performance.

She then made a film version of *Desk Set*, a play that had featured Shirley Booth on the stage. This Twentieth Century-Fox venture reteamed Kate and Tracy for the eighth time (their first together in color and CinemaScope) and was little more than William Marchant's trifle for the stage had been. What little interest there was stemmed from the playing of Tracy and Hepburn. Tracy's part for the film was built up and thus the love interest shifted his way.

The summer of 1957 took Hepburn to her native Connecticut as "Guest Star" of the American Shakespeare Festival at Stratford, for the salary of $350 per week. She played Portia in *The Merchant of Venice* and Beatrice in *Much Ado About Nothing*. Her "Guest Co-Star" was Alfred Drake. About *Much Ado About Nothing* Brooks Atkinson in *The New York Times* said: "The scenes between Miss Hepburn and Mr. Drake are thoroughly enjoyable, their respective senses of humor being pleasantly blended." Of *The Merchant of Venice*, Tom Donnelly in the *New York World-Telegram* remarked: "If Miss Hepburn is an ideal heroine of romance in the Belmont scenes, she falls short in the passages demanding depth of feeling, or unfettered eloquence. She is like a talented singer who can go three-quarters of the distance, captivatingly, and then must fail for want of breath at the climax of the aria. She makes an intelligent and gallant attempt to take the curse off the looming inevitability of the 'quality of mercy' speech by delivering it softly and simply, to Shylock, as a direct personal appeal, but, unhappily she loses control of it: it vanishes."

Hepburn went back to England in 1959 for director Joseph L. Mankiewicz (who had *produced* her *Woman of the Year*) in Sam Spiegel's production of *Suddenly, Last Summer*, to be released by Columbia. The Gore Vidal screenplay was adapted from the short play by Tennessee Williams, and Jack Hildyard (*Summertime*) was once again the photographer. This film, released in December 1959 for Academy Award consideration, caused a sensation. The notoriety which ensued marked it as one of the major films directly responsible for the changing trends in filmmaking, as well as for the various codes that developed during the 1960s. Both Hepburn and Elizabeth Taylor were nominated for Academy Awards as Best Actress, but neither won.

The American Shakespeare Festival at Stratford invited Kate back as "Guest Star" for its 1960 season and she accepted. She looked lovely as Viola in *Twelfth Night* but wasn't particularly effective—in what one would assume to be a perfect role for her. She then played Cleopatra to "Guest Co-Star" Robert Ryan's Marc Antony in *Antony and Cleopatra*, which was much better received. Said Miles Kastendieck in the *New York Journal-American*: "Cleopatra

may have died for her Antony but she also died that Caesar could not take her back to Rome. Thus the character of Cleopatra is more shrewdly underlined. Because Miss Hepburn caught that inflection, she gave one of her fine stage performances. It was when she played the role straight, grew fiery, and waxed furious that she was at her best. A touch of archness crept into the more romantic moments; both in voice and manner she became stagey. Mr. Ryan gave substance to his portrayal of Antony. This was a convincing characterization and served well to unify the story."

Tennessee Williams originally adapted his short story *Night of the Iguana* as a play for Hepburn, as a tribute to her performance in *Suddenly, Last Summer*, but she was tied up at Stratford when the play was ready for testing. Ironically enough, Hepburn was then absent from the stage for nine years.

Hepburn was next offered the plum role of dope-ravaged Mary Tyrone in the film version of Eugene O'Neill's *Long Day's Journey into Night* for independent producers Ely Landau and Jack J. Dreyfus, Jr. Sidney Lumet directed on a tight five-week schedule, using an old house on City Island in New York's Bronx, with interiors filmed at Production Center Studios on West 26th Street. When Kate asked Landau who did the screenplay, he replied "Eugene O'Neill." What better inducement could any actress have.

Taking a salary of $25,000 (and a percentage of the take, if any), the principals (Hepburn, Ralph Richardson, Jason Robards, Jr., and Dean Stockwell) rehearsed for three weeks before a camera turned. Lumet shot the *entire* play in sequence, instead of back and forth, the usual movie making practice. Hepburn remarked during rehearsals: "The more you work with this play, the better a writer he becomes. The play is so brilliant. I wanted to play it really without acting it. I did not want to be fascinating or colorful or exciting. I just wanted to keep out of its way and let it happen."

Kate worked long and hard on this role, and must have been justly proud of her contribution. O'Neill gave his actors long monologues, true tests of an actor's abilities. Hepburn's infinitely varied portrayal earned her another Academy Award nomination (her ninth) and won her her second Best Actress accolade from the Cannes Film Festival (her first had been *Little Women* in 1934).

Soon after *Long Day's Journey into Night* had been released, on November 20, 1962, her father, Dr. Hepburn, died at age eighty-two. (Her mother had passed away on March 17, 1951.) The following summer Tracy suffered a "congested lung condition" while picnicking with Kate. His brother Carroll and his sister-in-law accompanied Tracy to the hospital after Kate had called for a local emergency fire unit.

During the next five years, Hepburn left her career totally inactive and spent much of her time with ailing Spencer Tracy. Although she continually refused to consider any scripts whatsoever, she was constantly barraged with a flow of scripts. John Huston wanted her to co-star with Pat O'Brien in *The Lonely Passion of Judith Hearn,* from Brian Moore's novel. She was to do the movie version of a French play Ruth Gordon had adapted for Broadway, called *A Very Rich Woman.* Later, she was to co-star with Shirley Mac-Laine in a film version of the famed Broadway musical *Bloomer Girl,* but she withdrew because of Tracy's continued ill health.

At David O. Selznick's rites, Kate took part in the ceremony, along with Cary Grant and Joseph Cotten. George Cukor read a eulogy written by Truman Capote and Miss Hepburn gave a reading of Kipling's poem "If" to the gathering at Forest Lawn Cemetery.

In 1965 Hepburn turned writer, briefly, with an article "The Right of Privacy," which appeared in the *Virginia Law Weekly,* published by the University of Virginia.

Both public and press feel that they have an absolute right of access to the most intimate details of your life—and by life you must read largely sex life.

It was producer-director Stanley Kramer who convinced Hepburn to return—with Tracy—in William Rose's original screenplay *Guess Who's Coming to Dinner.* This was, indeed, big news, since Tracy's illness was a known fact and Kate's inactivity for five years because of that illness made many doubt if they would ever again see this brilliant team at work.

The ninth Tracy-Hepburn film, labeled a "social comedy" (whatever that means), cast them as liberal parents of a young girl who falls in love with—and wishes to marry—a fortyish

Discussing her filmed segment for the televised Oscar show, with the show's director Richard Dunlap

Negro doctor. The doctor was played with his accustomed polish by Sidney Poitier and the daughter was performed by Kate's niece, Katharine Houghton (her sister Marion's daughter).

Although the script sidestepped many pertinent issues, tending more toward soap opera than serious comedy-drama, *Guess Who's Coming to Dinner* was still the first big film from a major studio to deal with the question of interracial marriage. Acting honors belonged to Tracy but this was, sadly, his farewell. He died just a few weeks after its completion, on June 10, 1967.

The public wondered if Kate would withdraw from her career again, as she had done during Tracy's long illness, but was delighted when the lady began working on Joseph E. Levine's production of *The Lion in Winter.* Peter O'Toole played Henry II and Kate his burnished wife, Eleanor of Aquitaine. James Goldman's 1966 play offered her a marvelous role and she met the challenge with a finely shaded performance charged with fire and music. Anthony Harvey, the young British director of LeRoi Jones's *Dutchman,* began filming at interiors at Dublin's Ardmore Studios, moving to various location sites throughout the south of France.

Hepburn and O'Toole insisted on ten days' rehearsals before shooting began, and the results proved their worth. During the filming, Kate agreed to film a special segment to be used on the annual Academy Awards television presentations reviewing the four decades of the Oscar. In her costume of Eleanor of Aquitaine, Hepburn talked briefly about the first ten years and was followed, in turn, by Olivia de Havilland, Grace Kelly, and Anne Bancroft. This film clip was not only Hepburn's first venture into the media of television but marked her initial participation in an Awards ceremony. (For the record, Kate had previously narrated—without benefit of billing—a television film made on the Connecticut River for her brother-in-law Ellsworth Grant).

Both Tracy and Hepburn, as well as director Kramer, were nominated for Academy Awards for *Guess Who's Coming to Dinner.* The surprise came when the Academy members voted Kate her second Oscar. It was politely felt that this was really a Tracy-Hepburn presentation, rather than one for her performance alone. Her close friend George Cukor accepted for her.

Hepburn was filming *The Madwoman of Chaillot* in Nice when word reached her that she had won. She told the press at that time, "I am enormously touched." Later, in a cabled message to the Academy, she elaborated. "It was delightful, a total surprise. I feel I have received a big, affectionate hug from my fellow workers. They don't usually give these things to the old girls, you know."

John Huston had signed Kate in the fall of 1967 for Giraudoux's comedy-fantasy *The Madwoman of Chaillot* and, while she was in Dublin with *The Lion in Winter,* he began preparatory work in France. He began to assemble a large international cast, which included Irene Papas, Simone Signoret, and Catherine Allegret, all of whom were later replaced. In fact, Huston himself withdrew from the *Madwoman* project before Hepburn even stepped before a camera, due to differences of opinion on the "modernization" of the timeless fantasy, which Maurice Valency had adapted into English in 1948 for Martita Hunt.

No fewer than fourteen international names appeared with Hepburn in *The Madwoman of Chaillot* in mid-1968, under the direction of British director Bryan Forbes.

When released, *The Lion in Winter* was generally praised by critics and public alike. The acting was uniformly top-notch and Hepburn was nominated for her performance of Eleanor of Aquitaine, but no one in their right mind thought she would win it.

"It's a tie!" announced Ingrid Bergman—in a stunned, but excited, voice—on the night of April 14, 1969. Katharine Hepburn had split the Academy's 3,030 membership right down the middle to win her third Oscar (sharing the evening's honor with Barbra Streisand for *Funny Girl*). Miss Bergman later said, "I couldn't believe what I saw!"

Hepburn now holds the unofficial title of "Oscar Champion": the only star to be nominated 11 times (breaking a long-time record held by Bette Davis); the only star to win three Oscars in the major acting category; the third winner to collect the top prize in two consecutive years; and one of the few stars to win an Academy Award on first nomination (*Morning Glory*, 1933). In addition, this was only the second time in Academy history that a tie split the Academy vote.

After all this record-breaking activity, *The Madwoman of Chaillot* was released to lukewarm reviews from the first-string critics and good reviews from other reviewers. As always, however, the Hepburn name meant box office. Most felt that Kate's Madwoman wasn't really mad at all—only kind and warm and sentimental. Acting on a high plane was turned in by Danny Kaye, in the difficult role of the Ragpicker. It was Kate's eighth color film—out of thirty-seven—spanning thirty-seven years.

Hepburn then returned to Broadway, after an absence of seventeen years, to appear as Gabrielle (Coco) Chanel, the Queen of Paris Fashion, in Frederick Brisson's production of Alan Jay Lerner and Andre Previn's *Coco*. Said Clive Barnes in his *New York Times* review: "Miss Hepburn is a blithe spirit, a vital flame. Her voice is like vinegar on sandpaper; her presence is a blessing. She growls out the most ordinary lines as if they were pearls of great price, gems of wit, nuggets of wisdom. She grins and she is enchanting. She prowls gloweringly down to the footlights, mutters a word for ordure in an idiomatically terse fashion, and remains devastatingly charming.

"This is not acting in any of the accustomed fashions of acting. Her singing voice is unique—a neat mixture of

At the recording session of her Broadway hit *Coco* for Paramount Records

faith, love and laryngitis, unforgettable, unbelievable and delightful. Dear Miss Hepburn—perhaps they should have made a musical of your life rather than the dress designer. They say some beauty is ageless—yours is timeless."

Her first musical role proved a personal triumph and once again she was directed by Michael Benthall, who had guided her years earlier through Shakespeare and Shaw and her Australian tour of 1955. She became a recording artist when Paramount Records released the *Coco* album with Kate singing "The World Belongs to the Young," "Mademoiselle Cliché de Paris," "On the Corner of the Rue Cambon," "The Money Rings Out Like Freedom," "Coco," "Orbach's, Bloomingdale's, Best and Saks," and "Always Mademoiselle."

Nominated for the annual stage Tony (the Antoinette

Parry Award) Kate did a filmed clip of the number "Always Mademoiselle" on the televised proceedings—her second official appearance in that media, albeit on film, but she didn't win. Her close friend, Lauren Bacall, won the Best Musical Actress award for her performance in *Applause*, the dreary musical version of the noted film *All About Eve*.

If Katharine Hepburn's future is as unpredictable—and as rewarding—as her past achievements, large and small, few would venture to project what will appear next on her agenda.

Projections include the film of Josef Shaftel's *The Trojan Women* for director Michael Cacoyannis with co-stars Vanessa Redgrave and Irene Papas. She is slated to film *Coco* for Paramount Pictures and has indicated she may try her hand at film direction (and why not, she has done everything

else). She is most interested in Irene Mayer Selznick's production of *Martha*, an adaptation of Margery Sharp's 1964 novel *Martha, Eric and George* and its 1966 sequel *Martha in Paris*, which concerns the unusual career of a gifted English girl who goes to Paris to become a painter. Said Hepburn about this project: "The fact is I've always been interested in directing—Louis B. Mayer quite seriously asked me to direct films twenty years ago, as did John Ford—but I've never had a real opportunity to do so before this. *Martha*, I feel, is my first real chance, and I think I can do a damn good job of it."

FUTURE INDEFINITE

A musical-comedy star in the
Broadway production *Coco*

The Face

PORTRAITS FROM YESTERDAY TO
TODAY

*"I'm a personality as well
as an actress. Show me an
actress who isn't a personality,
and you'll show me a woman who
isn't a star. A star's
personality has to shine
through."*

30

36

Filmography

With Billie Burke

With John Barrymore

With David Manners

A Bill of Divorcement

AN RKO RADIO PICTURE   1932

CAST

Hillary Fairfield   John Barrymore
Margaret Fairfield   Billie Burke
Sydney Fairfield   Katharine Hepburn
Kit Humphrey   David Manners
Doctor Alliot   Henry Stephenson
Gray Meredith   Paul Cavanagh
Aunt Hester   Elizabeth Patterson
Bassett   Gayle Evers
Party Guest   Julie Haydon

CREDITS

Director   George Cukor
Executive Producer   David O. Selznick
Scenarists   Howard Estabrook, Harry Wagstaff Gribble
Based on the Play by   Clemence Dane
Photographer   Sid Hickox
Art Director   Carroll Clark
Editor   Arthur Roberts
Sound Recorder   George Ellis
Music Director   Max Steiner
Piano Concerto By   W. Franke Harling
Costumer   Josette De Lima
Makeup Artist   Mel Burns
Assistant Director   Dewey Starkey
Technical Director   Marion Balderstone

With John Barrymore

With Henry Stephenson and John Barrymore

With Elizabeth Patterson, Paul Cavanagh,
Julie Haydon, Billie Burke and David Manners

With David Manners

SYNOPSIS

Feeling himself well, shellshock victim Hillary Fairfield, whose streak of latent insanity was brought out by the strain of the World War, escapes from an asylum. He returns home on the very day his wife Margaret, who has since divorced him, plans to marry a healthy and sane man.

At first, Hillary is angered by this news, but he finally realizes that his love for his wife is great enough for him to give her up to this man. Letting her go, he remains with Sydney, his daughter. Sydney's is the real tragedy. When she learns of the insanity in her father's family and considers the possibility that if she marries her own children may be so afflicted, she sends her fiancé away and remains to look after her mentally tortured father.

CRITICS' CIRCLE

"Katharine Hepburn, who makes her screen debut here and who was last seen in New York on the stage in *A Warrior's Husband,* gives a beautiful performance as the luckless daughter."

—WILLIAM BOEHNEL
New York World-Telegram

"Mr. Barrymore, showing surprising restraint when you remember that he is a Barrymore playing a madman, is splendid as the escaped father, providing one of his finest cinema characterizations. Miss Billie Burke is youthful, radiant and moving in the brief role of the wife. The most effective portrayal of the film, however, is provided by Miss Katharine Hepburn, who is both beautiful and distinguished as the daughter, and seems definitely established for an important cinema career."

—RICHARD WATTS, JR.
The New York Herald Tribune

"The entire production maintains a high standard of excellence, and George Cukor is at his best in its direction."

—REGINA CREWE
New York American

"I liked the acting throughout; it's all very temperate and reasonable. Katharine Hepburn suggests the proper intensity without any undue trumpetings and alarums, and, with her general appearance of half Botticelli page and half bobbed-hair bandit, might well be the daughter of one of the old English families."

—*The New Yorker*

"Miss Hepburn has a harsh, grating voice, and there is a lot for her to learn, but she acts with sincerity and intelligence, and when she and Mr. Barrymore are alone together a dim reflection of the play's quality shines through the screen."

—*The (London) Times*

"The film is intelligent, moving, and capably acted."

—ALEXANDER BAKSHY
The Nation

"She (Hepburn) has dignity and an instinct for underplaying an emotion which are as valuable as they are, in a film actress, novel. In her ability and good looks, Miss Hepburn has the makings of a star. All she needs is a little more familiarity with the microphone, some worthy roles and a firm determination not to let her producers exploit her as a second Garbo, a second Joan Crawford, or a second anything."

—THORNTON DELEHANTY
New York Post

NOTES

Hepburn was an absorbing and touching Sydney Fairfield. Her strict determination to succeed in this difficult part overruled her basic screen inexperience. A decade earlier, the same role skyrocketed Katharine Cornell to fame on the stage and, in 1940, RKO thought it a perfect vehicle for their latest English import, Maureen O'Hara. Said *Time* magazine of the remake: "Lacking Cinemactress Hepburn's virile stride, Cinemactress Maureen O'Hara also lacks some of the neural stridency that made Hepburn effective. But Maureen O'Hara is just as resolutely eugenic and more tender."

Director Cukor later said: "Not the least of her gifts is intelligence. In *A Bill of Divorcement* she was most uncertain of screen technique. But she let no one know it. She watched herself carefully, felt her way cautiously and with that picture emerged as a top-rank film star, apparently in one easy lesson . . . but it was hard work for her."

Said Hepburn: "I learned a tremendous lot from Barrymore. One thing in particular has been invaluable to me—when you're in the same cast with people who know nothing about acting, you can't criticize them, because they go to pieces. He never criticized me. He just shoved me into what I ought to do before the camera. He taught me all that he could pour into one greenhorn in that short time."

With Billie Burke

With John Barrymore and Elizabeth Patterson

41

Christopher Strong

AN RKO RADIO PICTURE 1933

CAST

Lady Cynthia Darrington   Katharine Hepburn
Sir Christopher Strong   Colin Clive
Lady Elaine Strong   Billie Burke
Monica Strong   Helen Chandler
Harry Rawlinson   Ralph Forbes
Carrie Valentin   Irene Browne
Carlo   Jack La Rue
Bryce Mercer   Desmond Roberts
Bradford, the Maid   Gwendolyn Logan
Fortune Teller   Agostino Borgato
Girl at Party   Margaret Lindsay
Mechanic   Donald Stewart
Second Maid   Zena Savina

CREDITS

Director   Dorothy Arzner
Producer   David O. Selznick
Associate Producer   Pandro S. Berman
Scenarist   Zoë Akins
Based on the Novel by   Gilbert Frankau
Photographer   Bert Glennon
Art Director   Van Nest Polglase
Associate Art Director   Charles Kirk
Editor   Arthur Roberts

Sound Recorder   Hugh McDowell
Musical Score   Max Steiner
Costumer   Howard Greer
Makeup Artist   Mel Burns
Special Effects   Vernon Walker
Transitions   Slavko Vorkapich
Assistant Directors   Edward Killy, Tommy Atkins

SYNOPSIS

As the chance result of a "treasure hunt," a young woman, who is still a virgin, and a married man, who has always been a faithful husband, are introduced. She is Lady Cynthia Darrington, an enthusiastic aviatrix with no time for love in her young life. He is Sir Christopher Strong, a good husband and the father of a marriageable daughter, whose life has been completely absorbed in his political career. They are wracked by a love that neither can deny, and their lives become hopelessly entwined. Rather than hurt his wife, however, they decide to separate. Cynthia goes on an around-the-world trip while he goes to New York City on government business. They meet again in the city, rekindling the flame of their romance.

Cynthia promises Sir Christopher that after the world flight she will abandon her trips. However, soon after, learning that she is pregnant, she accepts a challenge to attempt to break the world altitude record. Her aircraft soars to 30,000 feet, where she takes off her oxygen mask and loses control of the plane.

With Colin Clive

CRITICS' CIRCLE

"In her first picture, *A Bill of Divorcement,* I did not care for Miss Hepburn at all. Her personality then struck me as hard, unsympathetic and shrewish. But by this, her second attempt, she has impressed me tremendously. Her sureness of touch, immense charm, purpose of character, win her way into all hearts. . . . This is a picture well worth a visit."
—*The (London) Times*

"She (Hepburn) fascinates by her strange beauty and inescapable magnetism, by her verve, her harshness and her tenderness, with the enormous advantage of making every mood reflect a mental state of utter sincerity and conviction. Easily the most important newcomer, although Mae West is the supreme box-office draw of the moment, Miss Hepburn is provocative and distinctive and her vibrant intelligence entitles her to the best and most carefully chosen story material."

—Herbert Lusk
Los Angeles Times

"That troubled, masque-like face, the high, strident, raucous, rasping voice, the straight, broad-shouldered boyish figure—perhaps they all may grate upon you, but they

With Billie Burke,
Helen Chandler and Ralph Forbes

43

compel attention, and they fascinate an audience. She is a distinct, definite, positive personality—the first since Garbo."

—REGINA CREWE
New York American

"Miss Hepburn is a fine actress, with rare technical equipment, a commanding personality and a golden voice, are facts which her performance leaves resolutely unverified. She has youth and an attractive appearance, but under the strained artificiality of her acting there is, unfortunately, no glimmer of the promise she showed in the dim dark past of several months ago when she made her screen debut in *A Bill of Divorcement.*"

—THORNTON DELEHANTY
New York Post

"Playing with a sort of harsh, gruff directness that manages to seem both gallant and tender, Miss Hepburn offers a characterization of a puzzled, grudging sentimentalist that combines emotional effectiveness with a certain air of level-headed sanity. . . . Thereupon *Christopher Strong*, for all its lack of dramatic power, becomes something more than the customary emotional orgy."

—RICHARD WATTS, JR.
New York Herald Tribune

"I suppose we are expecting more of Miss Hepburn than we are of any other newcomer in the movies today. There is a vitality, a special kind of beauty, in her appearance and her behavior on the screen; or, rather, there was in *A Bill of Divorcement.*"

—*The New Yorker*

"There is something finely natural about the acting of both Miss Hepburn and Mr. Clive. Miss Hepburn is thorough and believable and sometimes fascinatingly beautiful, especially when Lady Cynthia and Sir Christopher are in a motor boat which they have permitted to drift."

—MORDAUNT HALL
The New York Times

"Wearing aeronautical leggings, a white evening dress or a costume which, she says, makes her look like a moth, sleek Katharine Hepburn gives a performance in *Christopher Strong* which frequently brings Frankau's drawing room tragedy sharply to life."

—*Time*

"*Christopher Strong* . . . securely establishes the Katharine Hepburn of *A Bill of Divorcement* as an actress to be reckoned with. She has definitely *arrived*. A slim, gaunt-featured nymph, this actress, with her sharp, pleasantly unpleasant voice, and a penchant for the bizarre in outfits. True star material, she dominates each scene in which she figures."

—PHILIP K. SCHEUER
Los Angeles Times

NOTES

Under the astute direction of Dorothy Arzner, one of the few successful female directors in films, Hepburn began to develop her screen image as the independent woman in the twentieth century. She was persuasive and vivid as the career-minded aviatrix. Colin Clive was ideal as the stuffy happily married man who falls in love with her, and the supporting cast was also most effective.

Christopher Strong, whose working title was *A Great Desire*, was Hepburn's first starring film, but the story failed to generate the box-office business RKO had expected. It was a strange tale, which most critics found fascinating, but the public, obviously expecting another Sydney Fairfield did not warm up to Lady Cynthia Darrington.

On the set with Desmond Roberts,
Helen Chandler, Jack LaRue,
Irene Browne, director
Dorothy Arzner and Colin Clive

With Donald Stewart
and Desmond Roberts

With Helen Chandler

Morning Glory

AN RKO RADIO PICTURE   1933

CAST

Eva Lovelace   Katharine Hepburn
Joseph Sheridan   Douglas Fairbanks, Jr.
Louis Easton   Adolphe Menjou
Rita Vernon   Mary Duncan
Robert Harley Hedges   C. Aubrey Smith
Pepe Velez, the Gigolo   Don Alvarado
Will Seymour   Fred Santley
Henry Lawrence   Richard Carle
Charles Van Dusen   Tyler Brooke
Gwendolyn Hall   Geneva Mitchell
Nellie Navarre   Helen Ware
Maid   Theresa Harris

CREDITS

Director   Lowell Sherman
Producer   Pandro S. Berman
Executive Producer   Merian C. Cooper
Scenarist   Howard J. Green
Based on the Play by   Zoë Akins
Photographer   Bert Glennon
Art Director   Van Nest Polglase
Associate Art Director   Charles Kirk
Editor   George Nicholls, Jr.
Sound Recorder   Hugh McDowell
Musical Score   Max Steiner
Costumer   Walter Plunkett
Makeup Artist   Mel Burns
Assistant Director   Tommy Atkins

SYNOPSIS

Fresh from a small town in Vermont, stagestruck Eva Lovelace finds New York City a hard, unsympathetic place to find work as an actress. She is helped along by veteran actor Robert Harley Hedges, who gives her acting pointers and takes her to her first Broadway party, being given for Rita Vernon, a highly successful—and temperamental—actress. The famished newcomer gets drunk on champagne and causes a sensation by spouting Hamlet's famous soliloquy and the balcony scene from *Romeo and Juliet*.

Eva soon has an affair with Louis Easton, a theatrical manager, and later falls in love with Joseph Sheridan, a young playwright. The temperamental Miss Vernon, meanwhile, walks out of Sheridan's new play on opening night. Eva, up on the part, goes on and is an overnight sensation.

With Adolphe Menjou

CRITICS' CIRCLE

"In the present role, Miss Hepburn successfully gets away from that somewhat hard type that in *Christopher Strong* threatened to become a habit. The role of Eva Lovelace gives her plenty of opportunities to display her more mellow side, which is something for which to be exceedingly grateful."

—CHARLES PARKER HAMMOND
New York Post

"Miss Hepburn is supremely good, vivid, forthright, zestful and capable beyond praise."

—WILLIAM BOEHNEL
New York World-Telegram

With C. Aubrey Smith

"More an actress, less a 'personality,' Katharine Hepburn gives reason for rejoicing among the faithful, and cause for defection from the ranks of the skeptics, with a sure, skillful, sound performance."

—REGINA CREWE
New York American

"Miss Hepburn lives the part of the stage-struck girl, consequently her characterization automatically becomes perfect—a perfect blending of art, soul and intellect."

—*Hollywood Spectator*

"Lowell Sherman has done with Miss Hepburn much what he did with Mae West in *She Done Him Wrong*. He has transfigured her. Her *A Bill of Divorcement* and *Christopher Strong*, were but pale preludes to this. Sherman knows how to direct women and he knows life backstage—and in *Morning Glory* he deals with both."

—PHILIP K. SCHEUER
Los Angeles Times

"The striking and inescapably fascinating Miss Hepburn proves pretty conclusively in her new film that her fame in the cinema is not a mere flash across the screen. . . . It

With Douglas Fairbanks, Jr.

is, as I may have hinted, Miss Hepburn who makes *Morning Glory* something to be seen."

—RICHARD WATTS, JR.
New York Herald Tribune

"Miss Hepburn admirably mingles intellectual austerity with physical gaucherie, and, through all the vicissitudes of Eva's career, her grip on the part never falters, but those who most admire the perfection of her technique must have wished she could, for a few minutes, be free of the depressing limitations of a second-rate story."

—*The (London) Times*

"An ingratiating portrayal by Miss Hepburn and excellent acting by others in the cast, a fresh and imaginative development of most of its episodes, well-written dialogue and a generally handsome production."

—MORDAUNT HALL
The New York Times

"From this immemorial fairy tale, the delicate, muscled face of Heroine Hepburn shines out like a face on a coin. Of the brash little provincial she makes a strangely distinguished character, a little mad from hunger and dreams, absurdly audacious and trusting. Since *Christopher Strong*, she has toned down her strident voice, taken off some of her angular swank in gesture and strut, found other ways to register emotion than by dilating her nostrils. In *Morning Glory* she convinced Manhattan audiences that the playwright had good reason to feel she had the makings of a great actress. Flawless with women, Director Lowell Sherman tried to make all the men act in his own twitching style."

—*Time*

NOTES

Hepburn's third picture gave her a role that so resembled her own theatrical background and experiences that she gave the role of Eva Lovelace more depth and meaning than the script deserved. Howard J. Green's adaptation of Zoë Akins' play was superficially theatrical, as was the direction of Lowell Sherman.

The only other member of the cast who managed to rise above the material was Adolphe Menjou, who was excellent as the suave Broadway producer. Douglas Fairbanks, Jr., was appealing as the young playwright and Mary Duncan was allowed to overact the showy part of Rita Vernon.

Viewed today, the film's script limitations are even more apparent and, were it not for Hepburn's performance, the film would be almost unbearable to sit through. She won the Academy Award as Best Actress of the 1932–33 season, one of the few players to win on a first nomination. MORNING GLORY was remade in 1958 as STAGE STRUCK with Susan Strasberg and Henry Fonda, but did not fare much better.

With Adolphe Menjou

With Douglas Fairbanks, Jr.

With Adolphe Menjou

With Mary Duncan

Little Women

AN RKO RADIO PICTURE 1933

CAST

Jo   Katharine Hepburn
Amy   Joan Bennett
Professor Bhaer   Paul Lukas
Aunt March   Edna May Oliver
Beth   Jean Parker
Meg   Frances Dee
Mr. Laurence   Henry Stephenson
Laurie   Douglass Montgomery
Brooke   John Davis Lodge
Marmee   Spring Byington
Mr. March   Samuel S. Hinds
Hannah   Mabel Colcord
Mrs. Kirke   Marion Ballou
Mamie   Nydia Westman
Doctor Bangs   Harry Beresford
Flo King   Marina Schubert
Girls at Boarding House   Dorothy Gray, June Filmer
Mr. Davis   Olin Howland

CREDITS

Director   George Cukor
Executive Producer   Merian C. Cooper
Associate Producer   Kenneth MacGowan
Scenarists   Sarah Y. Mason, Victor Heerman
Based on the Novel by   Louisa May Alcott
Photographer   Henry Gerrard
Art Director   Van Nest Polglase
Set Decorator   Hobe Erwin
Editor   Jack Kitchin

With Henry Stephenson
and Douglass Montgomery

Sound Recorder Frank H. Harris
Musical Score Max Steiner
Costumer Walter Plunkett
Makeup Artist Mel Burns
Special Effects Harry Redmond
Assistant Director Edward Killy
Production Associate Del Andrews

SYNOPSIS

The four March sisters grow up in Concord, Massachusetts, during the difficult days of the Civil War. Their father is away fighting and their beloved mother, Marmee, holds the family together as best she can. Jo, the impulsive and headstrong daughter, wants desperately to write, but cannot break away from her sisters. When her sister Meg marries Mr. Brooke, despite her pleadings, Jo bitterly refuses a marriage proposal from her sweetheart, Laurie, and leaves for New York City, where she later meets Fritz Bhaer, a scholarly professor.

Under his influence, she loses her bitterness and grasps the true spirit of a writer. In Jo's absence, meanwhile, Laurie finds happiness with another sister, Amy, and they are married. Jo leaves New York for home to be with the fourth sister, Beth, who is dying. After Beth's death, Mr. March returns from the war and the March family is together again, including Fritz Bhaer, who has found that he cannot live without his dear Jo.

CRITICS' CIRCLE

"As an antidote to the febrile dramas of the underworld and backstage musical spectacles, *Little Women* comes as a reminder that emotions and vitality and truth can be evoked from lavender and lace as well as from machine guns and precision dances. . . . It is a tribute to those who shared in bringing it to the screen that there is no betrayal either of the spirit or feeling of the original. The hoydenish Jo is capitally performed by Katharine Hepburn; Joan Bennett is excellent as Amy, as are Frances Dee and Jean Parker as Meg and Beth. Also, George Cukor and the producers deserve praise for a production that has been carried out with taste as well as skill."

—THORNTON DELEHANTY
New York Post

"Miss Hepburn steps up the ladder, if anything, by her interpretation of Jo. She talks rather fast at times, but one feels that Jo did, and after all one does not wish to listen to dialogue in which every word is weighed when the part is acted by a Katharine Hepburn."

—MORDAUNT HALL
The New York Times

"It is, of course, the mood which is the important part of the work, and it is the unashamed straightforwardness of

51

With Jean Parker,
Frances Dee, Spring Byington
and Joan Bennett

With Paul Lukas

With Edna May Oliver

With Jean Parker

the writing, the unpatronizing shrewdness of George Cukor's direction and, above all, Miss Hepburn's beautiful playing which make *Little Women* an exquisite screen drama. It is one of the great feats of Mr. Cukor that he manages a screen play in which everyone is supposed to be charming all over the place and makes it all seem true."

—RICHARD WATTS, JR.
New York Herald Tribune

"That *Little Women* attains so perfectly, without seeming either affected or superior, the courtesy and rueful wisdom of its original is due to expert adaptation by Sarah Y. Mason and Victor Heerman, to Cukor's direction and to superb acting by Katharine Hepburn. An actress of so much vitality that she can wear balloon skirts and address her mother as 'Marmee' without suggesting quaintness, she makes Jo March one of the most memorable heroines of the year, a girl at once eager and puzzled, troubled, changing and secure.

"This picture, which critics last week pronounced the best that RKO has yet produced, is likely to place Katharine Hepburn near the top of the list of U.S. box-office favorites."

—*Time*

NOTES

George Cukor's production of the Louisa May Alcott classic blended all of the cinematic arts and crafts into one magnificent body. All of RKO's tremendous resources were carefully and skillfully employed, and the four men whose job it was to oversee this film are to be congratulated: director (Cukor), production chief (Selznick), executive producer (Cooper), and associate producer (MacGowan).

The hand-picked cast, from Hepburn to the smallest bit player, performed flawlessly. Hepburn's Jo was more like Hepburn than Alcott's heroine, but the blending of the two was in Cukor's capable hands. Hepburn later won the Cannes International Film Festival award as Best Actress of 1934.

Sarah Y. Mason and Victor Heerman's superb adaptation cannot be praised too highly. *Little Women* was filmed before as a silent and since (with Elizabeth Taylor and June Allyson) but no other version can compare in taste with this production. Selznick undertook a remake himself in the mid-forties with Jennifer Jones, Shirley Temple, Dorothy McGuire and Diana Lynn but plans were soon abandoned.

Little Women won three Academy Award nominations: Best Picture, Best Direction, and Best Screenplay Adaptation. Miss Mason and Mr. Heerman won an Oscar for their work.

With Joan Bennett, Mabel Colcord,
Jean Parker and Frances Dee

With Joan Bennett

With Jean Parker, Spring Byington, Douglass Montgomery,
Frances Dee and John Davis Lodge

Spitfire

AN RKO RADIO PICTURE   1934

CAST

Trigger Hicks   Katharine Hepburn
J. Stafford   Robert Young
G. Fleetwood   Ralph Bellamy
Eleanor Stafford   Martha Sleeper
Bill Grayson   Louis Mason
Etta Dawson   Sara Haden
Granny Raines   Virginia Howell
Mr. Sawyer   Sidney Toler
West Fry   High Ghere
Mrs. Sawyer   Therese Wittler
Jake Hawkins   John Beck

CREDITS

Director   John Cromwell
Executive Producer   Merian C. Cooper
Associate Producer   Pandro S. Berman
Scenarists   Jane Murfin, Lula Vollmer
Based on the Play TRIGGER *by*   Lula Vollmer
Photographer   Edward Cronjager
Art Director   Van Nest Polglase
Associate Art Director   Carroll Clark
Editor   William H. Morgan
Sound Recorder   Clem Portman
Musical Score   Max Steiner
Costumer   Walter Plunkett
Makeup Artist   Mel Burns
Assistant Director   Dewey Starkey

54

HEPBURN

in

SPITFIRE

Completely and daringly different from anything she has ever done.

With Robert Young

With Therese Wittler, High Ghere (Bob Burns) and Sidney Toler

SYNOPSIS

Trigger Hicks, a young tomboy faith healer in the Ozark mountains, believes that her prayers can heal the sick and raise the dead. However, she is feared by her neighbors, both for her temper and her strange religious fervor. After succumbing to the smooth speeches of two dam-building engineers, Stafford and his boss Fleetwood, she discovers that Stafford is married and becomes disillusioned.

In her confusion, Trigger impetuously kidnaps a dying baby, who grows better under her care. After the baby is returned to its parents, it weakens and dies. As a result, Trigger is cursed, stoned, and almost lynched, but she is saved by Fleetwood. Her courage does not fail her through this ordeal, but her faith is shaken. Accepting the exile decree of her neighbors, Trigger decides to leave, although she vows to return in a year—or perhaps sooner—to her mountain cabin, and Fleetwood.

CRITICS' CIRCLE

"The entertainment of the drama centers entirely on Miss Hepburn's characterization. And this is a thing of pristine beauty, lyric tenderness, fired with the flame of genius. Miss Hepburn is pretty definitely foremost, among American dramatic artists in the cinema. In *Spitfire* she holds the screen alone in an amazing histrionic *tour de force*."

—REGINA CREWE
New York American

"There is, unfortunately, nothing about Miss Hepburn's very modern, extremely urban personality to suggest a mystic healer from the far hills. John Cromwell, usually a lucid director, never makes quite clear the author's attitude toward young Trigger, whether she is to be accepted as a great healer or sympathized with as a self-deluded child. Miss Hepburn seemed equally bewildered."

—EILEEN CREELMAN
New York Sun

"Miss Hepburn plays so splendidly that she makes the girl a surprisingly real creation. . . . Her fine and straightforward work in *Spitfire*, however, should be pretty convincing proof that she is as striking a screen actress as those of us who have always admired her have insisted."

—RICHARD WATTS, JR.
New York Herald Tribune

"After the story of *Spitfire* is forgotten, memories of Miss Hepburn's performance will remain."

—*The (London) Times*

"The picture would suggest that Katharine Hepburn is condemned to elegance, doomed to be a lady for the rest of her natural life, and that her artistry does not extend to the interpretation of the primitive or the uncouth. That her producers have not bothered to give her a scenario of any interest or quality whatsoever is another aspect of the situation."

—*The New Yorker*

"Miss Hepburn attacks her part with a full appreciation of all the moods. She changes from a soulful religious mood to a violent outburst of rage in a really convincing fashion. She reveals Trigger's intelligence, her bright mind and also her hopeless ignorance. Dismal though the atmosphere of the picture is, Miss Hepburn never lacks the vivacity for the part and she speaks her lines with the necessary spontaneity, getting the full worth of humor out of them. As the director, Mr. Cromwell has done his task most commendably."

—MORDAUNT HALL
The New York Times

"John Cromwell, the director, has put the mountain around Trigger, rather than Trigger into the mountains. It is a wonder he gets as much feeling of the supernatural as he does; or it would be if he were less skillful with suggestion. He is, however, an expert in creating an almost intellectual mood; and in the deliberately retarded tempo he has adopted things, omens, acquire a portentousness they would not ordinarily possess.

"In spite of Miss Hepburn's handicap of an uncongenial role, she achieves one moment of ecstatic perfection in which her talent shines with the brilliance expected of her. This is the love sequence with Robert Young which has its climax in the girl's first kiss from a man. So completely does Miss Hepburn give of her best to this episode that she abandons entirely her attempted dialect."

—PHILIP K. SCHEUER
Los Angeles Times

"The Hepburn characterization of Trigger as a queer, hot-tempered warmhearted hoyden is wasted on the picture. In mood and manner *Spitfire* belongs to an obsolete era in the cinema. Typical shot: Trigger describing a lout who has tried to kiss her as 'consarned Son of Satan.'"

—*Time*

"In the wide world of the cinema, the art of Miss Katharine Hepburn has too small a place—small, perhaps, because she has never courted popularity by appearing in a quick succession of sophisticated and sentimental stories. Popularity means little to her; she is content with films that do not require her to throw away her rare gift of being able to touch in us an emotion usually free from the sentimentality which audiences have become accustomed to expect. She creates a feeling in her audience by a kind of vital expectation which causes a feeling to flow towards her."

—*The (London) Times*

NOTES

Spitfire, adapted from Lula Vollmer's play *Trigger*, offered Kate a different type of role than she had ever played. Trigger Hicks was a simple mountain girl, uneducated, and unfamiliar with the ways of the world outside her small community. Hepburn approached this part with tomboyish vigor and injected Trigger with a free and dynamic spirit.

The role of Trigger was originally set for Dorothy Jordan, before Hepburn agreed to take it.

She agreed to do this "outdoor" drama so she could return to the Broadway stage in *The Lake*. Director John Cromwell, whose handling of film actresses became a specialty, guided Hepburn into giving a splendid performance in this rural drama—only her nasal voice betrayed her.

The supporting cast included Robert Young and Ralph Bellamy and provided Sara Haden, a fine character actress, with the longest—and probably best—role of her career. Location shooting was done in the San Jacinto mountains in Southern California, near the Mexican border. Comedian Bob Burns acted in this film under the name High Ghere.

With Martha Sleeper and Robert Young

With Ralph Bellamy

With Sara Haden

With Sara Haden

The Little Minister

AN RKO RADIO PICTURE 1934

CAST

Babbie   Katharine Hepburn
Gavin   John Beal
Rob Dow   Alan Hale
Dr. McQueen   Donald Crisp
Thammas   Lumsden Hare
Wearyworld   Andy Clyde
Margaret   Beryl Mercer
Micah Dow   Billy Watson
Jean   Dorothy Stickney
Nanny   Mary Gordon
Lord Rintoul   Frank Conroy
Evalina   Eily Malyon
Captain Halliwell   Reginald Denny
Munn   Leonard Carey
Carfrae   Herbert Bunston
John Spens   Harry Beresford
Snecky   Barlowe Borland
Maid   May Beatty

CREDITS

Director   Richard Wallace
Producer   Pandro S. Berman
Scenarists   Jane Murfin, Sarah Y. Mason, Victor Heerman

With Andy Clyde

With John Beal

With Frank Conroy

59

With Billy Watson

With John Beal and Donald Crisp

Additional Scenes by Mortimer Offner, Jack Wagner
Based on the Novel and Play by Sir James M. Barrie
Photographer Henry Gerrard
Art Director Van Nest Polglase
Associate Art Director Carroll Clark
Set Decorator Hobe Erwin
Editor William Hamilton
Sound Recorder Clem Portman
Musical Score Max Steiner
Costumer Walter Plunkett
Makeup Artist Mel Burns
Special Photographic Effects Vernon Walker
Assistant Director Edward Killy
Technical Adviser Robert Watson, F.R.G.S.

SYNOPSIS

Lady Babbie often dresses as a gypsy wench and fraternizes with the poor weavers of the Auld Licht Kirk in the Thrums of 1840. Whenever the weavers begin to rebel against the city manufacturers, her guardian, Lord Rintoul, sends soldiers to quell the rebellion, but Babbie always warns them beforehand. During one of these jaunts, she meets Gavin Dishart, the conservative new minister of the kirk.

After an irritable beginning, the two become fast friends and soon find themselves in love. The minister tries, in vain, to fight against that emotion. He takes long walks with the gypsy lass, which causes a scandal among his parishioners. The elders are about to expel him from the pulpit when they discover that the wench is, in reality, the ward of Lord Rintoul, whereupon they forgive their little minister.

CRITICS' CIRCLE

"In the role of the wayward Babbie she (Hepburn) has attained a maturity which brings grace and tempered charm to a personality which, in the past, has been marred by a brittleness of voice and manner. . . . Though Miss Hepburn's contribution is both large and handsome, the virtues of the picture are generously distributed over the production, the direction and the performances of the supporting players. Of the many excellent performances, that of John Beal as the minister comes second to Miss Hepburn's. It is a straightforward and eloquently persuasive portrayal which goes direct to the heart of the character."

—THORNTON DELEHANTY
New York Post

"Miss Hepburn, gauntly handsome and spirited, makes no attempt to become that elusive, charming creature, a Barrie heroine. She is just Miss Hepburn, arch, vivid, varying little, adored by a vast public. Wistfulness is not a Hepburn characteristic. With so many other characters more suitable to her striking personality . . . it might be just a little kinder if she were to leave *Quality Street* and other Barrie plays to the Helen Hayeses and the Maude Adamses."

—EILEEN CREELMAN
New York Sun

"There is little doubt that the star (Hepburn) is one of the major wonder workers of Hollywood, with an unconquerable gift for turning lavender and old lace into something possessing dramatic vitality and conviction. Looking her handsomest and performing with considerable radiance, Miss Hepburn provides *The Little Minister* with much of the charm that went into the miracle of *Little Women*."

—RICHARD WATTS, JR.
New York Herald Tribune

"That quality, usually defined as whimsey, which admirers of Sir James M. Barrie find so charming in his prose, is impossible to reproduce upon the screen. For this reason *The Little Minister* lacks some of the effect of the novel from which it was derived. It attempts, therefore, to substitute charms of its own. Because of the delicacy with which Director Richard Wallace handled the story, and the peculiar grace of Katharine Hepburn in the role that Maude Adams created in 1897, the substitution is entirely satisfactory."

—*Time*

"The incomparable Katharine Hepburn is at top form in her portrayal of the elfin gypsy of the Thrums' woodlands. She makes the character leap alive from the pages of Barrie's book, and sways her audience with her through all the varied moods of the whimsical heroine. No other player of parts could have given Babbie the sprite-like wistfulness and gaiety with which Katharine endows her."

—REGINA CREWE
New York American

"Although dear Babbie's elfin whimsies are likely to cause minor teeth-gnashing among unsympathetic moderns, Miss Hepburn plays the part with likable sprightliness and charm. In its mild-mannered and sober way, *The Little Minister* proves to be a photoplay of genuine charm."

—ANDRE SENNWALD
The New York Times

NOTES

When Sarah Y. Mason and Victor Heerman, the brilliant adapters of *Little Women*, collaborated with Jane Murfin on Sir James M. Barrie's *The Little Minister* they changed it from tender comedy to emotional drama, obviously in a move to heighten its appeal to the larger, and less sophisticated, movie-going public.

Hepburn may not have been the ideal Babbie, but she approached the lass with winning conviction. Her enormous vitality and warmth worked well with both Babbie's boisterous flights of fancy and moods of tenderness. John Beal

On the set with assistant director Edward Killy, John Beal and director Richard Wallace

With John Beal

61

was convincing in the title role and the supporting players were well directed by Richard Wallace, whose chief claim to fame was the Nancy Carroll–Gary Cooper opus *The Shopworn Angel*. Wallace's career never seemed to generate any interest but he knew his craft and got good results.

Barrie's *The Little Minister* was first a novel (1891) and then a play (1897) before theatrical producer Charles Frohman brought it to America, in 1907. Maude Adams helped to make it a tremendous success on the stage and her 1915 revival duplicated that record. Miss Adams also did two broadcasts over the NBC network, in 1934, nine years after Ruth Chatterton revived it on Broadway.

In 1921 two silent movie versions were released: Vitagraph's, with Alice Calhoun and Jimmy Morrison, and Paramount's more sumptuous production, with Betty Compson and George Hackathorne.

Break of Hearts

AN RKO RADIO PICTURE 1935

CAST

Constance Dane   Katharine Hepburn
Franz Roberti   Charles Boyer
Johnny Lawrence   John Beal
Prof. Talma   Jean Hersholt
Marx   Sam Hardy
Miss Wilson   Inez Courtney
Sylvia   Helene Millard
Pazzini   Ferdinand Gottschalk
Elise   Susan Fleming
Schubert   Lee Kohlmar
Didi Smith-Lennox   Jean Howard
Phyllis   Anne Grey
and Inez Palange, Jason Robards, Egon Brecher, and Dick Elliott

CREDITS

Director   Philip Moeller
Producer   Pandro S. Berman
Scenarists   Sarah Y. Mason, Victor Heerman, Anthony Veiller
Based on a Story by   Lester Cohen
Photographer   Robert De Grasse
Art Director   Van Nest Polglase
Associate Art Director   Carroll Clark
Editor   William Hamilton
Sound Recorder   John Tribby
Musical Score   Max Steiner
Costumer   Bernard Newman
Makeup Artist   Mel Burns
Assistant Director   Edward Killy
Associate Editor   Jane Loring

With Charles Boyer

With Charles Boyer

With Helene Millard,
Jean Howard and Charles Boyer

With Charles Boyer

SYNOPSIS

The passionate Franz Roberti, a rich and eminent musical conductor, marries Constance Dane, an aspiring, yet poor and unknown composer. A blissful relationship exists for a short period until Constance discovers that Roberti is seeing another woman. She leaves him, only to be pursued by a clean-cut young man named Johnny Lawrence, who wants to take her away from it all.

Roberti soon goes in for heavy dipsomania, and his brilliant career is threatened. Constance returns to him to rouse him from his alcoholic stupor. Her successful plan for bringing him to his senses begins with her sitting down at the piano and playing "their song."

CRITICS' CIRCLE

"Philip Moeller's direction possesses the lifeless and static quality which marred his debut as a film director last winter in *Age of Innocence*. Miss Hepburn, like Mr. Boyer, works overtime in her courageous determination to find some freshness in the piece."

—ANDRE SENNWALD
The New York Times

"If further proof were needed of Miss Hepburn's genius, here it is. With absolutely no help from story or part, how superbly the actress surmounts all obstacles, equal to every emergency! Watching her you forget the story, its cheap emotionalism and shallow psychology. Her freshness is unimpaired. Her vitality glows. She plays in perfect sympathy with Boyer—an excellent partnership. She is impulsive and flame-like. He is tempered steel. Two remarkable personalities so strongly individual should harmonize well; they both have imagination, flexibility and variety."

—SYDNEY W. CARROLL
The (London) Times

"It is a painstaking, well-made drama, surprisingly conversational, however, in spite of its episodic quality. But, in spite of some capable acting, it lacks a certain compelling warmth. The audience's heart never quite breaks."

—EILEEN CREELMAN
New York Sun

"Still performing as the heroine of *Little Women*, Miss Hepburn makes it clear that unless her employers see fit to restore her to roles in keeping with her mannerisms, these will presently annoy cinemaddicts into forgetting that she is really an actress of great promise and considerable style. As the orchestra leader, Charles Boyer manages to make the defeat which he receives from his material comparatively graceful."

—*Time*

"Miss Hepburn is, of course, supremely good throughout the film—vivid, very beautiful and most believable. There are moments of great beauty and force in her playing—moments that definitely stamp her as the great actress she really is. The supporting cast is excellent. Indeed, it is a pity that such fine acting is frittered away on such labored and palpably fabricated writing."

—WILLIAM BOEHNEL
New York World-Telegram

With John Beal,
Jean Hersholt and Charles Boyer

With Charles Boyer

"Katharine Hepburn is not likely to enhance her reputation as one of the screen's first sorceresses in *Break of Hearts*. Her task of weaving a credible and moving characterization through the banalities of the new photoplay is, to be sure, prodigious. In spite of Philip Moeller's shrewd direction, an elaborately decorative mise-en-scène and a remarkably skillful performance by Charles Boyer, the synthesis of odds and ends that makes up the narrative defies a cohesive dramatic production. Mr. Boyer, who is rapidly taking a deserved place as one of the finest actors in the films, overshadows Miss Hepburn throughout much of *Break of Hearts* by the sheer force and subtlety of his performance."

—Howard Barnes
New York Herald Tribune

"It is expertly played by its stars, and the dialogue is far better than the tale deserves. Miss Hepburn has that certain something, that vague, illusive quality which reaches into the heart, and when there is drama she leaps upon it, holds it tight, and turns the illumination of her genius full upon it. . . . The musical direction of Max Steiner is superb, and the impressive harmony is a mighty help to the film."

—Regina Crewe
New York American

NOTES

Break of Hearts was intended as a vehicle for Hepburn and John Barrymore, but Mr. Barrymore must have read the script. Why Hepburn got involved in this excursion into trivia is anyone's guess. Charles Boyer, whose performances have usually been taken for granted, stepped into the role of the composer and, somehow, he managed to rise above the material.

Philip Moeller, a stage director who had made a reputation with his many Theatre Guild Productions, was unable to save this patently inept story from disaster. The studio gave it a fine production—technically—and the musical interludes of Max Steiner made things more bearable.

The failure of this modern-day romantic piffle prompted RKO to put Hepburn into more costume pieces, which they were now convinced was her forte.

On the set with
associate director Jane Loring,
assistant director Edward Killy,
photographer Robert de Grasse
and director Philip Moeller

Alice Adams

AN RKO RADIO PICTURE   1935

CAST

Alice Adams   Katharine Hepburn
Arthur Russell   Fred MacMurray
Mr. Adams   Fred Stone
Mildred Palmer   Evelyn Venable
Walter Adams   Frank Albertson
Mrs. Adams   Ann Shoemaker
Mr. Lamb   Charles Grapewin
Frank Dowling   Grady Sutton
Mrs. Palmer   Hedda Hopper
Mr. Palmer   Jonathan Hale
Henrietta Lamb   Janet McLeod
Mrs. Dowling   Virginia Howell
Mrs. Dresser   Zeffie Tilbury
Ella Dowling   Ella McKenzie
Malena   Hattie McDaniel

CREDITS

Director   George Stevens
Producer   Pandro S. Berman
Scenarists   Dorothy Yost, Mortimer Offner
Based on the Novel by   Booth Tarkington
Adaptation   Jane Murfin
Photographer   Robert De Grasse
Art Director   Van Nest Polglase
Editor   Jane Loring
Sound Recorder   Denzil A. Cutler
Musical Score   Max Steiner
Costumer   Walter Plunkett
Makeup Artist   Mel Burns

With Frank Albertson,
Ann Shoemaker and Fred Stone

With Frank Albertson

With Ann Shoemaker

With Evelyn Venable

Assistant Director   Edward Killy
Song: *"I Can't Waltz Alone" by*   Max Steiner, Dorothy Fields

SYNOPSIS

Young Alice Adams is ambitious for social recognition, but is merely tolerated by her wealthier girl friends. She longs to be a part of their world and to have them like her. Soon, at a party, she meets visiting Arthur Russell, who takes an interest in her and asks if he may call. They sit on the porch and chat.

Mrs. Adams, who wants her daughter to marry well, convinces her husband to leave his job at the glue factory, using a glue formula he has invented to open a business of his own. Alice's big night comes when Arthur arrives for dinner, but all is a disaster. Alice has fictionalized her life in a vain effort to impress him and the rest of her family follow suit, instead of being themselves. Further complications arise when her brother Walter admits that he has stolen from Mr. Lamb, his employer, and asks his father to cover it up. Later, after a heated argument, Mr. Lamb agrees to go into partnership with Adams.

CRITICS' CIRCLE

"From the beginning it was obvious that Miss Hepburn had conceived the part as a whole; that she was going to allow Alice to tell her story in her own way, and that she was not going to encompass poor Alice in a theatrical design of her own making. The result is that Miss Hepburn shows that there is a good deal more in Alice than mere vanity and man-hunting. Because of her insight into the part and the pathos she gives it it might appear to the superficial that Miss Hepburn has exaggerated the posings; what she really has done is to over-act as Alice over-acted every time she met a man or walked into a room."—*The (London) Times*

"In the title role Miss Hepburn gives a performance that is superb—a performance that captures all the loneliness and heartache of the character. Fred Stone, playing the part of the father, does a fine job—a job that easily might have become much too homespun and likable. In his hands it does not."

—WILLIAM BOEHNEL
New York World-Telegram

"For the purpose of exhibiting an actress in a variety of moods and situations *Alice Adams* could scarcely be surpassed—and Miss Hepburn has obviously taken possession of her task with sympathy and enthusiasm. Had the temptation to make the film a starring vehicle for Miss Hepburn been a little more strenuously resisted, *Alice Adams* could have achieved considerably more than its niche as merely a better-than-average romance."

—JOHN REDDINGTON
Brooklyn Daily Eagle

"Katharine Hepburn's Alice is as striking and sensitive a performance as any she has given . . . her performance holds that same quality of unexpected excitement which distinguished her first screen appearance in *A Bill of Divorcement*."

—ANDRE SENNWALD
The New York Times

"What was in 1922 a shrewd and observant novel, emerges in 1935 as a bitingly satiric portrait of an era. Of Hollywood's leading stars, Katharine Hepburn is possibly the least versatile. It is precisely this limitation which made her the ideal choice for the role of Alice. The woebegone grimaces, the expressions, half childish and half addle-headed, which she used to convey youth's nameless longings and which are often so startlingly misplaced in her portrayals of women of the world, are those which make her portrayal of a girl whom she really understands her masterpiece to date. The supremely difficult feat of characterizing a *poseuse* so as to mock the poses without mocking the person behind them she carries off with success. The direction of George Stevens, who at 30 is the youngest important director in Hollywood, is almost flawless."

—*Time*

"She (Hepburn) has never looked more stunning nor played with such distinction, authority and charm. It is a performance that is superb in every detail, well sustained, carefully modulated and accurately pitched to the keys of humor and wistful pathos which define the character."

—THORNTON DELEHANTY
New York Post

NOTES

Alice Adams was a klutz; try as she may, she never did anything right. Her continual dream world was a flimsy protection against the harsh realities of life. Hepburn found much of the sadness in Alice, as well as her boldness of spirit, and gave this strange creature an enthusiasm that was winning. Kate's Alice is touching, likable, thoughtful, and thoroughly believable, and her interpretation of the Booth Tarkington heroine won her a second Academy Award nomination.

George Stevens, directing his first major film, focused his attention on small-town America and middle-class society. He directed with sureness and spotted the proceedings with marvelous bits of humor—e.g., Hattie McDaniel as the slatternly Black maid Malena, whose cooking, gum-chewing, and disconcerting behavior at the dinner table were gems of comic acting.

The cast of players Stevens collected were each outstanding: Fred Stone was perfect as the father; Ann Shoemaker underplayed the nagging mother; Frank Albertson was fine as the younger brother; and Grady Sutton, who had

worked with Stevens in two-reelers, was funny as Kate's dancing partner. Fred MacMurray, as Alice's suitor, had little more to do than be charming and appealing.

RKO gave *Alice Adams* a first-rate production and Stevens supplied the proper atmosphere and accent. Besides Hepburn's nomination as Best Actress, the picture itself won an Academy Award nomination.

Alice Adams had been previously filmed, in 1923, with Florence Vidor.

With Ann Shoemaker (extreme left),
Fred MacMurray and Hattie McDaniel

With Grady Sutton

With Fred MacMurray

With Fred MacMurray

Sylvia Scarlett

AN RKO RADIO PICTURE 1936

CAST

Sylvia Scarlett   Katharine Hepburn
Jimmy Monkley   Cary Grant
Michael Fane   Brian Aherne
Henry Scarlett   Edmund Gwenn
Lily   Natalie Paley
Maudie Tilt   Dennie Moore
Drunk   Lennox Pawle
Bobby   Harold Cheevers
Sergeant Major   Lionel Pape
Turnkey   Robert (Bob) Adair
Stewards   Peter Hobbes, Leonard Mudie, Jack Vanair
Conductor   Harold Entwistle
Stewardess   Adrienne D' Ambricourt
Pursers   Gaston Glass, Michael S. Visaroff
Maid   Bunny Beatty
Customs Inspectors   E. E. Clive, Edward Cooper, Olaf
   Hytten
Russian   Dina Smirnova
Frenchman   George Nardelli
and Daisy Belmore, Elspeth Dudgeon, May Beatty, Connie
Lamont, Gwendolyn Logan, Carmen Beretta

CREDITS

Director   George Cukor
Producer   Pandro S. Berman
Scenarists   Gladys Unger, John Collier, Mortimer Offner
Based on the Novel The Early Life and Adventures of Sylvia
   Scarlett *By*   Compton MacKenzie

With Cary Grant,
Dennie Moore and Edmund Gwenn

Photographer   Joseph August
Art Director   Van Nest Polglase
Associate Art Director   Sturges Carne
Editor   Jane Loring
Sound Recorder   George D. Ellis
Musical Score   Roy Webb
Music Recorded By   P. J. Faulkner, Jr.
Costumer (For Miss Hepburn)   Muriel King
Costumer (For Miss Paley)   Bernard Newman
Makeup Artist   Mel Burns
Assistant Director   Argyle Nelson

SYNOPSIS

After Sylvia Scarlett's father commits larceny and is forced to flee France, she joins him, masquerading as a boy, so they will not easily be detected. They join up with a raffish cockney, Jimmy Monkley, soon practice a bit of swindling in London, and then take to the road with a Pierrot show, which also includes a daffy servant girl named Maudie Tilt, whom they picked up along the way.

By the time Sylvia becomes involved with a handsome, well-to-do artist, Michael Fane, Maudie has become Henry Scarlett's second wife. Meanwhile, Sylvia sheds her male disguise and attempts to become a woman again, to get Michael away from the austere presence of Lily, a strange Russian adventuress.

CRITICS' CIRCLE

"The dynamic Miss Hepburn is the handsomest boy of the season. I am forced to say that her vehicle is a sprawling and ineffective essay in dramatic chaos, with characters and situations enmeshed in vague obscurities, but for Miss Hepburn's performance I have only admiration. I don't care for *Sylvia Scarlett* a bit, but I do think Miss Hepburn is much better in it than she was as the small-town wallflower in *Alice Adams*."

—Richard Watts, Jr.
New York Herald Tribune

"Mr. Cukor's theatrical direction and the stars' artificial performances are among other unpleasant problems of the day. Miss Hepburn destroys her usual striking good looks by chopping off her hair and wearing highly unbecoming masculine garb, in which, since she still glides instead of walking, she makes a most unconvincing boy. The picture is a tragic waste of time and screen talent."

—Eileen Creelman
New York Sun

"Katharine Hepburn dons trousers, dances gypsy-like on the English countryside and achieves what is customarily if discouragingly referred to as a personal triumph in her new film. As the awkward, imaginative, tremulously frus-

With Cary Grant and Edmund Gwenn

With Brian Aherne,
Cary Grant and Natalie Paley

With Lennox Pawle and Brian Aherne

With Natalie Paley

trated heroine of the tale, Miss Hepburn is on her home grounds, and she plays the part with a richness of understanding that compares favorably with her performance in *Alice Adams*. There are several excellent performances under Mr. Cukor's management. Edmund Gwenn is completely satisfying, Dennie Moore plays with a freshness and a gift for humor that should quickly gain her attention in Hollywood. Cary Grant, whose previous work has too often been that of a charm merchant, turns actor in the role of the unpleasant cockney and is surprisingly good at it. Something fresh, touching and funny seems to have gone into *Sylvia Scarlett,* but it got caught in the machinery."

—ANDRE SENNWALD
The New York Times

"Under George Cukor's direction, the story of the novel has been transferred to the screen with remarkable ingenuity, in terms of whimsical and only occasionally sentimental comedy. . . . But despite its occasional overdrawn effects *Sylvia Scarlett* is a much more polished comedy than most, and consistently engaging."

—WINSTON BURDETT
Brooklyn Daily Eagle

"She (Hepburn) is something of the vital, forceful, straightforward young woman here that she was in *Christopher Strong*, but several degrees more magically vital and forceful. It is her special achievement that she makes the role of Sylvia, who for the sake of the plot must masquerade part of the time as a boy, both likable and believable when it might easily have been cloyingly annoying. It is, indeed, as fine a piece of warm and spirited, restrained and humble acting as you will see."

—WILLIAM BOEHNEL
New York World-Telegram

"*Sylvia Scarlett* reveals the interesting fact that Katharine Hepburn is better looking as a boy than as a woman. . . . One day on the beach she slips out of her male attire, steals the dress of a girl in swimming, goes up to his (Aherne's) house. What follows is one of those scenes which Miss Hepburn plays with her best intuition, a scene in which a woman who has played a man so long that she has abdicated her sex tries to become a woman for the man she loves. . . . (The film) is made memorable by a role that almost steals the show from Miss Hepburn's androgyne: Cary Grant's superb depiction of the cockney."

—*Time*

"It is a tour de force, made possible by her physical resemblance to the adolescent male. Her achievement is an accident of looks rather than a creative effort, and as such it belongs among those museum pieces which are ordinarily found under a glass case. . . . There is no justification for Miss Hepburn's throwing herself away on a part that demands little more than a studied imitation of gestures and

74

intonation. Cary Grant comes near to stealing the picture with his bitingly humorous portrait of a cockney ne'er-do-well."

—THORNTON DELEHANTY
New York Post

NOTES

Based on the 1918 Compton MacKenzie novel *The Early Life and Adventures of Sylvia Scarlett,* this film is one of George Cukor's most personal efforts. A beautifully made story of vagabond thieves, it was well ahead of its time.

Hepburn's Sylvia/Sylvester Scarlett was so radical a departure for her that the film proved most unpopular. Kate spent most of the time masquerading as a boy, which kept her fans away (no wonder Louis B. Mayer refused to allow Garbo to do *Hamlet*), although she gave a warm and revealing interpretation.

Cary Grant fared much better—and, as the cockney lout Jimmy Monkley, proved he was an actor and not just a handsome leading man. Edmund Gwenn was charmingly effective as Sylvia's father and Brian Aherne was good as the artist.

Also in the cast was Princess Natalie Paley, daughter of the Russian Grand Duke Paul (an uncle of the late Czar Nicholas). Miss Paley had previously appeared in the French version of *Folies Bergère* opposite Maurice Chevalier and in *L'Epervier* with Charles Boyer. Dennie Moore, an expatriate of the Ziegfeld Follies, was delightful as Maudie. Cukor later used her to advantage as Olga, the gossipy manicurist, in *The Women* (1939).

Despite its failure in 1936, *Sylvia Scarlett* should be seen, and studied, by those interested in acting art.

On the set with
director George Cukor
and visitor Hugh Walpole

Mary of Scotland

AN RKO RADIO PICTURE   1936

CAST

Mary Stuart   Katharine Hepburn
Earl of Bothwell   Fredric March
Elizabeth Tudor   Florence Eldridge
Darnley   Douglas Walton
David Rizzio   John Carradine
Morton   Robert Barrat
Leicester   Gavin Muir
James Stuart Moray   Ian Keith
John Knox   Moroni Olsen
Ruthven   William Stack
Randolph   Ralph Forbes
Throckmorton   Alan Mowbray
Mary Beaton   Frieda Inescort
Huntley   Donald Crisp
Lindsay   David Torrence
Mary Livingston   Molly Lamont
Mary Fleming   Anita Colby
Mary Seton   Jean Fenwick
Burghley   Lionel Pape
Donal   Alec Craig
Nurse   Mary Gordon
Messanger   Monte Blue
Maitland   Leonard Mudie
Arian   Brandon Hurst
Lexington   Wilfred Lucas
Kirkcaldy   D'Arcy Corrigan
Douglas   Frank Baker
Faudoncide   Cyril McLaglen
English Fisherman   Lionel Belmore
His Wife   Doris Lloyd

His Son   Bobby Watson
Sir Francis Knellys   Robert Warwick
Judges   Ivan Simpson, Murray Kinnell, Lawrence Grant,
   Nigel De Brulier, Barlowe Borland
Sir Francis Walsingham   Walter Byron
Sergeant   Wyndham Standing
Duke of Kent   Earle Foxe
Du Croche   Paul McAllister
Chatelard   Gaston Glass
Nobleman   Neil Fitzgerald
Prince James   Jean Kircher and Judith Kircher

CREDITS

Director   John Ford
Producer   Pandro S. Berman
Scenarist   Dudley Nichols
Based on the Play by   Maxwell Anderson
Photographer   Joseph H. August
Art Director   Van Nest Polglase
Associate Art Director   Carroll Clark
Set Decorator   Darrell Silvera
Editor   Jane Loring
Assistant Editor   Robert Parrish
Sound Recorder   Hugh McDowell, Jr.
Musical Score   Nathaniel Shilkret
Orchestrator   Maurice De Packh
Costumer   Walter Plunkett
Makeup Artist   Mel Burns
Special Photographic Effects   Vernon L. Walker
Assistant Director   Edward Donahue
Miss Hepburn's Hairdresser   Louise Sloan

SYNOPSIS

Mary Stuart's return to Scotland from France, in 1561, sparks Elizabeth Tudor's fear of a Stuart claim to her throne. Mary moves to strengthen her position by marrying Darnley, taking the loyal Earl of Bothwell as her protector. In time her son James is born, her beloved friend and secretary Rizzio is murdered before her eyes, and Darnley betrays her to the Scottish chiefs before he, too, is slain.

Her subsequent marriage to Bothwell precipitates a disastrous public reaction. To avert an uprising, Bothwell leaves the country so that Mary can continue her reign. However, the Scottish nobles betray their promise and imprison her. Smuggled out of prison to England, Mary throws herself on the mercy of an insincere Elizabeth I. Although imprisoned for some eighteen years, it is not until after Bothwell dies that Mary is condemned to death for treason. The Tudor queen offers her her freedom, provided she signs away all claims to her throne, but Mary refuses—and mounts the scaffold at Fotheringhay in 1586.

With Fredric March

CRITICS' CIRCLE

"In all the principal roles *Mary of Scotland* enjoys the luxury of accomplished actors. It is left to Miss Hepburn to bring Mary vividly, glowingly, to life. This she does. To be brief about it, she gives the part nobility. Acting with an unassuming pride, she has the courage and taste to underplay. As a result she represents grandeur without having to describe it. As the rough, tender and noble Bothwell, Fredric March does his best screen work, contributing a performance that is clear and forceful in every respect. Florence Eldridge catches both the dignity and the undercurrent of hypocrisy that are Elizabeth."

—WILLIAM BOEHNEL
New York World-Telegram

"John Ford's direction of the picture is a masterly job. He gets the maximum dramatic effect from every scene and his casting of the dramatic persons is an inspired piece of work."

—KATE CAMERON
New York Daily News

"It is also possible to object, and object forcibly, to the casting of Katharine Hepburn as Mary. But I will not protest too strenuously against the view that Miss Hepburn has succeeded beyond expectation, and that in her vital, sincere and impressive performance she registers a new triumph. That is not my own personal view, but I can understand it. Her accent was not of the Highlands, the Lowlands, nor a pure French equivalent. It was pure Hepburn, and nothing else. Still hers is a finely studied and artistic interpretation."

—SYDNEY W. CARROLL
The (London) Times

"A richly produced, dignified and stirringly dramatic cinematization of one of the most colorful periods and personalities in history. RKO Radio's *Mary of Scotland* must be considered one of the year's notable photoplays.

With Frieda Inescort

With Douglas Walton and Fredric March

With Florence Eldridge

On the set with
visitor Victor McLaglen
and director John Ford

77

"Too, although Katharine Hepburn's Mary Stuart shines brilliantly through most of the film's two-hour course, we were conscious of definite defects in her characterization. She may be a courageous Mary, perhaps a valiant one, but scarcely a fighter who gives no quarter and asks none. Almost we had forgotten Fredric March's Bothwell, which would have been unpardonable, for his is a first-rate portrayal of the bold, roistering, devil-may-care border Scot history shows him to have been. Florence Eldridge's Elizabeth is properly spiteful."

—FRANK S. NUGENT
The New York Times

"John Ford, who is Hollywood's No. 1 director at the moment, has managed the production with his customary gift for atmosphere, intelligent story-telling and the manipulation of his actors. Under his guiding hand Miss Hepburn, after a slightly strident opening scene, provides a lovely and touching characterization of the hapless Mary, while Fredric March has never been finer than he is as the bold, dashing and romanticized Bothwell."

—RICHARD WATTS, JR.
New York Herald Tribune

"The finish is a sad one and that is an old problem. It isn't always a bad idea but here, with the entire picture tending towards shadows, chatter and length, one wonders even more. There was, of course, nothing else the studio could do on that score, without completely corrupting history."
—*Variety*

"That, outside the narrow range in which she is superb, Katharine Hepburn often acts like a Bryn Mawr senior in a May Day pageant; that Fredric March's Scottish burr has Wisconsin overtones; and that Director John Ford tried to symbolize the sombre quality of his story by the over-simple expedient of shooting it in the dark, are circumstances which do not heighten the film's dramatic impact. If *Mary of Scotland* is still worth seeing, it is because the picture is based on one of those tremendous legends, which, projected to heroic proportions in their reflections in history, have a validity which not even the blunders of faulty narration can totally destroy. Best shot: Mary's infant son, who grows up to be James I, roaring at his foppish father."

—*Time*

NOTES

John Ford, considered the greatest American film director since D. W. Griffith, directed Hepburn in *Mary of Scotland.* The Dudley Nichols script eliminated Maxwell Anderson's blank verse but otherwise stayed close to the original work.

Ford's concentration went to the spectacle and historical pageantry of the period. The production was a visual delight, but the drama became static and at times dull.

Hepburn, recreating the role Helen Hayes did on Broadway, was a finely etched Mary Stuart while Fredric March gave a rich portrayal as the robust Bothwell. For obvious reasons the Earl of Bothwell's family name (Hepburn) was not referred to in the film version. Kate is a direct descendant.

Many actresses vied for the role of Elizabeth I. Warners' Bette Davis wanted to be loaned for it and RKO's own musical Ginger Rogers went to elaborate pains to convince producer Berman the role should be hers. However, Ford chose Florence Eldridge who gave the part great distinction.

The peak of the drama—when Mary Stuart and Elizabeth I meet—was the hit of the play and a stunning scene in the film, but as a matter of history it rang false. Dramatists writing of this period always contend that the two should have met—since it makes for better dramaturgy. The ladies never met.

With Robert Warwick and Walter Byron

79

A Woman Rebels

AN RKO RADIO PICTURE   1936

CAST

Pamela Thistlewaite   Katharine Hepburn
Thomas Lane   Herbert Marshall
Flora Thistlewaite   Elizabeth Allan
Judge Thistlewaite   Donald Crisp
Young Flora   Doris Dudley
Alan   David Manners
Betty Bumble   Lucile Watson
Gerald   Van Heflin
Piper   Eily Malyon
Aunt Serena   Margaret Seddon
Young Girl   Molly Lamont
Mr. White   Lionel Pape
Lady Gaythorne   Constance Lupino
Lady Rinlake   Lillian Kemble-Cooper
Signor Grassi   Nick Thompson
Signora Grassi   Inez Palange
Italian Boy   Tony Romero
Italian Bit   Joe Mack
Flora, Age 10   Marilyn Knowlden
Flora, Age 5   Bonnie June McNamara
Flora, As Infant   Marilyn French

CREDITS

Director   Mark Sandrich
Producer   Pandro S. Berman
Scenarists   Anthony Veiller, Ernest Vajda
Based on the Novel Portrait of a Rebel *by*   Netta Syrett
Photographer   Robert De Grasse
Art Director   Van Nest Polglase

Associate Art Director Perry Ferguson
Set Decorator Darrell Silvera
Editor Jane Loring
Sound Recorder George D. Ellis
Musical Score Roy Webb
Music Recorded by Clem Portman
Orchestrator Maurice De Packh
Musical Director Nathaniel Shilkret
Costumer Walter Plunkett
Ballroom Dances by Hermes Pan
Makeup Artist Mel Burns
Assistant Director Dewey Starkey

SYNOPSIS

This is the story of a woman's struggle for emancipation during the Victorian period. Pamela Thistlewaite fights against the strict conventions of the 1870s, a defiance which doesn't prove to be an easy or popular task. However, as a true rebel, she defies her autocratic father, Judge Thistlewaite; has an affair with Gerald, an amorous young man who leaves her with a child born out of wedlock; and refuses to marry Thomas Lane, a faithful suitor.

Pamela has brains and continually demands that she be allowed to use them. She soon proves her independence by becoming a crusading editor of a woman's magazine. Later, when she realizes that she really does love Thomas Lane, she decides to marry him.

CRITICS' CIRCLE

"Delving into the fascinating ugliness of Victorian England, Mark Sandrich and his producing fellows at RKO Radio have found material that is picturesque, humorous and tragic. Aided by an excellent source book, Netta Syrett's *Portrait of a Rebel,* and by a group of understanding players, they have fashioned it into a handsome period drama."

—FRANK S. NUGENT
The New York Times

"In it Katharine Hepburn gives an appealing if not altogether believable portrayal. Miss Hepburn plays the part in forthright and dynamic fashion, getting more out of the characterization than was put there by the authors."

New York Herald Tribune

"Ever since Katharine Hepburn set the cinema industry by the ears with *Little Women,* her employers have been trying doggedly to discover just what elusive factor, added to the stock formula of Lavender and Old Lace, made that picture so sensationally successful. *A Woman Rebels* represents an effort to discover if the element was the revolt of a young girl against convention. That the experiment is conducted with painstaking care only makes it the more apparent that the hypothesis is faulty.

With Elizabeth Allan

With Van Heflin

With Herbert Marshall

81

With Elizabeth Allan

With Doris Dudley

"Marked by none of the vitality of its predecessors in Katharine Hepburn's Victorian series, *A Woman Rebels* is saved from complete mediocrity by her well-modulated performance and by the admirable feeling for background and atmosphere implicit in Mark Sandrich's direction."
—*Time*

NOTES

Riding on the crest of the costume picture wave, RKO offered Hepburn *Portrait of a Rebel,* which later became *A Woman Rebels.* Her performance of a self-sustaining woman fighting her times gave Hepburn another opportunity to fight—on film—for women's rights. She was really quite good, but the meticulous direction of Mark Sandrich, while historically accurate, tended to slow the action down. If anything, a period piece should have pace.

It was shot in 54 days and Hepburn wore 22 different Walter Plunkett costumes covering styles from 1869 to 1890. In addition to co-star Herbert Marshall, a good actor but a dull one, the supporting cast included two young performers Hepburn had seen in Ina Claire's play *End of Summer* and recommended to RKO. Doris Dudley made only a few more films, but Van Heflin became in time a fine actor. He later appeared with Kate in *The Philadelphia Story* on stage and won an Academy Award for his supporting role in MGM's *Johnny Eager.*

With Margaret Seddon, Donald Crisp and Eily Malyon

82   With Herbert Marshall and Marilyn Knowlden

With Herbert Marshall

Quality Street

AN RKO RADIO PICTURE   1937

CAST

Phoebe Throssel   Katharine Hepburn
Dr. Valentine Brown   Franchot Tone
Susan Throssel   Fay Bainter
Sergeant   Eric Blore
Patty   Cora Witherspoon
Mary Willoughby   Estelle Winwood
Henrietta Turnbull   Florence Lake
Fanny Willoughby   Helena Grant
Isabella   Bonita Granville
Arthur   Clifford Severn
William Smith   Sherwood Bailey
Ensign Blades   Roland Varno
Charlotte Parratt   Joan Fontaine
Lieutenant Spicer   William Bakewell
Postman   York Sherwood
Student   Carmencita Johnson

CREDITS

Director   George Stevens
Producer   Pandro S. Berman
Scenarists   Mortimer Offner, Allan Scott
Based on the Play by   Sir James M. Barrie
Photographer   Robert De Grasse
Art Director   Van Nest Polglase
Set Decorator   Darrell Silvera
Editor   Henry Berman
Sound Recorder   Clem Portman
Musical Score   Roy Webb
Orchestrator   Maurice De Packh
Costumer   Walter Plunkett
Makeup Artist   Mel Burns
Assistant Director   Argyle Nelson

SYNOPSIS

Phoebe Throssel, whose beau Dr. Valentine Brown courts her but never quite gets around to proposing, is startled by his sudden departure for the Napoleonic wars. He is gone for ten long years, during which time Phoebe and her sister Susan turned their home into a school and themselves into old-maid schoolteachers.

Upon his return in 1805, Captain Brown fails to recognize his former seeetheart, whose bloom of youth is somewhat faded. To win him back—and get a dash of sweet revenge—she masquerades as the flirtatious Livvy, her own nonexistent niece.

CRITICS' CIRCLE

"It is strictly a self-propelled picture, tearing breathlessly, almost hysterically, through Barrie's quizzical account of a

With Fay Bainter
and Cora Witherspoon

With Franchot Tone

With Fay Bainter

With Florence Lake, Helena Grant,
and Estelle Winwood

84

man-hunt. . . . But we were exhausted by the intensity of Miss Hepburn's concentration on it. Her Phoebe Throssel needs a neurologist far more than a husband. Such flutterings and jitterings and twitchings, such hand-wringings and mouth-quiverings, such runnings about and eyebrow-raisings have not been seen on a screen in many a moon."

—FRANK S. NUGENT
The New York Times

"The production itself is pleasantly ornamented and Miss Hepburn's acting support is first-rate, but it is her quaint rendering of the leading role that does most towards animating a museum piece. Her fluttering movements and the strained intensity of her emotional scenes evoke the full flavor of the work's genteel whimsy, while she has the knack of falling in with the slightly bantering treatment of the play that fortifies this screen version with laughter. Miss Hepburn summons more variety of mood and manner for her performance than has been her custom in recent films."

—HOWARD BARNES
New York Herald Tribune

"Barrie wrote *Quality Street* in 1900. Some of the tired gaiety still clinging to its voluminous and lacy folds might have been revitalized if Producer Berman and his aids had overcome their reverence for Sir James Barrie."

—*Time*

"Katharine Hepburn, who seemed pretty far from an ideal Barrie heroine in *The Little Minister,* is exactly right in *Quality Street,* keeping the tone of her characterization always light, breaking her usual monotony of speech, and photographing effectively both as the drab unlovely Phoebe and the girlish, laughing Livvy she pretends to be. It is a pretty performance."

—EILEEN CREELMAN
New York Sun

With Franchot Tone

On the set
with director George Stevens
and producer Pandro S. Berman

With Roland Varno
and Joan Fontaine

"The film is clean and wholesome, both whole-heartedly. It is handsomely made, costumed and mounted. Mr. Stevens' direction is suitably sensitive and Miss Hepburn's performance is in the best Barrie tradition."

—BLAND JOHANESON
New York Daily Mirror

"Miss Hepburn, well photographed here, acquits herself ably in her prankish role, Mr. Tone is adequately dashing in soldier's uniform and Fay Bainter plays the part of Phoebe's mousy sister Susan with a gleam of humor."

—ROSE PELSWICK
New York Journal

"Three short years ago Katharine Hepburn rocketed to screen heights, but a succession of unfortunate selections of material has marooned a competent girl in a bog of box office frustration. There probably is no one in pictures who needs a real money film as much as this actress."

—*Variety*

"It is a play depending for its sweet and mild humor upon quaint customs of the past, for its drama upon romance taken from a scented album. Miss Hepburn does this sort of thing so well that she seems to belong in it. . . . Speaking for myself, I am beginning to be a little tired of seeing Miss Hepburn in such roles and I see no reason why the public shouldn't begin to tire also."

—ARCHER WINSTEN
New York Post

NOTES

Quality Street had less general appeal than most of Hepburn's previous films. Somewhat limited in scope by its period, it nevertheless had humor, tenderness, emotional appeal, and plenty of vigor. She provided the "vigor." Sir James M. Barrie's whimsical play was written in 1900 and brought to America the following year by Charles Frohman.

The property was a silent vehicle for Marion Davies in 1927, and one might think that the role of Phoebe Throssel better suited the talents and delicious humor of Miss Davies. However, Kate's Phoebe was a charming portrait indeed and she seemed to have a great deal of pleasure playing her.

George Stevens again directed her and his production is a tribute to his taste and talent. The cast was impeccable and the photography, sets, and costumes were splendid. Roy Webb's fine musical score was nominated for an Academy Award.

With Roland Varno, William Bakewell, and Franchot Tone

Stage Door

AN RKO RADIO PICTURE   1937

CAST

Terry Randall   Katharine Hepburn
Jean Maitland   Ginger Rogers
Anthony Powell   Adolphe Menjou
Linda Shaw   Gail Patrick
Catherine Luther   Constance Collier
Kaye Hamilton   Andrea Leeds
Henry Sims   Samuel S. Hinds
Judy Canfield   Lucille Ball
Richard Carmichael   Pierre Watkin
Harcourt   Franklin Pangborn
Mrs. Orcutt   Elizabeth Dunne
Hattie   Phyllis Kennedy
Butcher   Grady Sutton
Milbank   Jack Carson
Dukenfield   Fred Santley
Bill   William Corson
Stage Director   Frank Reicher
Eve   Eve Arden
Annie   Ann Miller
Ann Braddock   Jane Rhodes
Mary   Margaret Early
Dizzy   Jean Rouverol
Olga Brent   Norma Drury
Susan   Peggy O'Donnell
Madeline   Harriett Brandon
Cast of Play   Katherine Alexander, Ralph Forbes, Mary
    Forbes, Huntley Gordon
Aide   Lynton Brent
Elsworth   Theodore Von Eltz

With Constance Collier

87

With Andrea Leeds

With Adolphe Menjou

With Ginger Rogers

Playwright Jack Rice
Chauffeur Harry Strang
Baggageman Bob Perry
Theatre Patron Larry Steers
Actresses Mary Bovard, Frances Gifford
Eve's Cat Whitey the Cat

CREDITS

Director Gregory La Cava
Producer Pandro S. Berman
Scenarists Morrie Ryskind, Anthony Veiller
Based on the Play by Edna Ferber, George S. Kaufman
Photographer Robert De Grasse
Art Director Van Nest Polglase
Associate Art Director Carroll Clark
Set Decorator Darrell Silvera
Editor William Hamilton
Sound Recorder John L. Cass
Musical Score Roy Webb
Costumer Muriel King
Makeup Artist Mel Burns
Assistant Director James Anderson

SYNOPSIS

The Footlights Club houses a sincere group of poverty-stricken girls bent on show-business careers. Terry Randall, a smug, self-confident debutante, moves into the club for atmosphere and almost immediately her meticulous diction and extensive wardrobe far from endear her to the other girls. The antagonists include her acid-tongued roommate, Jean Maitland, a soft-hearted dancer with a gift for biting wisecracks.

Before long, Broadway producer Anthony Powell, a libertine who tires quickly of his girls, showers his attentions on the girls—first on Jean, then upon Terry. In fact, he signs Terry to star in his upcoming production *Enchanted April* which, unknown to both of them, is financed by her father Henry Sims. Also up for the same role is a fine little actress named Kaye Hamilton who, wasted by malnutrition, is crushed to see the dilettante Terry get the role she has lived to play and, on the opening night, commits suicide.

The tragedy of Kaye's death deeply affects Terry, raising her to the emotional heights required to put the play across. Shaken out of her brittle arrogance, she performs with inspiration and is an instant success. She also becomes, by dint of a martyr's curtain speech, the most popular girl around the Footlights Club.

CRITICS' CIRCLE

"It brings Katharine Hepburn back to the spot she occupied before a series of monotonous performances dimmed the memory of *Morning Glory*. It brings new laurels to Ginger Rogers who, coming through with a slick portrayal, proves her ability isn't confined solely to dancing. Under the expert guidance of director Gregory La Cava, this rewritten *Stage Door* takes its place as one of the season's best."

—ROSE PELSWICK
New York Journal

"It has less superficial brilliance and a more penetrating sincerity than the Kaufman-Ferber play."

—*Cue*

"Never has Miss Hepburn been more compelling, more spellbinding. In the powerful emotional climax in which, about to open in her first play, she learns of Kaye's suicide, she plays a tremendously effective scene which ranks as one of the best things she has done on the screen."

Brooklyn Daily Eagle

"Now and again Hollywood produces a version of a play that is superior to the parent work. RKO Radio has accomplished this feat in the picturization of the Kaufman-Ferber play, *Stage Door*. The film is more logical than the play and it has also more vitality. Although the picture has an abundance of smart repartee, a certain amount of wise-cracking and, for the most part, smooth comedy angles, the story is taken seriously and it results in an affecting, poignant drama, which has the added worth of being convincing.

". . . It is the type of role in which Miss Hepburn excels. Where most actresses in dealing with the part of a stage-struck girl might be tempted to over-act, Miss Hepburn realizes the need for restraint, evidenced by her brilliant work several years ago in *Morning Glory*, and in this current picture she is equally effective. Her Terry is a vivacious, honest, intelligent girl."

—MORDAUNT HALL
The New York Times

On the set
with director Gregory La Cava

With Ginger Rogers

With Lucille Ball and Ginger Rogers

89

With Samuel S. Hinds

"The leading roles are played with such magnificent flair by Katharine Hepburn, Ginger Rogers and Andrea Leeds that it would be easy to overlook the all-important work of director and scenarists. Miss Hepburn has never demonstrated more complete authority as an actress. Miss Rogers, as her caustic roommate, serves notice that she can act as well as dance. Her portrayal is straightforward, amusing and persuasive. To Miss Leeds has gone the difficult task of playing the suicide scene. She does it without faltering for an instant in a memorable screen passage. *Stage Door* . . . is a brilliant, witty and moving show."

—HOWARD BARNES
New York Herald Tribune

"It is artfully theatric in its emotionalism, balancing rough wit with lacy tenderness, sly sophistication with forthright sentimentality. In acting, directing, writing, it represents the finest flower of movie craftsmanship."

—BLAND JOHANESON
The New York Daily Mirror

"Cinemagoers welcomed the return of Katharine Hepburn from farthingales and tippets, were agreeably surprised at Ginger Rogers' versatility. But the actress who nearly stole the show was Andrea Leeds."

—*Time*

NOTES

Hepburn finally got to work with director Gregory La Cava in *Stage Door* (their earlier effort *Three Came Unarmed*

was abandoned in favor of her starring role in *Christopher Strong*). The Ryskind-Veiller scenario augmented the original Ferber-Kaufman dialogue with a great deal more brisk conversation. The results were better.

She had the difficult task of playing a determined *amateur* who becomes an actress of power through another's tragedy, but she gave a fine performance. Not the least of *Stage Door's* attractions was Ginger Rogers' emergence from dancing slippers as a lovely and lively comedienne. La Cava handled his actors with consummate skill, and Adolphe Menjou, Constance Collier, Gail Patrick, Eve Arden, and Lucille Ball were standouts. Andrea Leeds, on loan from Goldwyn, gave a delicately shaded portrayal of a high-strung yet dedicated tyro.

Stage Door was done on Broadway with Margaret Sullavan (Terry), Phyllis Brooks (Jean) and Frances Fuller (Kaye) and on tour with Joan Bennett in the lead.

The play-within-the-play sequence was a remodeled scene from the third act of *The Lake*. Hepburn's rendition of the line "The calla lilies are in bloom again" became a tag line for years.

The whole aura of noisy, glib, and wisecracking girls who keep on making the rounds of theatrical offices despite repeated rebuffs made *Stage Door* a grand box-office success. It received four Academy Award nominations: Best Picture, Best Supporting Actress (Andrea Leeds), Best Director and Best Screenplay.

90   With Andrea Leeds

Bringing Up Baby

AN RKO RADIO PICTURE   1938

CAST

Susan Vance   Katharine Hepburn
David Huxley   Cary Grant
Major Horace Applegate   Charles Ruggles
Aunt Elizabeth   May Robson
Constable Slocum   Walter Catlett
Gogarty   Barry Fitzgerald
Dr. Fritz Lehmann   Fritz Feld
Mrs. Gogarty (Hannah)   Leona Roberts
Alexander Peabody   George Irving
Mrs. Lehmann   Tala Birell
Alice Swallow   Virginia Walker
Elmer   John Kelly
George, the Dog   Asta
Baby, the Leopard   Nissa
Louis, the Headwaiter   George Humbert
Joe, the Bartender   Ernest Cossart
David's Caddy   Brooks Benedict
Roustabout   Jack Carson
Circus Manager   Richard Lane
Motor Cop   Ward Bond

CREDITS

Director   Howard Hawks
Producer   Howard Hawks
Associate Producer   Cliff Reid
Scenarists   Dudley Nichols, Hagar Wilde

With Cary Grant

With Cary Grant

With May Robson and Charles Ruggles

With Cary Grant, Asta,
May Robson, and Leona Roberts

With Cary Grant

With Tala Birell, Fritz Feld,
and Cary Grant

93

Based on a Story by   Hagar Wilde
Photographer   Russell Metty
Art Director   Van Nest Polglase
Associate Art Director   Perry Ferguson
Set Decorator   Darrell Silvera
Editor   George Hively
Sound Recorder   John L. Cass
Musical Score   Roy Webb
Costumer   Howard Greer
Makeup Artist   Mel Burns
Special Photographic Effects   Vernon L. Walker
Assistant Director   Edward Donahue

SYNOPSIS

David Huxley, a professor of zoology, intends to marry his secretary, Alice Swallow, as soon as he can take time off from his work of assembling the bones of a giant dinosaur. Everything is easy going with shy David and his very special world until Susan Vance, a madcap heiress, appears on the scene. Susan, a girl who always gets what she wants, wants David. She manages, in record time, to persuade the professor to take care of her tame Brazilian leopard "Baby." As a result, David loses his secretary; and a priceless dinosaur bone; alienates Susan's aunt Elizabeth, who had promised a million dollars to David's museum; and lands in jail. Needless to say, Susan gets David, the museum gets the money, and the giant dinosaur crashes to the floor.

CRITICS' CIRCLE

"Katharine Hepburn, as an heiress who goes after her man once she spots him, contributes one of her most invigorating screen characterizations as a madcap deb."

—*Variety*

"Cary Grant handles the role of the paleontologist with his usual comic skill but the real surprise of the picture is Katharine Hepburn. There has long been a delusion abroad that Miss Hepburn's dramatic talent was confined to a narrow range, and her recent costume pictures seemed to prove it. In *Bringing Up Baby* she leaps bravely into a new and daffy domain already conquered by Carole Lombard and equals Miss Lombard's best."

—*Life*

"*Bringing Up Baby* is undoubtedly the craziest, wackiest and screwiest farce that was ever saved from becoming idiotic by the talent of a delightful actress. Besides the new Miss Hepburn, who should find favor with a new audience as well as her old following, the supporting cast is splendid. Expertly directed by Howard Hawks who keeps the entire

With Cary Grant

production up to the pace set by his star, *Bringing Up Baby* earns its place among the comedy leaders of the screen, and is by far the funniest collection of nonsense of the young year."

—HERBERT COHN
Brooklyn Daily Eagle

"The film is rather frantically funny, relying on improbable situations and slapstick. Mr. Grant and Miss Hepburn, when in doubt, fall flat on their faces, trip over logs, knock each other down. Once was enough. The director, Howard Hawks, has been lazy about his editing. The film is much too long, stretching its title joke into 102 full minutes. In spite of all that, *Bringing Up Baby* still has its laughs."

—EILEEN CREELMAN
New York Sun

"Too farcical? Perhaps, but what joyous, unrestrained, sidesplitting fun! The acting of the entire cast, under Howard Hawks' bullet-speed direction, is superb. Having proved that she is the cinema's finest dramatic actress, Miss Hepburn now demonstrates that she is a comedienne of the highest order."

—WILLIAM BOEHNEL
New York World-Telegram

"When she was a college girl ten years ago, red-headed, Melpomene-mouthed Katharine Hepburn, in a trailing white nightgown cross-hatched with gold ribbon, regaled Bryn Mawr as Pandora in *The Woman in the Moone*. And since then most of Actress Hepburn's public appearances have been for the catch-in-the-throat cinema, playing alternately great ladies and emotional starvelings of brittle bravado. For '*Bringing Up Baby*' she plumps her broad A in the midst of a frantically farcical plot involving Actor Cary Grant, a terrier, a leopard, a Brontosaurus skeleton and a crotchety collection of Connecticut quidnuncs, proves she can be as amusingly skittery a comedienne as the best of them. . . . Under the deft, directorial hand of Howard Hawks, *Bringing Up Baby* comes off second only to last year's whimsical high spot, *The Awful Truth*. . . . *Bringing Up Baby's* slapstick is irrational, rough-&-tumble, undignified, obviously devised with the idea that the cinemaudience will enjoy (as it does) seeing stagy Actress Hepburn get a proper mussing up."

—*Time*

"To the Music Hall yesterday came a farce which you can barely hear above the precisely enunciated patter of Miss Katharine Hepburn and the ominous tread of deliberative gags. In *Bringing Up Baby* Miss Hepburn has a role which calls for her to be breathless, senseless and terribly, terribly fatiguing. She succeeds, and we can be callous enough to hint it is not entirely a matter of performance."

—FRANK S. NUGENT
The New York Times

"The players deserve the chief credit for the smattering of amusement in the offering. The part of a spoiled playgirl is perfectly suited to Miss Hepburn's talents, and she offers as breezy a performance as the script permits. Mr. Grant has more chance to create a burlesque, but he sometimes finds himself stranded while the plot makes good and sure that no one will miss a gag or a comical situation."

—HOWARD BARNES
New York Herald Tribune

NOTES

In *Bringing Up Baby* Hepburn proved that she could handle zany comic situations with ease. Her madcap heiress is pure bliss and one can tell she had the time of her life, while Cary Grant was hilarious as the shy anthropologist. Together they made a beautiful team—keeping up with the film's screwball pace.

Howard Hawks directed with complete abandon and the film made money despite the fact that the vogue for screwball farce had passed. Hawks said of Kate, "She has an amazing body—like a boxer. It's hard for her to make a wrong turn. She's always in perfect balance. She has that beautiful coordination that allows you to stop and make a turn and never fall off balance. This gives her an amazing sense of timing. I've never seen a girl that had that odd rhythm and control."

Also involved in the proceedings were Charles Ruggles, May Robson, Fritz Feld, and the dog Skippy, a wire-haired terrier who had won renown as "Asta" in the *Thin Man* series and was "Mr. Smith" in *The Awful Truth*.

The star of the title was an eight-year-old leopard named Nissa. Kate had no qualms about working with Nissa and got to know her a little each day before the shooting of their scenes began. Hepburn was told to douse herself with perfume "which always makes Nissa playful" and put resin on the soles of her shoes to prevent a sudden slip that might frighten the leopard. Said Nissa's trainer Mme. Olga Celeste, "I think if Miss Hepburn should ever decide to leave the screen she could make a very good animal trainer. She has control of her nerves and, best of all, no fear of animals."

With Cary Grant

With Cary Grant

Holiday

A COLUMBIA PICTURE   1938

CAST

Linda Seton   Katharine Hepburn
Johnny Case   Cary Grant
Julia Seton   Doris Nolan
Ned Seton   Lew Ayres
Nick Potter   Edward Everett Horton
Edward Seton   Henry Kolker
Laura Cram   Binnie Barnes
Susan Potter   Jean Dixon
Seton Cram   Henry Daniell
Banker   Charles Trowbridge
Henry   George Pauncefort
Thayer   Charles Richman
Jennings   Mitchell Harris
Edgar   Neil Fitzgerald
Grandmother   Marion Ballou
Man in Church   Howard Hickman
Woman in Church   Hilda Plowright
Cook   Mabel Colcord
Woman on Staircase   Bess Flowers
Scotchmen   Harry Allen, Edward Cooper
Farmer's Wife   Margaret McWade
Farmer   Frank Shannon
Farm Girl   Aileen Carlyle
Taxi Driver   Matt McHugh
Steward   Maurice Brierre
Mrs. Jennings   Esther Peck
Mrs. Thayer   Lillian West
Grandfather   Luke Cosgrave

With Jean Dixon, Lew Ayres,
and Edward Everett Horton

CREDITS

Director George Cukor
Associate Producer Everett Riskin
Scenarists Donald Ogden Stewart, Sidney Buchman
Based on the Play by Philip Barry
Photographer Franz Planer
Art Director Stephen Goosson
Associate Art Director Lionel Banks
Set Decorator Babs Johnstone
Editors Otto Meyer, Al Clark
Sound Recorder Lodge Cunningham
Musical Score Sidney Cutner
Musical Director Morris Stoloff
Costumer Kalloch
Jewelry by Paul Flato
Assistant Director Clifford Broughton

SYNOPSIS

Johnny Case, a terribly impractical young man, meets Julia Seton at Lake Placid and proposes to her. Later invited to her elegant New York mansion, he realizes that she is one of *the* Setons. At first, Julia appears to be his sort. However, when he outlines his plan about retiring young after making a bundle, and working again when he gets older, she balks.

Julia's unconventional sister Linda vainly tries to pull the two together but, in so doing, falls hopelessly in love with Johnny herself. Johnny finds a kindred soul in Linda for she not only understands him and takes to his closest friends, the Potters, but also has the courage to break away from her oppressively gilded existence to join him on his holiday.

CRITICS' CIRCLE

"By her performance as Linda, Katharine Hepburn seems highly likely to refute the argument of New York's Independent Theatre Owners Association, who claimed a month ago that her box-office appeal was practically nil. Highly responsive to the cajolings of pudgy, moon-faced Director Cukor, she gives her liveliest performance since appearing in his *Little Women*."

—*Time*

"There are notable characterizations by all the members of the cast as well as by Mr. Grant, whose performance is outstanding. Miss Hepburn is convincingly wistful as the rebellious Linda."

—Rose Pelswick
New York Journal-American

"George Cukor has directed it for Columbia with his customary suavity and precision, making the whole thing a sleek piece of screen comedy. . . . The comedy is full of the best of humor, edged with pathos never allowed to drop into sentimentality. And it is played with the greatest cheerfulness and a winning skill."

—Arthur Pollock
Brooklyn Daily Eagle

"It is a film to which Miss Hepburn is entirely suited. Surrounded by a splendid cast, placed in staggering settings and clothes, given bright dialogue which modernizes the Philip Barry play, Hepburn makes an acting carnival of *Holiday* and her most pleasing picture of the season. Grant is very good as the young man who refuses to trade his dream for easy wealth. Doris Nolan is splendid as father's true

With Cary Grant

With Doris Nolan and Cary Grant

daughter. Lew Ayres is beautifully touching as the frustrated younger brother."

New York Daily Mirror

"Miss Hepburn—the 'New Hepburn,' according to the publicity copy—is very mannish in this one, deep-voiced, grammatically precise, and is only a wee bit inclined to hysteria. Mr. Grant's Mr. Case is really the best role, although it is quite possible that neither Mr. Barry nor Columbia saw it that way. All told, what with George Cukor's sense of directorial balance, good dialogue, the amusing supporting presence of Edward Everett Horton, Jean Dixon, Lew Ayres and Binnie Barnes and others, *Holiday* comes satisfactorily close to being one. In fact, it is, and a pleasant one too."

—FRANK S. NUGENT
The New York Times

"George Cukor's expert direction and a vibrant, moving performance by Katharine Hepburn. Even though the comic edge of the original has been considerably blunted in translation, humor and romance have been skillfully blended to make a beguiling show. As a poor little rich girl, she sustains a dramatic suspense and emotional intensity which the narrative desperately needs. I call this first-class screen acting."

—HOWARD BARNES
New York Herald Tribune

NOTES

In 1936, Columbia had paid $80,000 to RKO for rights to a group of old RKO scripts. *The Awful Truth* and *Holiday* were two in that package.

With Cary Grant

With Doris Nolan

With Doris Nolan, Cary Grant, and Henry Kolker

Columbia hired George Cukor to direct the second film version of *Holiday,* Philip Barry's revolt against stuffed-shirt tradition and Cary Grant was given the role of Johnny Case. Hepburn, who was being offered second-rate material at RKO, bought herself out of her contract, and hastened over to Columbia to play the lovely nonconformist Linda Seton, the role she had been destined for since she first understudied Hope Williams back in 1928.

Donald Ogden Stewart, who had played Nick Potter in that production, wrote the scenario from which Cukor would work. Stewart injected his script with smart and literate

99

With Lew Ayres

dialogue. The result was a highly funny, urbane comedy—in the best of taste—in which Hepburn was simply radiant, forthright, and endlessly entertaining. Grant was marvelous as the man of principles.

Cukor worked his cast as an ensemble group and to this day, *Holiday* remains one of those special joys of the director's art. Excellent support was given by Doris Nolan, Lew Ayres, Edward Everett Horton, Jean Dixon, Henry Kolker, and others. Columbia spared no cost in giving this a top-notch production. The art direction of Stephen Goosson and Lionel Banks won an Academy Award nomination.

Holiday was first filmed by RKO-Pathe in 1930 with Ann Harding (Linda), Robert Ames (Johnny), and Mary Astor (Julia), but it was nothing more than a filmed stage play.

Co-star Cary Grant later said of Hepburn, "As an actress, she's a joy to work with. She's in there trying every minute. There isn't anything passive about her; she 'gives.' And as a person, she's real. There's no pretense about her. She's the most completely honest woman I've ever met."

On the set with Cary Grant, director George Cukor, production crew

With Cary Grant, Mary Nash, John Halliday, James Stewart and Ruth Hussey

The Philadelphia Story

A METRO-GOLDWYN-MAYER PICTURE   1940

CAST

C. K. Dexter Haven   Cary Grant
Tracy Lord   Katharine Hepburn
Mike Connor   James Stewart
Liz Imbrie   Ruth Hussey
George Kittredge   John Howard
Uncle Willie   Roland Young
Seth Lord   John Halliday
Dinah Lord   Virginia Weidler
Margaret Lord   Mary Nash
Sidney Kidd   Henry Daniell
Edward   Lionel Pape
Thomas   Rex Evans
John   Russ Clark
Librarian   Hilda Plowright
Manicurist   Lita Chevret
Bartender   Lee Phelps
Mac   David Clyde
Willie's Butler   Claude King
Dr. Parsons   Robert De Bruce
Elsie   Veda Buckland
First Mainliner   Dorothy Fay
Second Mainliner   Florine McKinney
Third Mainliner   Helene Whitney
Fourth Mainliner   Hillary Brooke

CREDITS

Director   George Cukor
Producer   Joseph L. Mankiewicz
Scenarist   Donald Ogden Stewart
Based on the Play by   Philip Barry
As Produced on the Stage by   The Theatre Guild, Inc.
Photographer   Joseph Ruttenberg
Art Director   Cedric Gibbons
Associate Art Director   Wade B. Rubottom
Set Decorator   Edwin B. Willis
Editor   Frank Sullivan
Sound Recorder   Douglas Shearer
Musical Score   Franz Waxman
Hair Stylist   Sidney Guilaroff
Costumer   Adrian
Makeup Artist   Jack Dawn
Assistant Director   Edward Woehler

SYNOPSIS

On the eve of Tracy Lord's second marriage, to a stuffy Philadelphia blueblood, her ex-husband, C. K. Dexter Haven, equally well born, but more down to earth and something of a drunk, makes an appearance. Haven has arranged for Mike Connor, a reporter from *Spy* magazine,

With James Stewart

With James Stewart,
John Howard, and Mary Nash

With John Howard

and Liz Imbrie, the magazine's photographer, to write up the wedding festivities. The reportorial duo are allowed to stay on in the exalted Lord household only after Tracy discovers that she can buy off a scandalous story detailing her father's illicit affair with an actress by consenting to pose for *Spy* herself.

In the next twenty-four hours, Tracy faces a variety of new experiences. Her ex-husband shows her up as a prig and an icicle. Reporter Connor, who has deeper ambitions as a writer, gets Tracy drunk on champagne and they go for a nude swim. Hours later, her father appears and justifies his conduct by asserting he is just an aging man trying to hold on to his youth. Next morning, Tracy is a changed girl and remarries husband number one.

CRITICS' CIRCLE

"Discarding the profanity of the original they have followed so skillfully Mr. Barry's blueprint for an adult, often subtle, and mature entertainment that the spectator would find it hard to detect the alterations without hints from the roving camera. *The Philadelphia Story* is that good. . . .

"Miss Hepburn is a more distinguished, a more deeply understanding Tracy Lord now than she was when we saw the play in New York last Spring. Whether one regards Miss Hepburn as an important actress or just a glamorous lady with a harshly musical voice, one can accept her warmth, her sincerity, her sensitivity. There is a sheen now to her vividness, and her abrupt, electric style of motion has taken on flow and grace. There is no doubt of her validity in the role of Tracy Lord."

—*The Christian Science Monitor*

"For *The Philadelphia Story* fits the curious talents of the redheaded Miss Hepburn like a coat of quick-dry enamel. It is said to have been written for her. Its shiny surface reflects perfectly from her gaunt, bony face. Its languid action becomes her lean, rangy body. Its brittle smart-talk suits her metallic voice. And when Katharine Hepburn sets out to play Katharine Hepburn, she is a sight to behold. Nobody is then her equal."

—*Life*

"George Cukor has directed it with tonic imagination, the acting of every member of the cast is flawless, the lines sparkle and bubble and the script is so artfully contrived that the wit is seldom of the wisecrack variety, but the kind that results naturally and effectively from shrewdly observed characterization. It is a sagacious, literate and scampish entertainment."

—William Boehnel
New York World-Telegram

"*The Philadelphia Story* is first and above all a Katharine Hepburn triumph. Not only does she know her character

With Cary Grant and James Stewart

With Virginia Weidler,
Mary Nash and Cary Grant

With John Halliday and Mary Nash

intimately, but she portrays her with humor, wisdom, and an emotional intensity that she hasn't displayed to screen audiences since *A Bill of Divorcement*."

—ELSIE FINN
Philadelphia Record

"Cary Grant plays the ex-husband with dignity and a sharp humor, making an excellent contrast to James Stewart's slow, easy-going comedy. Miss Hepburn, more natural than she has ever been on screen or stage, misses neither the fun nor the tender qualities of Tracy's character."

—EILEEN CREELMAN
New York Sun

"*The Philadelphia Story* is much more entertaining. . . . That is because performances, moods, and feelings are beautifully rendered."

—ARCHER WINSTON
New York Post

"*The Philadelphia Story* was made in 1940, with Katharine Hepburn, Cary Grant, and James Stewart. All three give performances of such calm comic judgment that one wonders whether Cukor's legendary reputation as an actress's director does him honour enough. . . . Donald Ogden Stewart's

owlishly witty screenplay . . . embodies a view of life as critical and formed as one would expect of any serious dramatic writer."

—PENELOPE GILLIATT
The (London) Observer (1961)

NOTES

The screen version of Hepburn's notable stage hit not only brought her back into the front ranks as a screen actress, but made her a respected businesswoman as well. She bought the film rights from Barry and received many offers to sell them. Warners offered $225,000 but Kate was not included in the bargain. Finally MGM came across with the best deal—$75,000 for her services, $175,000 for the rights, her choice of director (Cukor) and co-stars (Grant and Stewart) and reasonable script supervision. In order to get Grant, MGM had to promise him top billing and agree to pay his salary of $137,500 to the British War Relief Fund.

Under Cukor's adroit guidance, Hepburn added new dimension and freshness to the role that had been especially tailored for her. Grant's C. K. Dexter Haven was delivered

With James Stewart

in his own impeccable style and James Stewart completed the trio, giving a grand account of himself.

Who can forget the tears welling up in her eyes as her father says, "You have a good mind, a pretty face, and a disciplined body that does what you tell it. You have everything it takes to make a lovely woman except the one essential—an understanding heart. Without it, you might just as well be made of bronze."

The Philadelphia Story won six Academy Award nominations: Best Picture, Best Actor (Stewart), Best Actress (Hepburn), Best Supporting Actress (Ruth Hussey), Best Screenplay (Donald Ogden Stewart), and Best Director (Cukor). Both Stewarts won! Kate was honored with the New York Film Critics' award.

With James Stewart

104

Woman of the Year

A METRO-GOLDWYN-MAYER PICTURE   1942

CAST

Sam Craig   Spencer Tracy
Tess Harding   Katharine Hepburn
Ellen Whitcomb   Fay Bainter
Clayton   Reginald Owen
William Harding   Minor Watson
Pinkie Peters   William Bendix
Flo Peters   Gladys Blake
Gerald   Dan Tobin
Phil Whittaker   Roscoe Karns
Ellis   William Tannen
Dr. Martin Lubbeck   Ludwig Stossel
Matron at Refugee Home   Sara Haden
Alma   Edith Evanson
Chris   George Kezas
Reporter   Jimmy Conlin
Justice of the Peace   Henry Roquemore
Harding's Chauffeur   Cyril Ring
Punchy   Ben Lessy
Pal   Johnny Berkes
Reporter   Ray Teal
Football Player   Duke York
Adolph   Edward McWade
Building Superintendent   Joe Yule
Chairlady   Winifred Harris
Man at Banquet   William Holmes

With Spencer Tracy

CREDITS

Director George Stevens

Producer Joseph L. Mankiewicz

Original Screenplay Ring Lardner, Jr., Michael Kanin

Photographer Joseph Ruttenberg

Art Director Cedric Gibbons

Associate Art Director Randall Duell

Set Decorator Edwin B. Willis

Editor Frank Sullivan

Sound Recorder Douglas Shearer

Musical Score Franz Waxman

Costumer Adrian

Makeup Artist Jack Dawn

Hair Stylist Sydney Guilaroff

Assistant Director Robert Golden

SYNOPSIS

International affairs columnist Tess Harding and Sam Craig, a sportswriter for the same newspaper, have a running feud over the game of baseball. Violating the sanctity of the press box, Sam introduces Tess to baseball and they become fast friends. Although extreme opposites, they are soon married, much to the amazement of their friends.

Tess goes along as the same as before, putting her career ahead of wifely duties. Sam, who expected at least a little domesticity from his wife, eventually walks out. On the evening that Tess discovers her failure as a wife, she is named the Woman of the Year. Soon, when her father remarries, she listens to the wedding vows with new understanding and determines to make a go of her marriage.

CRITICS' CIRCLE

"*Woman of the Year* is particularly fortunate in having Miss Hepburn and Mr. Tracy teamed for the first time in a film. For they are both so competent in the field of screen performing that they rarely miss in realizing all the potentialities of a script or in realizing all the conception of an able director."

—HOWARD BARNES
New York Herald Tribune

"*The Philadelphia Story,* it is now clear, marked a turning point in Miss Hepburn's career; gone for good are the mannerisms, the tricks, the superficiality which marred much of her previous work. Her performance in *Woman of the Year* shows even more subtlety and depth, despite the light nature of the story. Her performance is a constant pleasure to watch. Mr. Tracy is an excellent foil for her in this particular instance. His quiet, masculine stubbornness and prosaic outlook on life is in striking contrast with her sparkle and brilliance. They make a fine team, and each complements the other."

—DONALD KIRKLEY
Baltimore Sun

"Actors Hepburn and Tracy have a fine old time in *Woman of the Year.* They take turns playing straight for each other, act one superbly directed love scene, succeed in turning several batches of cinematic corn into passable moonshine. As a lady columnist, she is just right; as a working reporter, he is practically perfect. For once, strident Katharine Hepburn is properly subdued." —*Time*

"This is a sound script to start with. Spencer Tracy's steady skillful, quietly humorous characterization contrasted with Katharine Hepburn's tense, rather shrill portrait of an egotistic woman. The principals are excellent. George Stevens has directed with so light and sure a touch that the Sam Craigs become very real people."

—EILEEN CREELMAN
New York Sun

With Spencer Tracy

With Spencer Tracy

"The title part is played by Miss Hepburn, who has never looked more beautiful. It is played with such humor, resourcefulness and contagious spirit that I think it is even better than her performance in *The Philadelphia Story*, and that was just as fine as anything could be. No less satisfactory is Mr. Tracy. There isn't a false note in his characterization of the sports writer. And the things he can do with gesture, with a smile, are nobody's business. . . . What an actor!"

—William Boehnel
New York World-Telegram

"Miss Hepburn and Mr. Tracy are admirably paired. Mr. Tracy's easy style with an undertone of firmness convinces one that his Sam is the man to cope with Miss Hepburn's combination of detachment and restlessness as Tess, the career woman."

—*The Christian Science Monitor*

With Henry Roquemore,
Fay Bainter and Spencer Tracy

On the set with
director George Stevens

NOTES

In *The Philadelphia Story* Hepburn was a goddess in high society: cold, pristine, distant. In *Woman of the Year* her new co-star, Spencer Tracy, toppled her from that lofty perch—to the delight of millions of movie goers. Tracy was just the man Hepburn needed to come along at this time for their individual styles were well suited to one another.

At first news of this unique casting, one began to conjure up a picture of an odd couple, but the match could not have been more apt. Their screen partnership was to take them through eight more films spanning nearly twenty-eight years. They were, indeed, the perfect American couple in all their moods, settings, and experiences.

Woman of the Year was one of the brightest comedies of 1942 (it was completed just prior to Pearl Harbor) and was expertly directed by George Stevens. The script, by two relatively unknown writers, was deft and amusing. Adding to the luster of its technical crew, the supporting cast included Fay Bainter, Reginald Owen, William Bendix, Gladys Blake, and Sara Haden.

Hepburn received her fourth Academy Award nomination but only the Ring Lardner, Jr.–Michael Kanin original screenplay won an Oscar.

With Spencer Tracy

With Spencer Tracy
and Reginald Owen

109

With Spencer Tracy

Keeper of the Flame

A METRO-GOLDWYN-MAYER PICTURE 1942

CAST

Steven O'Malley Spencer Tracy
Christine Forrest Katharine Hepburn
Clive Kerndon Richard Whorf
Mrs. Forrest Margaret Wycherly
Mr. Arbuthnot Donald Meek
Freddie Ridges Horace (Stephen) McNally
Jane Harding Audrey Christie
Dr. Fielding Frank Craven
Geoffrey Midford Forrest Tucker
Orion Percy Kilbride
Jason Rickards Howard Da Silva
Jeb Rickards Darryl Hickman
Piggot William Newell
John Rex Evans
Anna Blanche Yurka
Janet Mary McLeod
William Clifford Brooke
Ambassador Craufurd Kent
Messenger Boy Mickey Martin
Reporters Manart Kippen, Donald Gallaher, Cliff Danielson
Men Major Sam Harris, Art Howard, Harold Miller
Pete Jay Ward
Susan Rita Quigley

Auctioneer Dick Elliott
Lawyer Edward McWade
Boy Reporter Irvin Lee
Girls Diana Dill (Diana Douglas), Gloria Tucker
Minister's Voice Dr. Charles Frederick Lindsley
Tim Robert Pittard
Gardener Louis Mason

CREDITS

Director George Cukor
Producer Victor Saville
Associate Producer Leon Gordon
Scenarist Donald Ogden Stewart
Based on the Novel by I. A. R. Wylie
Photographer William Daniels
Art Director Cedric Gibbons
Associate Art Director Lyle Wheeler
Set Decorator Edwin B. Willis
Associate Set Decorator Jack Moore
Editor James E. Newcom
Sound Recorder Douglas Shearer
Musical Score Bronislau Kaper
Costumer Adrian
Makeup Artist Jack Dawn
Special Effects Warren Newcombe
Assistant Director Edward Woehler

SYNOPSIS

Steven O'Malley, a noted correspondent just back from Europe, is sent by his newspaper to write a story on the death of Robert V. Forrest, an American national hero. Christine Forrest, the widow, is unapproachable and the dead man's secretary, Clive Kerndon, behaves suspiciously. O'Malley overhears a conversation between Christine and Jeb Rickards, the son of the gateman, which convinces him she played a part in her husband's murder. He accuses her of having killed her husband and says he must write his story despite his love for her.

Later, through his probing, O'Malley discovers that Forrest's supernationalism was merely star-spangled fascism. When Christine finally decides to tell him the truth, the murderer sets fire to the evidence, and they are trapped in a burning building. O'Malley now realizes that Christine has lied only to shield her husband's name, motivated by what the name represented to so many Americans.

CRITICS' CIRCLE

"Mr. Tracy relies heavily on the pursed lips and crinkled forehead of his talent, but he turns in a rounded, effective performance. Miss Hepburn once more is the actress over whom it is easiest to start an argument. She parades all the

With Spencer Tracy

With Richard Whorf

With Richard Whorf

111

elaborate mannerisms that engulf her characterization for some watchers and sends others out of the place ecstatic over the superb art of the lady, you take your choice of reactions, but one thing is certain: either reaction will be strongly felt."

—ALTON COOK
New York World-Telegram

"Tracy is fine as the reporter and Miss Hepburn, except in the last few scenes, is very persuasive as the widow."
New York Daily News

"*Keeper of the Flame* is an expensive testimonial to Hollywood's inability to face a significant theme, i.e., that Fascism might offer itself to the U.S. behind a handsome and disarming face. . . . For stars Hepburn and Tracy and all concerned, it is the high point of a significant failure."
—*Time*

"In *Keeper of the Flame*, George Cukor has made a psychological thriller with a sociological message. The new MGM film is unorthodox and, on the whole, absorbing drama. Mr. Cukor has filled it with ominous portents and overtones which take the place of physical action. . . . Mr. Cukor has not Alfred Hitchcock's facility with psychological thrills but he has turned out an important and arresting film. Katharine Hepburn is not an altogether happy choice for the heroine

With Spencer Tracy

With Darryl Hickman

With Howard da Silva
and Spencer Tracy

of this story. She is an admirable subject for interesting photography and her mannerisms are suited to certain roles, but she lacks the technical skill required to register the character complexities of a heroine like Christine."
—*The Christian Science Monitor*

"The heroine of the film is as lovely and poised as ever and she (Hepburn) gives a magnificent portrayal of a grief-stricken widow with something to hide from the reporters. Spencer Tracy gives a somewhat restrained but completely winning performance."

—JOHN U. STURDEVANT
New York Journal-American

"That the two principal players, Mr. Tracy and Miss Hepburn, give *Keeper of the Flame* its full values, goes without saying. They are a beautifully matched team, as witness *Woman of the Year,* and they bring to the current business their finest efforts."

—LEO MISHKIN
New York Morning-Telegraph

NOTES

In the late thirties, RKO Radio bought the "idea for an unwritten novel" from I. A. R. Wylie but never did anything with it. MGM bought the rights and it ultimately became the second Tracy-Hepburn picture. Donald Ogden Stewart turned *Keeper of the Flame* into a fascinating and suspenseful antifascist film.

George Cukor directed the pair and endeavored to employ the same moody suspense technique at which Alfred Hitchcock was a master. William Daniels' camera work, Cedric Gibbons' sets, and Bronislau Kaper's musical score helped keep the mood and proper tone of the piece—but Hitchcock it was not.

Tracy employed his best understatement in the role of the inquiring reporter and Hepburn, looking radiant in gowns by Adrian, was arresting as the widow with a secret.

With Donald Meek

On the set with director George Cukor and photographer William Daniels

113

On the set with director Frank Borzage

Stage Door Canteen

A SOL LESSER PRODUCTION
RELEASED THRU UNITED ARTISTS   1943

CAST

Eileen   Cheryl Walker
Ed "Dakota" Smith   William Terry
Jean   Marjorie Riordan
"California"   Lon McCallister
Ella Sue   Margaret Early
"Texas"   Michael Harrison
Mamie   Dorothea Kent
"Jersey"   Fred Brady
Lillian   Marion Shockley
The Australian   Patrick O'Moore
Girl   Ruth Roman

And, the Stars at the Stage Door Canteen:

Judith Anderson, Henry Armetta, Benny Baker,
Kenny Baker, Tallulah Bankhead, Ralph Bellamy,
Edgar Bergen & Charlie McCarthy, Ray Bolger,
Helen Broderick, Ina Claire, Katharine Cornell,
Lloyd Corrigan, Jane Cowl, Jane Darwell,
William Demarest, Virginia Field, Dorothy Fields, Gracie
Fields, Lynn Fontanne, Arlene Francis, Vinton Freedley,
Billy Gilbert, Lucile Gleason, Vera Gordon,
Virginia Grey, Helen Hayes, Katharine Hepburn,
Hugh Herbert, Jean Hersholt, Sam Jaffe, Allen Jenkins,
George Jessel, Roscoe Karns, Virginia Kaye,

114

With director Frank Borzage (on her right) and the production crew

With Selena Royle

With Cheryl Walker

115

Tom Kennedy, Otto Kruger, June Lang, Betty Lawford, Gertrude Lawrence, Gypsy Rose Lee, Alfred Lunt, Bert Lytell, Harpo Marx, Aline MacMahon, Elsa Maxwell, Helen Menken, Yehudi Menuhin, Ethel Merman, Ralph Morgan, Alan Mowbray, Paul Muni, Elliott Nugent, Merle Oberon, Franklin Pangborn, Helen Parrish, Brock Pemberton, George Raft, Lanny Ross, Selena Royle, Martha Scott, Cornelia Otis Skinner, Ned Sparks, Bill Stern, Ethel Waters, Johnny Weissmuller, Arleen Whelan, Dame May Whitty, Ed Wynn

And:

Count Basie and His Band
Xavier Cugat and His Orchestra, with Lina Romay
Benny Goodman and His Orchestra, with Peggy Lee
Kay Kyser and His Band
Freddy Martin and His Orchestra
Guy Lombardo and His Orchestra

CREDITS

Director Frank Borzage
Producer Sol Lesser
Associate Producer Barnett Briskin
Original Screenplay by Delmer Daves
Photographer Harry Wild
Art Director Hans Peters
Set Decorator Victor Gangelin
Editor Hal Kern
Sound Recorder Hugh McDowell
Musical Score Freddie Rich
Musical Director C. Bakaleinikoff
Production Designer Harry Horner
Assistant Production Designer Clem Beauchamp
Costumer Albert Deano
Talent Coordinator Radie Harris
Assistant Directors Lew Borzage, Virgil Hart

SONGS:

"She's a Bombshell from Brooklyn"
  Sol Lesser, Al Dubin, Jimmy Monaco
"The Girl I Love to Leave Behind"
  Lorenz Hart, Richard Rodgers
"We Mustn't Say Goodbye"
"The Machine Gun Song"
"American Boy"
"Don't Worry Island"
"Quick Sands"
"A Rookie and His Rhythm"
"Sleep Baby Sleep in Your Jeep"
"We Meet in the Funniest Places"
"You're Pretty Terrific Yourself"
  Al Dubin, Jimmy Monaco

"Why Don't You Do Right?"
  Joe McCoy
"Bugle Call Rag"
  Elmer Schoebel, Billy Meyers, Jack Pittis
"Ave Maria"
  Franz Schubert
"Flight of the Bumble Bee"
  Rimsky-Korsakov

SYNOPSIS

Eileen, a canteen junior hostess at New York's Stage Door Canteen, meets Private Ed Smith, nicknamed "Dakota" after his home state by his three buddies. They don't hit it off, because Eileen is really seeking out Broadway producers, not mere soldiers. Next day, the sailing is postponed and the boys are back at the Canteen, but Eileen is abrupt with "Dakota" and he soon leaves. Later, her roommates upbraid her behavior and the next evening, she receives him warmly. Both soon find they are in love.

The couple plan to get married and agree to meet at the Canteen at 5:00 P.M. However, since she has broken the rule about dating servicemen, the Canteen takes Eileen's pass away. Katharine Hepburn, who is Officer of the Day, suggests that Eileen be allowed to wait inside. Shortly, an Australian soldier brings word that the boys sailed that morning. Miss Hepburn consoles Eileen, giving her the strength to go on doing her important morale work at the Canteen until "Dakota" comes back.

With Cheryl Walker and Selena Royle

Between takes with Cheryl Walker, Selena Royle, Lon McCallister, director Frank Borzage, Marjorie Riordan, and Margaret Early

CRITICS' CIRCLE

". . . Katharine Hepburn, whose sequence toward the end with Eileen (Cheryl Walker) is as moving in warmth as it is gripping in sentiment."

—LAWRENCE PERRY
Baltimore Sun

"The story devised by Delmer Daves as a basis for demonstrating the fine work being done by the canteen for service men, and on which the innumerable sketches and variety acts of the stars are strung like a set of sparkling jewels, is simple and unpretentious."

—KATE CAMERON
New York Daily News

"*Stage Door Canteen* is a skillful admixture by two casts. . . . Scripter Delmer Daves did a deft writing job, and Frank Borzage's direction smoothly splices the sum total into a very palatable cohesive entity . . . the film catches the generous spirit of the show folk's desire to do their bit. There is something very poignant and very noble in the aspect of famous people giving of themselves, often in a spirit of humility, that parting youngsters may have a few, brief, happy hours."

—BOSLEY CROWTHER
The New York Times

NOTES

No fewer than sixty-five stars contributed their services in *Stage Door Canteen*. Hepburn agreed to appear as herself when she learned that 80 percent of the profits would go to the canteens operated by the American Theatre Wing in New York City, Washington, D.C., Philadelphia, Cleveland, Hollywood, San Francisco, Boston, and Newark.

Director Frank Borzage worked with Delmer Daves's original screenplay in both Hollywood and New York. The lead was played by Cheryl Walker, a twenty-two-year-old former movie extra who had been a stand-in for Veronica Lake and Claudette Colbert.

While most of the stars were in fleeting cameo bits, Hepburn—along with about ten others—had quite a bit of footage. One of the highlights was the film debut of Katharine Cornell who recited a scene from *Romeo and Juliet* (one of her biggest stage hits) with young Lon McCallister while in the serving line.

Stage Door Canteen received two Academy Award nominations: Best Song ("We Mustn't Say Goodbye" by Al Dubin and Jimmy Monaco) and Best Scoring of a Musical Picture (Frederic E. Rich).

Dragon Seed

A METRO-GOLDWYN-MAYER PICTURE   1944

CAST

Jade   Katharine Hepburn
Ling Tan   Walter Huston
Mrs. Ling Tan   Aline MacMahon
Wu Lien   Akim Tamiroff
Lao Er   Turhan Bey
Lao San   Hurd Hatfield
Orchid   Frances Rafferty
Third Cousin's Wife   Agnes Moorehead
Third Cousin   Henry Travers
Captain Sato   Robert Lewis
Japanese Kitchen Overseer   J. Carrol Naish
Lao Ta   Robert Bice
Mrs. Wu Lien   Jacqueline De Wit
Fourth Cousin   Clarence Lung
Neighbor Shen   Paul E. Burns
Wu Sao   Anna Demetrio
Major Yohagi   Ted Hecht
Captain Yasuda   Abner Biberman
Old Peddler   Leonard Mudie
Japanese Diplomat   Charles Lung
Student   Benson Fong
Japanese Guard   Philip Van Zandt
Japanese Officer   Al Hill
Japanese Soldier   J. Alex Havier
Leader of City People   Philip Ahn
Speaker with Movies   Roland Got
Young Farmer   Robert Lee
Old Clerk   Frank Puglia
Hysterical Woman   Claire Du Brey

Innkeeper Lee Tung Foo
Japanese Soldier Jay Novello
Japanese Official Leonard Strong
Narrator Lionel Barrymore

CREDITS

Directors Jack Conway, Harold S. Bucquet
Producer Pandro S. Berman
Scenarists Marguerite Roberts, Jane Murfin
Based on the Novel by Pearl S. Buck
Photographer Sidney Wagner
Art Director Cedric Gibbons
Associate Art Director Lyle R. Wheeler
Set Decorator Edwin B. Willis
Associate Set Decorator Hugh Hunt
Editor Harold F. Kress
Sound Recorder Douglas Shearer
Musical Score Herbert Stothart
Makeup Artist Jack Dawn
Special Effects Warren Newcombe
Costume Supervisor Irene
Costumer Valles
Assistant Director Al Shenberg
Technical Director Wei F. Hsueh

SYNOPSIS

Lao Er, a young Chinese farmer, does not understand his wife Jade. She is idealistic and at the same time realistic about the new China. Lao Er's father, Ling Tan, discusses the then-distant threat of Japanese aggression as if there is nothing much to worry about. When the Japanese actually are approaching, Jade and Lao Er go to the interior with Chinese patriots who plan to set up munitions factories there. Jade visits Wu Lien, Ling Tan's son-in-law, a wealthy merchant, who is spying for the Japanese. Jade makes eyes at the Japanese kitchen overseer and poisons the food being prepared for a banquet Wu Lien is giving for his Japanese masters. Wu Lien is suspected and killed.

Ling Tan makes a difficult decision for an old man who has known only his valley and his peaceful farm life: he consents to burn down his farmhouse and his crops and, with his faithful wife, accompanies Lao Er and Jade to the mountains to continue the fight against the invaders.

CRITICS' CIRCLE

"As Katharine Hepburn, Walter Huston, Aline MacMahon, Akim Tamiroff, Turhan Bey, Hurd Hatfield, Frances Rafferty and all the rest of the very competent cast troupe is, they make *Dragon Seed*, for all its 2½ hours, a compelling saga. Misses Hepburn and MacMahon and Huston are especially

With Jacqueline de Wit
and Akim Tamiroff

Pearl Buck's best seller has become one of the truly fine motion pictures of our time...

The glorious story of a girl with a fighting heart and the man who fought by her side...

Katharine Hepburn as the brave and lovely "Jade" gives THE performance of her career...

For its tremendous drama and great tenderness, a triumph that exceeds even "The Good Earth"!

M-G-M's
DRAGON SEED

KATHARINE HEPBURN
WALTER HUSTON
ALINE MacMAHON
AKIM TAMIROFF
TURHAN BEY

Hurd Hatfield · J. Carrol Naish
Agnes Moorehead · Henry Travers
Robert Bice · Jacqueline de Wit
Frances Rafferty · Robert Lewis

Screen Play by Marguerite Roberts and Jane Murfin · Based on the Novel by Pearl S. Buck · Directed by Jack Conway and Harold S. Bucquet · Produced by Pandro S. Berman

M-G-M
Twenty Years Of
Screen Leadership

119

With Turhan Bey

With Turhan Bey

With Aline MacMahon,
Walter Huston and Turhan Bey

120

With J. Carrol Naish

effective histrionically, and one soon forgets Tamiroff's vodka accent in the Chinese setting."

—*Variety*

"Miss Hepburn's gulping elocution bothered me at the outset, but she went on to make Jade a rather wondrous character. Huston is splendid as Ling Tan and Miss MacMahon never fails to be restrained and right."

—Howard Barnes
New York Herald Tribune

"*Dragon Seed* is a kind of slant-eyed *North Star*. A two-and-a-half-hour picturization of Pearl Buck's best-selling novel about China at war. Often awkward and pretentious, it nevertheless has moments of moral and dramatic grandeur."

—*Time*

"The film is rich with warmth and wit and humor, as well as stark drama and a profound sense of comradeship for all peoples. And the cast could hardly have been bettered, though it may be a little hard to accept Katharine Hepburn's New England twang and sharply Anglo-Saxon features as Chinese. She contributes, however, an excellent job as Jade."

—Jesse Zunser
Cue

"Katharine Hepburn, even with her makeup, is still nobody but Katharine Hepburn, but she is in herself such a splendid actress, when given the opportunity, that she even overcomes her own personality to give a shining, glowing performance."

—Leo Mishkin
New York Morning Telegraph

"The strong mannerisms of Katharine Hepburn make the pretense very difficult in her case, but beneath them emerges a vigorously conceived character, a girl who grows from flower-like fragility to rugged, warrior womanhood."

—Alton Cook
New York World-Telegram

NOTES

For this super-production of Pearl S. Buck's best-selling novel, Hepburn played the Chinese peasant girl Jade with great sincerity, warmth, and feeling. It is really a tribute to her acting ability that she managed to pull it off—a performance often overlooked by those who attacked the occidental cast's oriental makeup.

Dragon Seed was filmed largely on location in the San Fernando Valley by Jack Conway and Harold S. Bucquet. The lengthy picture was immensely popular with audiences, who were then reading about the suppression of Chinese peasants by Japanese oppressors in the newspapers.

The cast was above average. Turhan Bey, borrowed from Universal, was Hepburn's husband and Aline MacMahon's depiction of an old Chinese farmer's wife was nominated for a Supporting Academy Award. The film's other nomination went to Sidney Wagner, for his unusually stunning photography.

With Frances Rafferty

On the set with Pearl S. Buck
and co-director Jack Conway

With Spencer Tracy

Without Love

A METRO-GOLDWYN-MAYER PICTURE   1945

CAST

Pat Jamieson   Spencer Tracy
Jamie Rowan   Katharine Hepburn
Kitty Trimble   Lucille Ball
Quentin Ladd   Keenan Wynn
Paul Carrell   Carl Esmond
Edwina Collins   Patricia Morison
Professor Grinza   Felix Bressart
Anna   Emily Massey
Flower Girl   Gloria Grahame
Caretaker   George Davis
Elevator Boy   George Chandler
Sergeant   Clancy Cooper
Professor Thompson   Wallis Clark
Professor Ellis   Donald Curtis
Colonel Braden   Charles Arnt
Driver   Eddie Acuff
Porter   Clarence Muse
Headwaiter   Franco Corsaro
Pageboy   Ralph Brooks
Doctor   William Forrest
Soldier   Garry Owen
Soldier   Joe Devlin
Soldier   William Newell
Sergeant   James Flavin
Girl on Elevator   Hazel Brooks

CREDITS

Director   Harold S. Bucquet
Producer   Lawrence A. Weingarten

With Spencer Tracy

With Emily Massey

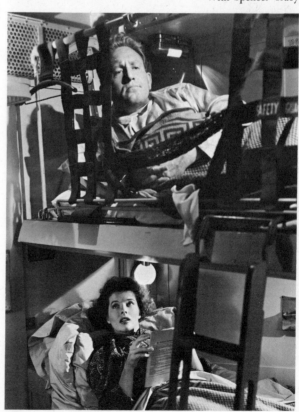

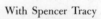

With Spencer Tracy

With Spencer Tracy

With Spencer Tracy,
and Charles Arnt

With Spencer Tracy

Scenarist   Donald Ogden Stewart
Based on the Play by   Philip Barry
As Produced on the Stage by   The Theatre Guild, Inc.
Photographer   Karl Freund
Art Director   Cedric Gibbons
Associate Art Director   Harry McAfee
Set Decorator   Edwin B. Willis
Associate Set Decorator   McLean Nisbet
Editor   Frank Sullivan
Sound Recorder   Douglas Shearer
Musical Score   Bronislau Kaper
Costume Supervision   Irene
Associate Costumer   Marion Herwood Keyes
Special Effects   A. Arnold Gillespie, Danny Hall
Montage   Peter Ballbusch
Assistant Director   Earl McEvoy
Makeup Artist   Jack Dawn

SYNOPSIS

Jamie Rowan, an attractive widow, has a large house in wartime Washington, D.C. Pat Jamieson, a scientist who is having difficulties with the housing shortage in the capital, desperately needs a place where he can conduct his experiments. Jamie proposes a "platonic" marriage and the woman-hating bachelor accepts.

Pat struggles to perfect a helmet for high-altitude flying and Jamie, throughout these experiments, becomes his assistant. After a while, it becomes apparent to them—as it has to their friends—that their "without-love" policy is fading from their marriage.

CRITICS' CIRCLE

"A very witty and engaging picture, recommended here without hesitation. Miss Hepburn and Mr. Tracy succeed brilliantly in the leading parts. The somewhat metallic and stylized quality of Miss Hepburn's acting is almost perfectly suited to a role that is largely a vehicle for fashionable humor, and Mr. Tracy's homespun behavior seems just about right for a man who really prefers airplanes to dames."

—*The New Yorker*

"Hollywood has taken considerable liberties with Philip Barry's stage comedy *Without Love*. They are all to the good. With Katharine Hepburn and Spencer Tracy playing house in a deliberately loveless marriage and Donald Ogden Stewart's glib underlining of the situation in his adaptation, the show is great good fun, no matter how far-fetched. The performances are, of course, the chief attractions of the film. Miss Hepburn, playing her original stage role in the production, is superb, in addition to being a star. She runs right through the scale of make-believe with brilliant authority and humor. Tracy is right behind her in making it a matter of consequence that the 'without' is dropped from the title of the picture."

—HOWARD BARNES
New York Herald Tribune

"Mr. Tracy handles a farce scene as competently as he does a good drama. *Without Love* still seems a waste of a fine actor's time. Miss Hepburn caricatures her part, perhaps not always intentionally. It still was as good a way as any to play the neurotic young widow."

—EILEEN CREELMAN
New York Sun

"Though it's all pretty much on the coy and contrived side, the film offers diverting comedy for the Tracy-Hepburn admirers. (It) is one of those glossy conversation pieces that MGM does up so handsomely."

—ROSE PELSWICK
New York Journal-American

"*Without Love* (is) a completely successful projection of the Philip Barry play. . . . There is a nice love-story hidden somewhere in the picture, and though there is practically no attempt really to explore or explain its possibilities, it somehow gets itself satisfactorily told. To a great extent Philip Barry, and Donald Ogden Stewart, who wrote the skillful screen play, are to be thanked for this. Spencer Tracy is as good as their words, and Miss Hepburn, whose Bryn Mawr drawl and tailored walk sometimes get in her way, brings this sort of lady to life more convincingly than could anybody else in pictures. Lucille Ball handles her lowly wisecracks so well as to set up a new career for herself."

—*Time*

"*Without Love* is a satiny translation of a Philip Barry play; I like it all right and have very little to say for or against it. Unlike Mr. Barry, I don't find the expression 'by gum' charming on lips which use it for charm's sake, and enjoy even less the heroine's recalling, of her dying husband, that he 'grinned that grin of his.' But a good deal of the dialogue is happy to hear and happier in its skill; Katharine Hepburn and Spencer Tracy are exactly right for their jobs; (and) it is good to see Lucille Ball doing so well with a kind of role new to her."

—JAMES AGEE
The Nation

NOTES

Despite whatever faults there may have been in Philip Barry's play, scenarist Donald Ogden Stewart streamlined the comedy into a first-class vehicle for Tracy and Hepburn. Harold S. Bucquet, who had co-directed *Dragon Seed*, handled the directorial chores in this urbane comedy.

As Jamie Rowan, Hepburn was never better and she enriched the proceedings with her vigor, humor, and candor.

With Spencer Tracy

With Spencer Tracy, Lucille Ball,
Keenan Wynn and Carl Esmond

Tracy also seemed to be enjoying himself; his subtle approach to even the simplest of situations was always a joy. The byplay of these two pros was once again utilized to its fullest, and the audiences responded.

The cast included Lucille Ball and Keenan Wynn in roles that were to do much for their careers in later years.

125

Undercurrent

A METRO-GOLDWYN-MAYER PICTURE   1946

CAST

Ann Hamilton   Katharine Hepburn
Alan Garroway   Robert Taylor
Michael Garroway   Robert Mitchum
Prof. "Dink" Hamilton   Edmund Gwenn
Lucy   Marjorie Main
Sylvia Lea Burton   Jayne Meadows
Mr. Warmsley   Clinton Sundberg
Prof. Joseph Bangs   Dan Tobin
Mrs. Foster   Kathryn Card
George   Leigh Whipper
Justice Putnam   Charles Trowbridge
Henry Gilson   James Westerfield
Uncle Ben   Billy McLain
Julia Donnegan   Bess Flowers
Cora   Sarah Edwards
Saleslady   Betty Blythe

CREDITS

Director   Vincente Minnelli
Producer   Pandro S. Berman
Scenarist   Edward Chodorov

Based on a Story by Thelma Strabel
Photographer Karl Freund
Art Director Cedric Gibbons
Associate Art Director Randall Duell
Set Decorator Edwin B. Willis
Associate Set Decorator Jack D. Moore
Editor Ferris Webster
Sound Recorder Douglas Shearer
Musical Score Herbert Stothart
Costumer Irene
Hair Stylist Sydney Guilaroff
Makeup Artist Jack Dawn
Assistant Director Norman Elzer

SYNOPSIS

Ann Hamilton, daughter of a little-known college professor, falls in love with wealthy, dynamic industrialist Alan Garroway. When they marry, she is not immediately accepted into his social status, but the couple are happy just the same. After a while, Ann discovers that Alan has a brother whom he never mentions and will not discuss. In time, his behavior becomes strange and frightening.

As time goes on, their relationship becomes haunted by a strange undercurrent of doubt and suspicion and Ann fears for her marriage. She is told many conflicting stories about the mysterious brother Michael, but is confronted by a completely different image when one day he suddenly appears. Is he really a psychopath, a murderer, a dangerous man? Or is it her husband that fits these descriptions?

CRITICS' CIRCLE

"Miss Hepburn gives a crisp and taut performance. Mr. Taylor accelerates a brooding meanness. For Vincente Minnelli, the director, has used atmosphere and mood to build up some rather fateful moments in which you wait for the unknown to occur."

—BOSLEY CROWTHER
The New York Times

"The valid reasons for witnessing *Undercurrent* are all contained in the performing. Miss Hepburn handles (her role) with skill and a variety of expression which does her great credit. Either as a bobby-soxer or a curious *femme fatale*, she gives a resounding portrayal. Taylor is far less successful."

—HOWARD BARNES
New York Herald Tribune

"Miss Hepburn plays the young wife with stunning effect, converting a country girl into a sophisticated woman without supplanting her honest charm."

—HERBERT COHN
Brooklyn Daily Eagle

"In the generally decorative vein of the picture, Katharine Hepburn fills an authentic niche of her own, her clean cut outlines, deft movements and molded features handsomely decked out in costumes by Irene. Her playing is volatile, mannered, nasal as always; it is never negligible. This in itself is a virtue in a world compounded of celluloid imagery."

—*Theatre Arts*

With Edmund Gwenn

With Robert Taylor

127

With Leigh Whipper

With Jayne Meadows

With Robert Taylor

128

With Robert Mitchum

NOTES

Undercurrent was Robert Taylor's first postwar film assignment, and also marked Hepburn's initial venture into the world of melodrama. The role of Ann Hamilton gave her the opportunity to develop from a shy young girl to a sophisticated wife. Taylor was most effective as the brooding husband and Robert Mitchum was properly mysterious as the brother—a role that gave his career quite a boost.

Vincente Minnelli, who usually directed musicals—except for the tender story *The Clock*—worked hard in a genre that was foreign to him. His use of music to intensify the action of the film is noteworthy. *Undercurrent* is not great melodrama, but it is a well-made, well-performed film.

The supporting cast included Edmund Gwenn, playing Kate's father, as he had done a decade earlier in *Sylvia Scarlett*; Marjorie Main, adding comic relief; and Clinton Sundberg, whom Kate had seen in Tracy's play *The Rugged Path*. She was directly responsible for his being signed by MGM.

With Kathryn Card

"The indigestible plot, full of false leads and unkept promises, is like a woman's magazine serial consumed at one gulp."

—*Time*

"*Undercurrent* is loaded with entertainment, suspense and fine acting, with Katie stealing the honors as to the latter. Taylor comes across with a fine job in his unaccustomed role, and Robert Mitchum wallops in a couple of swell scenes. It's a grand meller."

—LEE MORTIMER
New York Daily Mirror

"Hepburn has grown still more set in her ways. Taylor has deepened in his. He is now more integrated. . . . But though the story and some of the actors rarely deserve it, Vincente Minnelli directs them as sensitively and truthfully as though he were working out Henry James."

—CECELIA AGER
PM

"Miss Hepburn, carefully avoiding her usual mannerisms, this time looks like herself, and not, as she sometimes does, like her imitators."

—EILEEN CREELMAN
New York Sun

On the set with director
Vincente Minnelli

With Spencer Tracy

The Sea of Grass

A METRO-GOLDWYN-MAYER PICTURE 1947

CAST

Lutie Cameron   Katharine Hepburn
Colonel James Brewton   Spencer Tracy
Brice Chamberlain   Melvyn Douglas
Sara Beth Brewton   Phyllis Thaxter
Brock Brewton   Robert Walker
Jeff   Edgar Buchanan
Doc Reid   Harry Carey
Selena Hall   Ruth Nelson
Banty   William "Bill" Phillips
Sam Hall   James Bell
Judge White   Robert Barrat
George Cameron   Charles Trowbridge
Major Harney   Russell Hicks
Floyd McCurtin   Robert Armstrong
Andy Boggs   Trevor Bardette
Crane   Morris Ankrum
Nurse   Nora Cecil

CREDITS

Director   Elia Kazan
Producer   Pandro S. Berman
Scenarists   Marguerite Roberts, Vincent Lawrence
Based on the Novel by   Conrad Richter
Photographer   Harry Stradling
Art Director   Cedric Gibbons
Associate Art Director   Paul Groesse
Set Decorator   Edwin B. Willis
Editor   Robert J. Kern

With Spencer Tracy

Sound Recorder   Douglas Shearer
Musical Score   Herbert Stothart
Costumer   Walter Plunkett
Makeup Artist   Jack Dawn
Assistant Director   Sid Sidman

SYNOPSIS

Cattle tycoon Colonel James Brewton owns the magnificent St. Augustine plains of New Mexico Territory, known as the "Sea of Grass." Homesteaders pour into these fertile grazing ranges after Colonel Brewton loses a court decision to keep them out. Unhappy over Jim's obsession with his sea of grass, his wife Lutie leaves him and goes to Denver, where she has an affair with her husband's bitterest enemy, Brice Chamberlain, the lawyer who championed the homesteaders' cause. Lutie returns to Jim and within months a son is born. The colonel cherishes the child, Brock, as his own but after Lutie presents him with a daughter, he throws her off his ranch.

Not until their children are grown, and in difficulty, does Lutie return, but she is almost too late. Dashingly irresponsible Brock is shot in a gun duel and dies in Jim's arms and, at her daughter's urging, Lutie goes back to Jim.

CRITICS' CIRCLE

"There is some honest historical conflict, and a bit of honest unhappiness, in this movie. Spencer Tracy too often gazes stonily at God's sea of grass to show that he is both rugged individualist and nature mystic, but he plays with consid-

erable force and style. Miss Hepburn looks tense, but arouses interest chiefly through her beautiful turn-of-the-century costumes. In spite of all the sincerity and talent involved in it, *The Sea of Grass* is an epically dreary film."

—*Time*

"In *The Sea of Grass*, Mr. Tracy is grim, purposeful, and, I'm afraid, occasionally ludicrous, while Miss Hepburn is as pert as a sparrow. As the lawyer responsible for Miss Hepburn's trouble, Melvyn Douglas, is as gloomy as if *he* were the wronged husband, instead of being the worm in the domestic apple. The picture is much too long, but there are a lot of good shots of Western scenery, and I suppose the general confusion of the plot isn't any worse than usual."

—JOHN MCCARTEN
The New Yorker

"The scenes are spectacular and the photography irreproachable. But the script is weak, and the acting varies between dramatically effective and artificially slick—with Miss Hepburn chief offender in her lately acquired highly stylized, patronizing fashion. Tracy is, as usual, rough-hewn; Melvyn Douglas is excellent as the life-long lover who waits for the girl who never comes; and Robert Walker does well enough by an unusual (for him) role—a two gun killer."

—JESSE ZUNSER
Cue

NOTES

The major reason *The Sea of Grass* failed was its lame script. Elia Kazan's direction—no matter how hard he tried—

131

With Melvyn Douglas

With Harry Carey

With Edgar Buchanan

With Morris Ankrum

With Phyllis Thaxter

never managed to breathe life into it. The characterizations were ineptly drawn and one suspects that the stars, too, were trying anything in their power to give their roles substance.

Hepburn came off in an overacting fashion, while Tracy's underacting resembled boredom. This was, with little doubt, the weakest of the Tracy-Hepburn films.

The picture's one great asset was Harry Stradling's breathtakingly beautiful photography of the wild land just outside of Valentine, Nebraska—where the location work was done. Walter Plunkett's costumes were excellent, and Kate wore some thirty gowns.

At best, *The Sea of Grass* is an actionless Western drama that never should have been offered to stars of the caliber of Tracy and Hepburn without a first-rate script.

On location
with director Elia Kazan

With Melvyn Douglas, James Bell and Ruth Nelson

133

With Paul Henreid

Song of Love

A METRO-GOLDWYN-MAYER PICTURE 1947

CAST

Clara Wieck Schumann   Katharine Hepburn
Robert Schumann   Paul Henreid
Johannes Brahms   Robert Walker
Franz Liszt   Henry Daniell
Professor Wieck   Leo G. Carroll
Bertha   Else Janssen
Julie   Gigi Perreau
Felix   "Tinker" Furlong
Marie   Ann Carter
Eugenie   Janine Perreau
Ludwig   Jimmie Hunt
Ferdinand   Anthony Sydes
Elsie   Eilene Janssen
Dr. Hoffman   Roman Bohnen
Haslinger   Ludwig Stossel
Princess Valerie Hohenfels   Tala Birell
Judge   Kurt Katch
King Albert   Henry Stephenson
Reinecke   Konstantin Shayne
Court Officer   Byron Foulger
Lady in Box   Josephine Whittell

CREDITS

Director   Clarence Brown
Producer   Clarence Brown

With Robert Walker
and Henry Daniell

Scenarists Ivan Tors, Irmgard Von Cube, Allen Vincent, Robert Ardrey
Based on the Play by Bernard Schubert, Mario Silva
Photographer Harry Stradling
Art Director Cedric Gibbons
Associate Art Director Hans Peters
Set Decorator Edwin B. Willis
Editor Robert J. Kern
Sound Recorder Douglas Shearer
Musical Director Bronislau Kaper
Piano Recordings Artur Rubinstein
Orchestra MGM Symphony Orchestra
Conductor William Steinberg
Costume Supervision Irene
Women's Costumer Walter Plunkett
Men's Costumer Valles
Makeup Artist Jack Dawn
Hair Stylist Sydney Guilaroff
Chorus St. Luke's Boy Choir
Musical Adviser Laura Dubman
Special Effects Warren Newcombe
Assistant Director Al Raboch

SYNOPSIS

Despite their poverty and her parent's objections, strong-willed Clara Wieck, a brilliant pianist, weds a struggling and unappreciated composer, Robert Schumann. After several difficult years, she retires to devote her entire life to him and their seven children. The young Johannes Brahms comes to live and study with the Schumanns and ultimately falls in love with Clara. When she refuses him, he departs.

Eventually, Schumann, tormented by his lack of success, breaks down while conducting his "Cantata from *Faust*." Later, he dies in an asylum. Clara returns to the concert stage to bring her husband's magnificent music to the public.

CRITICS' CIRCLE

"The screen drama which Mr. Brown concocts from these real people and their problems is one of the outstanding

With Paul Henreid

135

With Robert Walker

With Paul Henreid

With Leo G. Carroll and Paul Henreid

films of 1947. This department may have been too harsh of late in exposing the thespian tricks and stylized mannerisms of Katharine Hepburn. But when Miss Hepburn gets a real part, she knows what to do with it. In *Song of Love* the accent is on acting. Katie stops playing Katharine Hepburn and becomes Clara Wieck with a skill that places her in the first rank among screen performers. It is an interpretation in which you'll find echoes of your wife and mother and every woman who ever encouraged you."

—JACK MOFFITT
Esquire

"In the role of Schumann's wife, Katharine Hepburn, whose romantic appeal is rather lessened by the circumstance that the script has given her seven children, behaves as if she had just been wreathed with the Vassar daisy chain, and Paul Henreid, as Schumann, refuses to register anything but torpor. The third major character is Robert Walker, who plays Brahms as though he were a musician whose fate depended on bobby-soxers. Some very skilled recordings by Artur Rubinstein are wasted on the picture, along with some excellent imitations by Miss Hepburn of a pianist at work. She even manages to stay in the same section of the keyboard as the sound track."

—JOHN MCCARTEN
The New Yorker

"Miss Hepburn portrays Clara with skill and feeling. She is fascinating to watch at the piano, using the clawlike 19th Century style; her 'reactions' to the men's music, in various dramatic contexts, are the backbone of the picture. . . . The lives and the music are somewhat distorted, as is usual—and never entirely forgivable—in such pictures. But this is how Brahms and the Schumanns might very possibly have acted if they had realized that later on they would break into the movies."

—*Time*

"It will be news to music lovers that Brahms cherished a profound and enduring passion for Mrs. Schumann, and proposed marriage to her after she became a widow. This portion of the picture is akin to soap, rather than grand opera, and deserves a muted musical raspberry in B minor. There is a fine, sympathetic, earnest performance of Katharine Hepburn as Clara Wieck Schumann. We suspect that, aside from the Brahms aberration, this portrait is reasonably close to the truth; it adheres to fundamentals at least, and is very pleasant to watch."

—DONALD KIRKLEY
Baltimore Sun

"Miss Hepburn is fine as Clara, showing in her work touches of the expert direction of Clarence Brown. She progresses neatly from emotion to emotion and registers solidly in both comedy and pathos."

—*Variety*

NOTES

For her portrayal of Clara Wieck Schumann, Hepburn studied many hours a day with pianist Laura Dubman, a pupil of Artur Rubinstein (who did the piano recordings

On the set
with director Clarence Brown

for the picture). Miss Dubman coached Kate in fundamentals and taught her the proper techniques of playing difficult compositions for close-up shooting. Her hard work paid off for the musical interludes were perfectly timed and coordinated to give the illusion that Hepburn was actually playing.

Clarence Brown directed the Hollywood-ized script with flair and Harry Stradling contributed immeasurably to the success of this production with his outstanding photography. Paul Henreid was effective as Robert Schumann and Henry Daniell was a fine Franz Liszt, but Robert Walker seemed a bit silly as the great Johannes Brahms, even though he was playing a young Brahms.

State of the Union

A LIBERTY FILM PRODUCTION
A METRO-GOLDWYN-MAYER PICTURE 1948

With Spencer Tracy

CAST

Grant Matthews   Spencer Tracy
Mary Matthews   Katharine Hepburn
Spike McManus   Van Johnson
Kay Thorndyke   Angela Lansbury
Jim Conover   Adolphe Menjou
Sam Thorndyke   Lewis Stone
Sam Parrish   Howard Smith
Lulubelle Alexander   Maidel Turner
Judge Alexander   Raymond Walburn
Bill Hardy   Charles Dingle
Grace Orval Draper   Florence Auer
Senator Lauterback   Pierre Watkin
Norah   Margaret Hamilton
Buck   Irving Bacon
Joyce   Patti Brady
Grant, Jr.   George Nokes
Bellboy   Carl Switzer
Barber   Tom Pedi
Waiter   Tom Fadden
Blink Moran   Charles Lane
Leith   Art Baker
Jenny   Rhea Mitchell
First Reporter   Arthur O'Connell

With Spencer Tracy
and Adolphe Menjou

Blonde Girl   Marion Martin
Wrestler   Tor Johnson
Senator   Stanley Andrews
Pilot   Dave Willock
Politician   Russell Meeker
Joe Crandall   Frank L. Clarke
Rusty Miller   David Clarke
Broder   Dell Henderson
Bradbury   Edwin Cooper
Crump   Davison Clark
Josephs   Francis Pierlot
Editor   Brandon Beach

CREDITS

Director   Frank Capra
Producer   Frank Capra
Associate Producer   Anthony Veiller
Scenarists   Anthony Veiller, Myles Connolly
Based on the Play by   Howard Lindsay, Russel Crouse
Photographer   George J. Folsey
Art Director   Cedric Gibbons
Associate Art Director   Urie McCleary
Set Decorator   Emile Kuri
Editor   William Hornbeck
Sound Recorder   Douglas Shearer
Musical Score   Victor Young
Costumer   Irene
Special Effects   A. Arnold Gillespie
Assistant Director   Arthur S. Black, Jr.

With Adolphe Menjou

With Angela Lansbury
and Howard Smith

SYNOPSIS

Mary Matthews joins her estranged husband-candidate Grant to bolster his political chances for the Republican nomination by pretending they enjoy a happy marriage. Pushed by people like Kay Thorndyke, a shrewd newspaperman's daughter, who also loves him, and Jim Conover, a sharp old-line politician, Grant gradually sacrifices all of his principals in favor of his "White House fever."

At a dinner party, fearing that she's lost her husband to Kay, Mary blasts away at the politicians present. Her speech jars her husband into the realization that he has almost forfeited everything he believed in. During a political broadcast, Grant admits his dishonesty with the voters and, calling himself "unworthy," retires from the race.

CRITICS' CIRCLE

"Mr. Tracy is glib and delightful as the gentleman who would rather be right than be the Republican candidate for President and Miss Hepburn is charming as his wife."
—BOSLEY CROWTHER
The New York Times

"To sustain the illusion of interest, Wonder-Worker Capra relied on a blaze of star-power: Spencer Tracy, Katharine Hepburn, Van Johnson, Adolphe Menjou, Angela Lansbury. But Tracy, as in all his recent pictures, lacks fire; Hepburn's affectation of talking like a woman trying simultaneously to steady a loose dental brace sharply limits her range of expression; Johnson, playing a Drew Pearsonish columnist, is no more effective than Pearson would be playing Johnson; Menjou (in a double-breasted vest) is rather more Menjou than politician. Only Lansbury, whom Metro has long dieted on lean parts, does any real acting. As the adderish lady publisher, she sinks a fine fang." —*Time*

"Hepburn knowingly plays the wise wife who restores his (Tracy's) integrity and bests her rival." —*Look*

"When *State of the Union* most closely follows the Lindsay-Crouse play from which it derives, it is a fairly enjoyable business, but when it lights out on its own, it becomes a sad spectacle. Still, Mr. Tracy is often persuasive, and Katharine Hepburn, as his wife, manages to say as if she meant them such lines as 'Grant likes to get up on the mountains and slap the hurricanes down.' Among the others in the cast, Adolphe Menjou, as a conniving politician, is most prominent."
—JOHN McCARTEN
The New Yorker

"If there is any lingering notion that the director is not the most important person in the business of film-making, it should be dispelled by *State of the Union.* In this Frank Capra job of producing and directing, a fine play has been

With Spencer Tracy

With Spencer Tracy

With Spencer Tracy

superlatively translated to the screen. . . . With his (Tracy's) forthright acting and his knowledge of the nuances which make a screen scene click, he brings a satirical and very human account of political skulduggery into sharp focus. Aiding and abetting him no end is Katharine Hepburn. She is restrained, persuasive and altogether delightful. . . . *State of the Union* is a triumphant film, marked all over by Frank Capra's artistry."

—HOWARD BARNES
New York Herald Tribune

NOTES

Originally slated for Gary Cooper and Claudette Colbert, this Pulitzer Prize–winning play got a timeless treatment from director Frank Capra which still retains its sting and bite when viewed today. The names have changed but the game of politics is still the same.

The Howard Lindsay–Russel Crouse play, which kept up on current events weekly while running on Broadway, provided Hepburn and Tracy with roles into which they could get their teeth. And they did. Tracy was strong and honorable; Hepburn was ever charming, with a sting all her own, by his side.

The all-star cast worked well—especially Angela Lansbury as the domineering Kay Thorndyke. Her scenes with Hepburn sizzle with excitement.

On the set with director
Frank Capra and Spencer Tracy

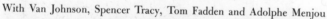

With Van Johnson, Spencer Tracy, Tom Fadden and Adolphe Menjou

Adam's Rib

A METRO-GOLDWYN-MAYER PICTURE   1949

CAST

Adam Bonner   Spencer Tracy
Amanda Bonner   Katharine Hepburn
Doris Attinger   Judy Holliday
Warren Attinger   Tom Ewell
Kip Lurie   David Wayne
Beryl Caighn   Jean Hagen
Olympia La Pere   Hope Emerson
Grace   Eve March
Judge Reiser   Clarence Kolb
Jules Frikke   Emerson Treacy
Mrs. McGrath   Polly Moran
Judge Marcasson   Will Wright
Dr. Margaret Brodeigh   Elizabeth Flournoy
Mary, the Maid   Janna Da Loos
Dave   James Nolan
Roy   David Clarke
Court Clerk   John Maxwell Sholes
Court Stenographer   Marvin Kaplan
Police Matron   Gracille La Vinder
Benjamin Klausner   William Self
Emerald   Paula Raymond
Photographer   Ray Walker
Reporter   Tommy Noonan
Adam's Assistants   De Forrest Lawrence, John Fell
Amanda's Assistant   Sid Dubin
Mr. Bonner   Joe Bernard
Mrs. Bonner   Madge Blake
Mrs. Marcasson   Marjorie Wood
Judge Poynter   Lester Luther

With Spencer Tracy

143

With Judy Holliday

With Eve March and Judy Holliday

With Spencer Tracy

144

Mrs. Poynter Anna Q. Nilsson
Hurlock Roger David
Elderly Elevator Operator Louis Mason
Fat Man Rex Evans
Young District Attorney Charles Bastin
Subway Rider E. Bradley Coleman

CREDITS

Director George Cukor
Producer Lawrence Weingarten
Scenarists Garson Kanin, Ruth Gordon
Based on an Original Story by Garson Kanin, Ruth Gordon
Photographer George J. Folsey
Art Director Cedric Gibbons
Associate Art Director William Ferrari
Set Decorator Edwin B. Willis
Associate Set Decorator Henry Grace
Editor George Boemler
Sound Recorder Douglas Shearer
Musical Score Miklos Rozsa
Costumer Walter Plunkett
Special Effects A. Arnold Gillespie
Assistant Director Jack Greenwood
Song:"Farewell, Amanda" by Cole Porter

SYNOPSIS

Amanda Bonner, a lawyer with a fierce belief in women's rights, defends Doris Attinger, a dumb blonde who has shot her two-timing spouse. Amanda's husband Adam, a sharp assistant district attorney, has been assigned prosecutor in the case. Eventually, the trials and tribulations of the trial, along with the nagging question of female equality, fill the air and envelop Adam and Amanda—not only on the job, but at home as well.

CRITICS' CIRCLE

"*Adam's Rib* again presents Katharine Hepburn and Spencer Tracy as the ideal U.S. Mr. and Mrs. of upper-middle income. This time, besides being wittily urbane, both are lawyers. . . . Hepburn's elegantly arranged bones and Tracy's assurance as an actor make them worth looking at in any movie, but the stars are called on for some aggressive cuteness in this one.

"*Adam's Rib* is acted as though the players found it funny, but actually, like many 'sophisticated' movie comedies, it is more absurd than comical. Its chief asset: a high-toned song called 'Farewell, Amanda,' with dismal lyrics which Cole Porter must have written while waiting for a bus."
—*Time*

"As we say, Mr. Tracy and Miss Hepburn are the stellar performers in this show and their perfect compatibility in

With Tom Ewell

With Jean Hagen

With Polly Moran

With Spencer Tracy
and David Wayne

comic capers is delightful to see. A line thrown away, a lifted eyebrow, a smile or a sharp, resounding slap on a tender part of the anatomy is as natural as breathing to them. Plainly, they took great pleasure in playing this rambunctious spoof. Miss Holliday . . . is simply hilarious as a dumb but stubborn dame."

—BOSLEY CROWTHER
The New York Times

"Here again is the famous battle of the sexes, strictly without benefit of August Strindberg and waged in the home and courtroom shared by Adam Bonner (Tracy) and his wife Amanda (Hepburn). Although both are lawyers and given to calling each other Pinky in their kittenish moments, there is no confusing their respective pronouncements on a woman's right to take a few compulsive potshots at a philandering husband."

—*Newsweek*

NOTES

Adam's Rib rescued the sagging box-office ratings of both its stars and was the shot-in-the-arm they all needed. Kate's close friends Garson Kanin and his wife Ruth Gordon—together with director George Cukor—provided a laugh-a-minute comedy that owes as much of its success to the outstanding supporting cast as it does to its stars.

Tracy and Hepburn as a pair of married attorneys were utterly delightful when they found themselves on opposite sides in a trial. Judy Holliday was brilliantly effective as a dumb blonde—the role directly responsible for getting her the screen assignment of her Broadway hit *Born Yesterday*. Tom Ewell, Jean Hagen, David Wayne, and Hope Emerson all made their presence known. They couldn't have been bettered. It was also good to see old-time comedy star Polly Moran as a witness in the trial.

The production was first-class all the way. Its only sour grape was a dour song written by Cole Porter, called "Farewell, Amanda." The Kanin-Gordon screenplay was nominated for an Oscar.

With Joe Bernard, David Wayne,
Spencer Tracy, Paula Raymond
and Madge Blake

The African Queen

A HORIZON-ROMULUS PRODUCTION
RELEASED THRU UNITED ARTISTS
IN TECHNICOLOR 1951

CAST

Charlie Allnut   Humphrey Bogart
Rose Sayer   Katharine Hepburn
Reverend Samuel Sayer   Robert Morley
Captain of Louisa   Peter Bull
First Officer   Theodore Bikel
Second Officer   Walter Gotell
Petty Officer   Gerald Onn
First Officer of Shona   Peter Swanick
Second Officer of Shona   Richard Marner

CREDITS

Director   John Huston
Producer   S. P. Eagle
Scenarists   James Agee, John Huston
Based on the Novel by   C. S. Forester
Photographer   Jack Cardiff
Production Managers   Leigh Aman, T. S. Lyndon-Haynes,
    Wilfred Shingleton, John Hoesli
Editor   Ralph Kemplen
Sound Recorder   John Mitchell
Musical Score   Alan Gray

With Humphrey Bogart

147

With Humphrey Bogart

With Humphrey Bogart

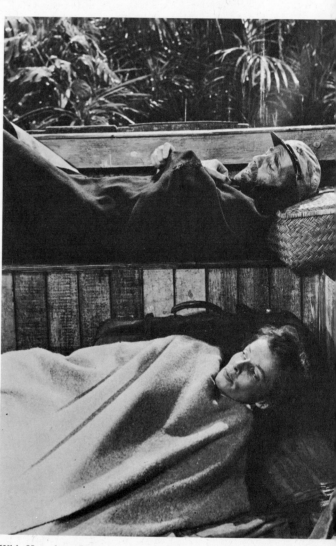

With Humphrey Bogart

Orchestra   Royal Philharmonic Orchestra
Conductor   Norman Del Mar
Sound Editor   Eric Wood
Miss Hepburn's Costumer   Doris Langley Moore
Film Costumer   Connie De Pinna
Makeup Artist   George Frost
Second Unit Photography   Ted Scaife
Special Effects   Cliff Richardson
Camera Operator   Ted Moore
Assistant Director   Guy Hamilton
Hairdresser   Eileen Bates
Wardrobe Mistress   Vi Murray
Continuity   Angela Allen

SYNOPSIS

In German East Africa, during the early days of World War I, German soldiers burn a native village, destroying the church and causing the death of the Reverend Samuel Sayer. The missionary's old-maid sister, Rose, is offered sanctuary by a gin-swilling ne'er-do-well riverboat pilot, named Charlie Allnut, who proposes sitting out the war in the backwaters. Rose strongly suggests a daring plan to go downriver and try to sink a 100-foot German gunboat commanding the area, which blocks a British invasion.

Rose handles the tiller of the riverboat, the *African Queen,* and helps take it down the perilous rapids, past a well-armed German fort at Shona into a peaceful cove. In relief, they fall into each other's arms. For three days they hide in reeds while Allnut creates two torpedoes from oxygen cylinders and blasting gelatine and attaches them to the launch, intending to ram the enemy. The *African Queen* is swamped in a gale and the pair are hauled aboard the gunboat and sentenced to hang. Allnut asks the Captain to marry them first and, as the ceremony ends, the ship runs into the derelict launch and blows up. Thrown into the water, Rose and Charlie begin swimming to shore.

CRITICS' CIRCLE

"Filmed in the Congo, the movie, rich in pictorial beauty, is virtually a Technicolor Cook's tour of jungle wonders, further enriched by performances unmatched by anything Hepburn and Bogart have yet contributed to the screen. *The African Queen* is one of the best pictures of the year—a mature, deeply touching, adult romance linked to a first-rate thriller."

—JESSE ZUNSER
Cue

"Performance-wise, Bogart has never been seen to better advantage. Nor has he ever had a more knowing, talented film partner than Miss Hepburn. . . . In the lady missionary role Katharine Hepburn is fluttery and airy in her very best comedy style, and Humphrey Bogart is humorously sodden

and resentful as the river-boat tramp. In her maidenly anxiety about bathing in proximity to this outlandish man, Miss Hepburn tips off the brand of humor that Mr. Huston originally conceived. It is, indeed, wholly reminiscent of the sort that was richly and roundly employed by Charles Laughton and Elsa Lanchester in *The Beachcomber.*"

—BOSLEY CROWTHER
The New York Times

"The movie is not great art, but it is great fun. Essentially it is one long, exciting, old-fashioned movie chase. Filmed in the Belgian Congo and Uganda by Director John Huston, it tells its adventure yarn in a blaze of Technicolor, fine wild scenery and action. Bogart, cast as a Canadian instead of a Cockney, does the best acting of his career as the badgered rumpot who becomes a man and a lover against his will. Katharine Hepburn is excellent as the gaunt, freckled, fanatic spinster. Their contrasting personalities fill the film with good scenes, beginning with Bogart's tea-table agony as the indelicate rumbling of his stomach keeps interrupting Missionary Robert Morley's chitchat about dear old England."

—*Time*

"The duel between this woman, as played by Miss Hepburn, and the dirty amiable ne'er-do-well played by Mr. Bogart, is a masterpiece of acting, directing, and dialogue. . . . They have descended the river in order to reach a lake whose far shore is British territory. They are at the end of their tether and she prays: 'Oh God, tomorrow, when we are dead, judge us not by our failures but by our love.'

"That is a very powerful line, and Miss Hepburn reads it flawlessly. After she has spoken it her strength, her pride and her will are all gone. The back that had once been so straight crumpled and the head that had always been so high doddered to the deck and was still. She had been indeed laid low. One accepts not only her end, but the end of the film.

"But the camera lifts up from the deck of the dirty boat, up from the almost lifeless man and woman, up from the swamp reeds and the jungle grass, up from the tops of the tropical trees, and there, a few hundred yards away, is the lake. The effect is breathtaking. It is an instance of the perfect utilization of pure cinema."

—HENRY HART
Films in Review

NOTES

This was Hepburn's first experience in color and was her twenty-seventh film. Director John Huston signed her when her Shakespearean tour (*As You Like It*) was over. Humphrey Bogart was co-star, Huston and James Agee prepared the scenario, and Sam Spiegel (under the pseudonym S. P. Eagle) produced.

With Humphrey Bogart

With Humphrey Bogart

The director and stars—accompanied by Lauren Bacall and thirty-four British technicians—did location shooting for two months in British Uganda. They received additional aid from Banyaro tribesmen, who doubled as helpers and film extras. The intrepid group fought heat, sun, wild life, and illness until they were forced—by sheer loss of numbers—to retreat to England to complete filming.

Said director Huston later, in a *New York Times* interview, "Bogie and Katie expanded as actors. They were both playing roles strictly against type, and for me they were a revelation. The spontaneity, the instinctive subtle interplay between them, the way they climbed inside of the people they were supposed to be—all of this made it better than we had written it, as human, as comprehending as we had any right to expect from any two actors."

The beautiful love story which evolved from this highly incongruous couple will never be forgotten. *The African Queen* won four Academy Award nominations: Best Actor (Bogart), Best Actress (Hepburn), Best Director (Huston), and Best Screenplay (Huston and Agee). Bogart won.

With Humphrey Bogart

150

Pat and Mike

A METRO-GOLDWYN-MAYER PICTURE 1952

CAST

Mike Conovan Spencer Tracy
Pat Pemberton Katharine Hepburn
Davie Hucko Aldo Ray
Collier Weld William Ching
Barney Grau Sammy White
Spec Cauley George Mathews
Mr. Beminger Loring Smith
Mrs. Beminger Phyllis Povah
Hank Tasling Charles Buchinski (Bronson)
Sam Garsell Frank Richards
Charles Barry Jim Backus
Police Captain Chuck Connors
Gibby Joseph E. Bernard
Harry MacWade Owen McGiveney
Waiter Lou Lubin
Bus Boy Carl Switzer
Pat's Caddy William Self
Caddies Billy McLean, Frankie Darro, Paul Brinegar,
    "Tiny" Jimmie Kelly
Women Golfers Mae Clarke, Helen Eby-Rock,
    Elizabeth Holmes
Commentator Hank Weaver
Sportscaster Tom Harmon
Line Judge, Tennis Court Charlie Murray
Themselves Gussie Moran, Babe Didrikson Zaharias,
    Don Budge, Alice Marble, Frank Parker, Betty Hicks,
    Beverly Hanson, Helen Dettweiler

151

CREDITS

Director   George Cukor
Producer   Lawrence Weingarten
Scenarists   Ruth Gordon, Garson Kanin
Based on an Original Story by   Ruth Gordon, Garson Kanin
Photographer   William Daniels
Art Director   Cedric Gibbons
Associate Art Director   Urie McCleary
Set Decorator   Edwin B. Willis
Associate Set Decorator   Hugh Hunt
Editor   George Boemler
Sound Recorder   Douglas Shearer
Musical Score   David Raskin
Miss Hepburn's Wardrobe by   Orry-Kelly
Makeup Artist   William Tuttle
Special Effects   Warren Newcombe
Montage   Peter Ballbusch
Assistant Director   Jack Greenwood

SYNOPSIS

Pat Pemberton, a college physical education teacher, is signed as an all-around professional athlete by Mike Conovan, a smooth, fast-talking sports promoter. When it comes to golf, however, Pat just cannot reach the top of her game when her fiancé, Collier Weld, is watching her. This situation gives bright ideas to a pair of petty racketeers, who own part of her contract. It seems they want her to throw a golf tournament.

CRITICS' CIRCLE

"One of the season's gayest comedies, *Pat and Mike* benefits by George Cukor's shrewd direction, the sprightly lines of Authors Ruth Gordon and Garson Kanin, and the comic capering of Old Hands Hepburn and Tracy. Aldo Ray is amusing as a dumb boxer with a foghorn voice."

—*Time*

"This trifling money-maker successfully provides the following opportunities; for Katharine Hepburn to display her golf and tennis prowess; for Spencer Tracy to prove that he can be illiterate and still have his heart of gold; for Ruth Gordon and Garson Kanin to write specious, amusing dialogue and to kid Miss Hepburn's spare physique; for Director George Cukor to kid film gangsters, pugilists and other stereotypes. It also provides an opportunity for almost anyone to have an entertaining hour and a half."

—*Films in Review*

"Katharine Hepburn and Spencer Tracy, who lost their amateur standing years ago so far as their popular rating as theatrical entertainers goes, are proving themselves equally able as a couple of professional sports in *Pat and Mike*. . . ."

152

With Babe Didrikson Zaharias

With William Ching and Spencer Tracy

With Spencer Tracy and Sammy White

With Charles Buchinski (Bronson),
Spencer Tracy and George Mathews

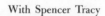

With Spencer Tracy

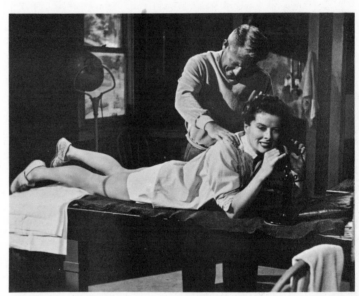

With Spencer Tracy

Miss Hepburn always has been an actress whose competence with a line or with a tensile dramatic situation has been well above the margin of surprise. But this is the first time she has shown us—at least, on the motion-picture screen—that she can swing a golf club or tennis racquet as adroitly as she can sling an epigram. In the role of the tough-guy sports promoter . . . Mr. Tracy, too, makes happy pretense of being a sporting type—a type several pegs below the lady but none the less a sport. . . . It is smoothly directed by George Cukor and slyly, amusingly played by the whole cast, especially by its due of easy, adroit, experienced stars. Mr. Ray, Sammy White, William Ching, George Mathews and Charles Buchinski are also fun."

—BOSLEY CROWTHER
The New York Times

NOTES

Hepburn's final film on her MGM contract was waiting for her return from location shooting on *The African Queen.* It seems that the *Adam's Rib* crowd was at it again—this time with a comedy called *Pat and Mike.* Tracy was delightful as a sports promoter while Hepburn was given every opportunity to display her athletic skills—including swimming, hiking, golf, basketball, and tennis.

Cukor brought in many notable sports figures to add authenticity to the proceedings, and the Garson Kanin–Ruth Gordon script even brought in sports racketeers. It was a mad funfest for all concerned.

Aldo Ray headed a supporting cast that included Phyllis Povah (so delightful in Cukor's *The Women*) and Chuck Connors, first baseman of the Los Angeles Angels, who went on to become a television series star.

Pat and Mike won the Kanins another Academy Award nomination and was a critical and commercial success.

With Aldo Ray

With Spencer Tracy

Summertime

A LOPERT FILM PRODUCTION
RELEASED THRU UNITED ARTISTS
IN TECHNICOLOR 1955

CAST

Jane Hudson   Katharine Hepburn
Renato Di Rossi   Rossano Brazzi
Signora Fiorini   Isa Miranda
Eddie Yaeger   Darren McGavin
Phyl Yaeger   Mari Aldon
Mrs. McIlhenny   Jane Rose
Mr. McIlhenny   MacDonald Parke
Mauro   Gaitano Audiero
Englishman   Andre Morell
Vito Di Rossi   Jeremy Spenser
Giovanna   Virginia Simeon

CREDITS

Director   David Lean
Producer   Ilya Lopert
Associate Producer   Norman Spencer
Scenarists   David Lean, H. E. Bates
Based on the Play The Time of the Cuckoo *by*
  Arthur Laurents
Photographer   Jack Hildyard
Art Director   Vincent Korda
Associate Art Directors   W. Hutchinson, Ferdinand Bellan
Editor   Peter Taylor
Sound Recorder   Peter Handford

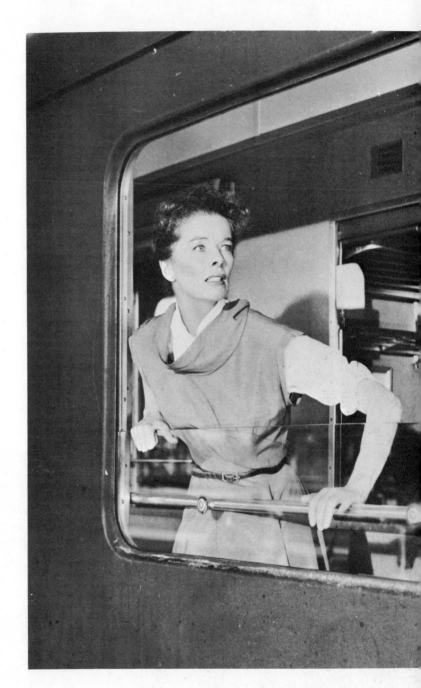

With MacDonald Parke and Jane Rose

With Mari Aldon and Isa Miranda

With Rossano Brazzi

With Rossano Brazzi

Sound Editor   Winston Ryder
Musical Score   Alessandro Cicognini
Camera Operator   Peter Newbrook
Hair Stylist   Grazia De Rossi
Makeup Artist   Cesare Gamberelli
Assistant Directors   Adrian Pryce-Jones, Alberto Cardone
Production Managers   Raymond Anzarut, Franco Magli
Assistant to the Producer   Robert Kingsley
Continuity   Margaret Shipway

Location Photography in Eastman Color

SYNOPSIS

Jane Hudson, a middle-aged American spinster, arrives in Venice, fulfilling a lifelong dream. On her first evening, she has an encounter with Mauro, an enterprising little street urchin, who becomes her unofficial guide. While sightseeing with him the next day, she meets Renato Di Rossi, the proprietor of an antique shop, and soon the pair are hopelessly in love and seemingly inseparable.

One evening, while she is waiting for Renato in the Piazza St. Marco, a young man named Vito tells Jane that Renato will be late. She asks him to join her and learns that he is Renato's son. Even though she is hurt, Jane agrees to spend a few days with Renato on the lovely island of Burano and all is carefree and idyllic, until she is reminded of the futility of their relationship. She leaves Venice a little richer for what she has found there; a little sadder, because she couldn't take it with her.

CRITICS' CIRCLE

"As the secretary, Katharine Hepburn has an air of stylized hysteria that is somewhat unsettling when we first meet her. After she quiets down, though, she is wonderfully effective, making the most of her opportunities for registering pathos and passion, and turning in a couple of first-rate slapstick sequences as well."

—*The New Yorker*

"Miss Hepburn has labored long in the service of her art and, like many grand actress personalities, she has now created herself in her own image. Everything superfluous is gone, the elements are refined and complete—the sad mouth, the head-back laugh, the snap of *chic* in shirtmaker dresses, the dream of enchantment behind wistful eyes, the awakened puritan passion of the girl in love, the 'regular' way with children, the leggy stride, and always the bones—the magnificent, prominent, impossible bones which a visiting journalist, made somewhat exuberant by the deceptively mild local wine, described as the 'greatest calcium deposit since the white cliffs of Dover.'"

—LEE ROGOSIN
The Saturday Review

With director David Lean
and Gaitano Audiero

"Both Miss Hepburn and Brazzi are excellent in their roles, with the former making the most of her characterization as the shy and lonely dreamer and Brazzi scoring as the realistic charmer."

—ROSE PELSWICK
The New York Journal-American

"Miss Hepburn is clever and amusing as a spirited American old maid who turns up in Venice with her guide books and a romantic gleam in her eye. She makes a convincing summer tourist. And her breathlessly eager attitude is just right for the naive encounters and farcical mishaps that have been arranged."

—BOSLEY CROWTHER
The New York Times

"Few actresses in films could equal Hepburn's evocation of aching loneliness on her first night in Venice as she wanders, forlorn and proud, like a primly starched ghost in a city of lovers. . . . The script has dropped overboard many of the plot gimmicks that Playwright Arthur Laurents used as cogs for stage action. With them go some of the harsher truths about the career girl's character and therefore any possibility of comparing Hepburn's performance with that of Shirley Booth in the stage play. The Eastman Color and the camerawork by Jack Hildyard are superb."

—*Time*

158

NOTES

In the summer of 1954 Hepburn joined director David Lean and a crew of British technicians in Venice to film *Summertime,* based loosely on Arthur Laurents' play *The Time of the Cuckoo.* The David Lean–H. E. Bates screenplay removed the harsh realities of the original and, utilizing the magnificent beauty of Venice through the lens of Jack Hildyard, made a superior tear-jerker.

Hepburn, as spinster Jane Hudson, was eloquent in her depiction of a lonely woman who finds her dream romance only to discover that it is a thing of the moment and cannot last. Rossano Brazzi, whom Hepburn helped attain co-starring status, was handsome and suave as the antique dealer who romances the spinster. Isa Miranda, whose American film career was short-lived, was an understanding Signora Fiorini. The best supporting acting was contributed by Jane Rose and MacDonald Parke, as the McIlhennys, a pair of obnoxious American tourists that were given painfully accurate characterizations. Young Gaitano Audiero was charming as Hepburn's guide through the canals and streets of Venice.

Hepburn made newspaper headlines during the filming of her famous fall in the Venice canal, which is a perfect example of creative film editing. Tourists visiting Venice are still shown that very spot. *Summertime,* called *Summer Madness* in England, premiered in Venice on May 29, 1955.

With Gaitano Audiero

The Rainmaker

A PARAMOUNT PICTURE   1956

CAST

Starbuck   Burt Lancaster
Lizzie Curry   Katharine Hepburn
File   Wendell Corey
Noah Curry   Lloyd Bridges
Jim Curry   Earl Holliman
H. C. Curry   Cameron Prud'Homme
Sheriff Thomas   Wallace Ford
Snookie   Yvonne Lime
Belinda   Dottie Bee Baker
Deputy   Dan White
Townsmen   Stan Jones, John Benson, James Stone,
   Tony Merrill, Joe Brown
Phil Mackey   Ken Becker

CREDITS

Director   Joseph Anthony
Producer   Hal B. Wallis
Associate Producer   Paul Nathan
Scenarist   N. Richard Nash
Based on the Play by   N. Richard Nash
Photographer   Charles Lang, Jr.
Art Director   Hal Pereira
Associate Art Director   Walter Tyler
Set Decorator   Sam Comer
Associate Set Decorator   Arthur Krams

With Burt Lancaster,

With Burt Lancaster

With Cameron Prud'Homme, Lloyd Bridges, Earl Holliman
and Burt Lancaster

With Burt Lancaster

With Burt Lancaster

Editor Warren Low
Sound Recorders Harold Lewis, Winston Leverett
Musical Score Alex North
Costumer Edith Head
Makeup Artist Wally Westmore
Hair Stylist Nellie Manley
Special Photographic Effects John P. Fulton
Assistant Director C. C. Coleman, Jr.
Technicolor Color Consultant Richard Mueller

SYNOPSIS

Lizzie Curry, a frightened spinster who has a father and two brothers to care for in their drought-plagued farm outside a small southwestern town, is seemingly content in her day-to-day existence. Into Lizzie's world comes a sweet-talking, brash young conman, named Starbuck, who not only boasts that he can bring rain to the area for just $100, but also convinces Lizzie that she is more of a woman than she herself believes. He transforms her into a woman ready for love.

CRITICS' CIRCLE

"Miss Hepburn is superb as she brings elderly, barren despair to a blossoming of radiant, girlish bliss. . . . Lancaster's flights of fancy talk are an achievement in comic art, in fanatical grandiloquence and in overpowering emotional plea."

—ALTON COOK
New York World-Telegram

"In her portrait of a cow-town spinster, Miss Hepburn never entirely convinces us that she really is just a homely little primitive, but she does succeed in obtaining full lachrymal measure from the plight of a woman who wants a man in the worst way and doesn't know how to go about capturing one. As her clodhopping Svengali, Mr. Lancaster is most engaging and whether he is enlightening her about her formidable potentialities as a female or shilling the yokels into believing that he can make rain, he is a believable character."

—*The New Yorker*

"Burt Lancaster has never played the mountebank more sweetly, and Miss Hepburn's performance as the plain, unwanted woman who finds that it is within her own power to become both beautiful and desired, again compels admiration for her qualities as an actress and the choice architecture of her face."

—*The (London) Observer*

"Most important, there are the awkward, pathetic Lizzie, so intelligently and warmly played by Katharine Hepburn, and the swaggering pitchman with his own unexpected humility, a part wonderfully suited to Burt Lancaster's

With Burt Lancaster

talents and personality. . . . *The Rainmaker* adds up to a first-rate picture."

—ELINOR HUGHES
Boston Herald

"In the hands of Katharine Hepburn, who plays this impressionable dame; Burt Lancaster, who plays the faker, and three or four other would-be clowns, this simple and saucy country whimsy gets squeezed so strenuously that it squirts in a dozen directions and splashes humor and sentiment all over the place. . . . Miss Hepburn, who has done her farce performing on a somewhat higher social scale, is nothing daunted by the requirement of doing it as a rube. And even though her manners are quite airy for the Corn Belt and her accent suspiciously Bryn Mawr, she holds her own better than even with a bunch of voracious clowns."

—BOSLEY CROWTHER
The New York Times

"Director Joseph Anthony keeps his actors moving nimbly along. Actor Lancaster does a businesslike job as the rainmaker. Prud'Homme and Holliman are excellent as the father and the younger brother. Actress Hepburn does not always surely suggest the stages in Lizzie's life, as she passes from emotional chrysalis to vivid imaginal maturity, but she holds the eye in scene after scene like a brilliant moth as she batters wildly about one or another light o' love. Most welcome in her performance is the restraint put on the all-too-well-known Hepburn mannerisms—apparently by Director Anthony, a man who once heated up an old chestnut and hurled it at another overactive actress: 'Look, dear, don't just DO something, STAND there!'"

—*Time*

161

On the set with designer Edith Head, writer N. Richard Nash, and producer Hal B. Wallis

Kate added depth and perception to the already vividly written character of Lizzie Curry in this film version of N. Richard Nash's 1954 Broadway hit. She also benefited immeasurably from the boisterous performance of Burt Lancaster as the charlatan Starbuck. Both actors delved deep for the roots of these individuals and came up with winning portrayals.

Joseph Anthony, who had directed Geraldine Page in the stage version, repeated his assignment as director. Stage actor Cameron Prud'Homme recreated his original role of Lizzie's father perfectly. Also turning in fine performances were Lloyd Bridges, Wendell Corey, and Earl Holliman.

The opening up of this stage piece owes much to the photography of Charles Lang, Jr., and editor Warren Low. Alex North's musical score won him an Academy Award nomination as did Hepburn's Lizzie—her seventh.

The Rainmaker later returned to the Broadway stage as a musical called *110 in the Shade.*

With Cameron Prud'Homme

162

The Iron Petticoat

A BENHAR PRODUCTION
RELEASED BY METRO-GOLDWYN-MAYER
IN VISTAVISION AND TECHNICOLOR 1956

CAST

Chuck Lockwood Bob Hope
Vinka Kovelenko Katharine Hepburn
Colonel Sklarnoff James Robertson Justice
Ivan Kropotkin Robert Helpmann
Dubratz David Kossoff
Colonel Tarbell Alan Gifford
Lewis Paul Carpenter
Connie Noelle Middleton
Tony Mallard Nicholas Phipps
Paul Sidney James
Senator Alexander Gauge
Maria Doris Goddard
Sutsiyawa Tutte Lemkow
Tityana Sandra Dorne
Lingerie Clerk Richard Wattis
Sklarnoff's Secretary Maria Antippas
Grisha Martin Boddey

CREDITS

Director Ralph Thomas
Producer Betty E. Box

With Bob Hope

With Bob Hope

Scenarist   Ben Hecht (name removed from credits)
Based on an Original Story by   Harry Saltzman
Photographer   Ernest Steward
Art Director   Carmen Dillon
Set Decorator   Vernon Dixon
Editor   Frederick Wilson
Sound Recorders   John W. Mitchell, Gordon K. McCallum
Musical Score   Benjamin Frankel
Sound Editor   Roger Cherrill
Production Manager   R. Denis Holt
Costumer   Yvonne Caffin
Makeup Artist   W. T. Partleton
Camera Operator   H. A. R. Thompson
Assistant Director   James H. Ware
Continuity   Joan Davis

SYNOPSIS

Captain Vinka Kovelenko, of the Russian Air Force, angered at being passed over for military awards, flies a MIG to an American base in Germany. Flier Chuck Lockwood is assigned to convert her to democracy but she tries, simultaneously, to show him the advantages of communism. They go to London where she succumbs to the fleshpots of capitalism and soon abandons her uniform for frilly feminine things, drinks champagne and vodka, and ends up falling in love. Alerted to the situation, the Russian Embassy arranges to have her kidnapped and take her back to Moscow.

With Bob Hope and Noelle Middleton

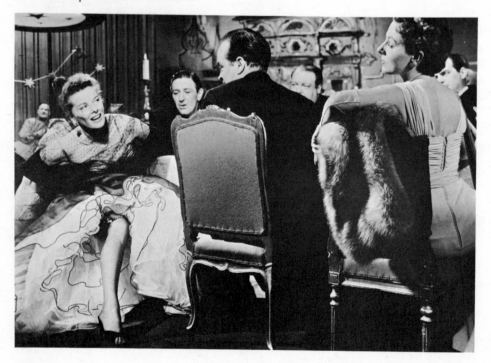

CRITICS' CIRCLE

"*The Iron Petticoat* is practically a remake of the old Greta Garbo—Melvyn Douglas comedy about how Lenin's glass-of-water theory is vanquished by Hollywood's slipper-of-champagne theory, and the world is saved for black lace undies. . . . Katharine Hepburn, doing her smooth-cheeked, trim-legged best to look like a Soviet with sex appeal. . . . For a couple of reels the leading comedian plays it, not for guffaws, but for the quiet snickers he is really better at getting; yet in the last half of the picture he goes right back to the cheap tricks that in recent years have made many moviegoers give up Hope."

—Time

"Miss Hepburn makes an impressive showing as the Soviet pilot; she looks the part as well as playing it; and the gradual transition in outlook, accompanied by the change in style of her wardrobe, is accomplished with considerable sensitivity. Hope maintains the spirit of the piece at a lively pace, but never quite forgets his work habits as a gagman."

—Variety

With Bob Hope and Robert Helpmann

With Noelle Middleton and Bob Hope

"There were rumors that some of Miss Hepburn's stuff was cut out, and there were reports of feuding between Hope and Hecht, who was originally engaged for the screenplay. At any rate, the screenplay credit on the picture goes begging. Everyone else is on hand to face the music."

—HOLLIS ALPERT
The Saturday Review

"'Vy you are smilink?' Katharine Hepburn asks Bob Hope, trying her best to sound like a Russian, in *The Iron Petticoat*. Nobody's smilink. In fact, for Hepburn and Hope fans, this should be a day of cryink.

"They seem amazed to find themselves in a comedy that has no humor, and they go through the motions grimly, like children at dancing school, hoping it will all be over soon. When Miss Hepburn, encased in an army uniform that does nothing for her lissom figure, turns to Hope and says 'I was vorried,' she has good reason."

—WILLIAM K. ZINSSER
New York Herald Tribune

On the set with director Ralph Thomas

"*The Iron Petticoat*, which encloses Katharine Hepburn and Bob Hope, is about as inflexible and ponderous as the garment its title describes. . . . *Ninotchka*, you say. It should be half as humorous as that old film! It should be even half as funny as the successive *Comrade X*.

"Furthermore, the hopeful off-beat teaming of Miss Hepburn and Mr. Hope as the ideological opposites who get together has resulted in something grotesque. Miss Hepburn's Russian affectations and accent are simply horrible, and Mr. Hope's wistful efforts with feeble gags to hold his franchise as a funny man are downright sad."

—BOSLEY CROWTHER
The New York Times

"Bob Hope and Katharine Hepburn are finding plenty of fun still left in the old Greta Garbo–Melvyn Douglas comedy. The new version is broader farce, but the laughter runs high and hearty. The picture does not properly belong to Bob Hope, but that does not bother him in taking charge of most of the laughter. Miss Hepburn does a giddy caricature of her own behavior in romantic and dramatic roles. In advance the pairing sounded unlikely, but they make a hilarious team."

—ALTON COOK
New York World-Telegram

NOTES

Ben Hecht called his "original story" *Not for Money* when filming began but it was released as *The Iron Petticoat*. Even the most casual of moviegoers noticed the similarities to Melchior Lengyel's *Ninotchka* which Garbo made memorable in 1939.

Despite good direction by Ralph Thomas and good supporting actors like James Robertson Justice and Robert Helpmann, among others, this film proved quite a disaster.

Kate overemphasized her Russian accent and Hope pushed too hard to steal the picture from Kate—with the help of his entourage of gag writers—and when Hope's footage began to swell and Hepburn's shrink, Ben Hecht pulled out. This explains why the final film ambiguously states, "Based on an Original Story."

Hecht, in an open letter published in *The Hollywood Reporter*, said in part, "Although her magnificent comic performance has been blow-torched out of the film, there is enough left of the Hepburn footage to identify her for her sharpshooters. I am assured by my hopeful predators that *The Iron Petticoat* will go over big with people 'who can't get enough of Bob Hope.' " Hope retaliated in the same publication, saying, in part, "As for Kate Hepburn, I don't think she was depressed with the preview audience rave about her performance."

The Iron Petticoat was first shown at the Berlin Film Festival in June 1956 and was in general release in England long before it arrived in the United States in late December.

Desk Set

A TWENTIETH CENTURY-FOX PICTURE
IN CINEMASCOPE AND COLOR BY DE LUXE   1957

CAST

Richard Sumner   Spencer Tracy
Bunny Watson   Katharine Hepburn
Mike Cutler   Gig Young
Peg Costello   Joan Blondell
Sylvia   Dina Merrill
Ruthie   Sue Randall
Miss Warringer   Neva Patterson
Smithers   Harry Ellerbe
Azae   Nicholas Joy
Alice   Diane Jergens
Cathy   Merry Anders
Old Lady   Ida Moore
Receptionist   Rachel Stephens
Kenny   Sammy Ogg

CREDITS

Director   Walter Lang
Producer   Henry Ephron
Scenarists   Phoebe Ephron, Henry Ephron
Based on the Play The Desk Set *by*   William Marchant
As Produced on the Stage by   Robert Fryer, Lawrence Carr
Photographer   Leon Shamroy
Art Director   Lyle Wheeler
Associate Art Director   Maurice Ransford
Set Decorator   Walter M. Scott
Associate Set Decorator   Paul S. Fox
Editor   Robert Simpson

With Spencer Tracy

With Joan Blondell,
Dina Merrill and Sue Randall

With Gig Young

168

With Gig Young

With Spencer Tracy

With Joan Blondell and Spencer Tracy

169

Sound Recorders   E. Clayton Ward, Harry M. Leonard
Musical Score   Cyril J. Mockridge
Musical Director   Lionel Newman
Orchestrator   Edward B. Powell
Costumer   Charles Le Maire
Makeup Artist   Ben Nye
Special Photographic Effects   Ray Kellogg
Assistant Director   Hal Herman
Color Consultant   Leonard Doss
Hair Stylist   Helen Turpin
Cinemascope Lenses by   Bausch & Lomb

SYNOPSIS

Bunny Watson, who possesses a formidable brain and memory, is head of a large TV network's reference library. Together with her quite capable staff, she can answer almost any question. Along comes Richard Sumner, a methods engineer, who has invented an electronic brain called Emerac—or "Emmy," for short—that can answer anything.

The girls fear that this cold machine will replace them, sooner or later, and rivalries spring up between Bunny and the inventor. Her constant contact with Richard inspires a suitor of seven years, Mike Cutler, to propose. However, the canny engineer succeeds in making it quite clear that Emmy isn't going to do Bunny out of her job, but leave her more time for research—and him.

CRITICS' CIRCLE

"Solely through their (Hepburn and Tracy's) efforts a second-rate movie becomes tolerable and sometimes even amusing. Miss Hepburn is as beguiling as always. She is at her best disarming the engineer with feats of memory and thrusts of wit. She manages to bring some depth to a character that really has none. Tracy accomplishes the same trick, mainly by underplaying his role."

—WILLIAM K. ZINSSER
New York Herald Tribune

"Best of all, there are Miss Hepburn and Mr. Tracy. They can tote phone books on their heads or balance feathers on their chins and be amusing—which is about the size of what they do here. Under Walter Lang's relaxed direction, they lope through this trifling charade like a couple of oldtimers who enjoy reminiscing with simple routines. Mr. Tracy is masculine and stubborn, Miss Hepburn is feminine and glib. The play is inconsequential. The sets and color are good."

—BOSLEY CROWTHER
The New York Times

"Although Katharine Hepburn and Spencer Tracy are both getting on, they are expertly directed by Walter Lang, fresh from his triumphs with *The King and I,* in their first screen

romp together in five years. . . . On the stage *Desk Set* was no great shakes, in fact it was little, if anything, more than a personal victory for its star, Shirley Booth. On the screen it is a victory for Lang, and for Hepburn and Tracy. Without them, and without an excellent supporting cast, *Desk Set* would not be the successful entertainment it is. She (Hepburn) looks younger in *Desk Set,* and very much better, than she did in her last two films, and has many more opportunities to show off her acting skill. She plays a semi-drunken scene convincingly and often seems to be enjoying the fun in the script."

—ROMANO V. TOZZI
Films in Review

"The people all do their jobs well, with special salutes to Hepburn for her crisp efficiency, and Tracy for his air of science, so deep that it becomes wholly unfathomable. *Desk Set,* let us conclude, is a shining piece of machinery brought to a high polish, and, delivered with appropriate performances, flourishes, affection, though, it cannot inspire."

—ARCHER WINSTEN
New York Post

"Hepburn and Tracy are a highly effective comedy team well worth watching, he chewing his lip and she baring her teeth."

—*Newsweek*

"Based on William Marchant's 1955 Broadway comedy about the milder terrors of technological unemployment, *Desk Set* has been expanded by a sizable pigeonhole, in which Katharine Hepburn and Spencer Tracy intermittently bill and coo. . . . Though Actress Hepburn tends to wallow in the wake of Shirley Booth, who played the part on Broadway, she never quite sinks in the comic scenes, and in the romantic ones she is light enough to ride the champagne splashes of emotion as if she were going over Niagara in a barrel. Spencer Tracy has one wonderful slapstick scene, and Gig Young does very well with a comic style for which he is much beholden to William Holden."

—*Time*

NOTES

William Marchant's cute little play *The Desk Set* was hardly ready—or capable—for the expanded treatment that the screen version warranted once it became known that Tracy and Hepburn were interested in it. It almost burst at the seams. What held the whole thing together was the familiar playing of the all-American couple who deftly added touches of sheer brilliance whether in both comic moments and serious scenes. Gig Young and Joan Blondell contributed more laughs and what finally evolved was a fun-filled light entertainment.

This was the first time Tracy and Hepburn had appeared *together* in (1) color and (2) CinemaScope. *Desk Set* was their eighth film—and the next-to-last.

With Joan Blondell, Sammy Ogg,
Spencer Tracy, Sue Randall and
Dina Merrill

With Spencer Tracy

Suddenly, Last Summer

A HORIZON (G. B.) LIMITED PRODUCTION
IN ASSOCIATION WITH ACADEMY PICTURES
AND CAMP FILMS
RELEASED BY COLUMBIA PICTURES   1959

CAST

Catherine Holly   Elizabeth Taylor
Mrs. Venable   Katharine Hepburn
Dr. Cukrowicz   Montgomery Clift
Dr. Hockstader   Albert Dekker
Mrs. Holly   Mercedes McCambridge
George Holly   Gary Raymond
Miss Foxhill   Mavis Villiers
Nurse Benson   Patricia Marmont
Sister Felicity   Joan Young
Lucy   Maria Britneva
Dr. Hockstader's Secretary   Sheila Robbins
Young Blonde Interne   David Cameron
A Patient   Roberta Woolley

CREDITS

Director   Joseph L. Mankiewicz
Producer   Sam Spiegel
Scenarists   Gore Vidal, Tennessee Williams
Based on the Short Play by   Tennessee Williams

On the set

With Montgomery Clift
and Mercedes McCambridge

Photographer Jack Hildyard
Production Supervisor Bill Kirby
Production Designer Oliver Messel
Art Director William Kellner
Set Decorator Scott Slimon
Editorial Consultant William W. Hornbeck
Editor Thomas G. Stanford
Sound Recorders A. G. Ambler, John Cox
Sound Editor Peter Thornton
Musical Score Buxton Orr, Malcolm Arnold
Assembly Editor John Jympson
Costumer for Miss Taylor Jean Louis
Costumer for Miss Hepburn Norman Hartnell
Associate Costumer Joan Ellacott
Makeup Artist David Aylott
Hair Stylist Joan White
Special Photographic Effects Tom Howard
Assistant Director Bluey Hill
Camera Operator Gerry Fisher
Construction Manager Dewey Dukelow
Continuity Elaine Schreyeck

SYNOPSIS

In North Africa, Sebastian Venable, a rich and cosseted American poet, dies suddenly during the summer. The death certificate declares it a heart attack, but mentions that the body "was somewhat damaged." Catherine Holly, the poet's beauteous cousin, who was with him at the time, babbles about "dreadful things," but she is incoherent and unclear. Her aunt, Mrs. Violet Venable—determined to protect her son's reputation at any cost—has her committed to an insane asylum and demands that she be given a lobotomy, which may turn her into an imbecile, but will end her ravings about Sebastian's life—and death.

Mrs. Venable offers $1,000,000 to the hospital where the deed is to be done, but its brilliant young neurological

With Montgomery Clift
and Elizabeth Taylor

With Albert Dekker
and Montgomery Clift

surgeon, Dr. Cukrowicz, prefers to administer a truth serum to Catherine. Under the influence of the serum, in the presence of the collected family, the whole sordid tale comes out. Sebastian was a homosexual who used, first his beautiful mother, until her beauty faded, and then his young cousin, to procure boys for him. The way he died represents a grisly sort of vengeance.

CRITICS' CIRCLE

"Elizabeth Taylor, as the beleaguered heroine of a New Orleans nightmare, works with an intensity beyond belief; hers is unquestionably one of the finest performances of this or any year. Katharine Hepburn uses every ounce of the Hepburn charm (and every one of the Hepburn mannerisms) to make her portrait of an egocentric matron and too-doting mother ring true. . . . It is, in short, a wholly admirable rendering into film of a work that is at once fascinating and nauseating, brilliant and immoral. Its reception at the box office unquestionably will have an important bearing on the future of 'adult' film in this country."

—ARTHUR KNIGHT
The Saturday Review

"Katharine Hepburn, as Sebastian's mother, acts brilliantly but privately, as though she'd never realised there were other persons in the picture. . . . I loathe this film. I say so candidly. To my mind it is a decadent piece of work, sensational, barbarous, and ridiculous."

—C. A. LEJEUNE
The (London) Observer

"Katharine Hepburn's role is one that even in its evil has a perverted charm. As to (her) performance, it is splendid, as one might expect. Words in this film are dominant, not merely one tool but the adze with which the mood, the action, and the characterization are shaped. One can relish the exquisite way in which Miss Hepburn reads them, but one cannot forget that it is the word, not her actions, that makes the film."

—PAUL V. BECKLEY
New York Herald Tribune

"The source of the pressure, Katharine Hepburn, projects a strange, highly personal character but lacks that old Southern charm."

—ARCHER WINSTEN
New York Post

"It's no criticism of Katharine Hepburn as the devouring mother to say that she acts as if on a stage, because given this over-life-size part, imagined and (I suppose) largely as written for the stage, no one could do anything else with it. Elizabeth Taylor as the unhappy girl comes best out of the whole affair."

—*Punch*

"The doctor, smoothy played by Montgomery Clift, has been allowed a shade of romantic feeling. The mother remains her implacable self; and though in the glittering performance of Katharine Hepburn she looks, except for a few vicious seconds, improbably youthful. I shall not complain of the chance of seeing the lovely creature. The triumph, however, belongs to Elizabeth Taylor—a wild bird trapped: there are moments when she gives the character of the girl the true dimensions of despair."

—DILYS POWELL
The (London) Sunday Times

"Hocus-pocus that this symbol-ridden confection certainly is, made more silly still by its implicit claim to be ranked as high art, it still exercises a certain fascination. This is due partly to the immense gusto and self-confidence of the writing, partly to the stylish direction by Joseph L. Mankiewicz, Oliver Messel's sultry settings and some highly polished performances. Katharine Hepburn is frighteningly imperious as Mrs. Venable and Elizabeth Taylor's Catherine is an exciting study making up in spirit what it lacks in compassion. As the doctor Montgomery Clift has little to do except to look pained and puzzled, as well he might."

—PATRICK GIBBS
London Daily Telegraph

"Obviously, the big problem in such a picture is to pat all the various bits of dirt into some sort of significant mud pie,

and Director Joseph L. Mankiewicz has done the patting with considerable skill and taste. . . . Katharine Hepburn, even though she is all dolled up like a cross between Auntie Mame and the White Queen, does an intelligent job of portraying the devouring mother."

—*Time*

"Miss Hepburn, with her surer techniques, is dominant, making her brisk authority a genteel hammer, relentlessly crushing the younger woman. Miss Taylor is most effective in her later scenes."

—*Variety*

NOTES

In 1958 Tennessee Williams' one-act play *Suddenly, Last Summer* was produced on the stage along with another one-acter called *Something Unspoken* under the collective title *Garden District*. Anne Meacham was Catherine Holly, Robert Lansing was Dr. Cukrowicz, and Hortense Alden was Mrs. Venable. It was the same Hortense Alden that

With Montgomery Clift, Albert Dekker, Gary Raymond, Mavis Villiers, Patricia Marmont, Mercedes McCambridge and Elizabeth Taylor

With Montgomery Clift and Elizabeth Taylor

With Montgomery Clift

With Montgomery Clift

176

Hepburn replaced in the role of the maid in *A Month in the Country* on Broadway in 1930. Now Hepburn, in the expanded film version, was playing a role that Alden had created off-Broadway.

Gore Vidal worked on the screenplay with Williams to produce a bizarre yet utterly fascinating work. Hepburn's salary was $175,444. It was filmed in England for producer Sam Spiegel (*The African Queen*), director Joseph L. Mankiewicz (*Woman of the Year*), and photographer Jack Hildyard (*Summertime*).

Mankiewicz evoked from Elizabeth Taylor what was probably her finest piece of acting; her handling of the long and difficult monologues was outstanding. Hepburn's Mrs. Venable blended love, decadence, and insanity into a shattering experience that never failed to excite.

This was the first major film to give a hint of what was to come from filmmakers in the sixties and seventies. It succeeded in smashing old taboos concerning untouchable subjects when its box-office returns grew and grew.

Hepburn and Taylor were both nominated for Best Actress honors, but canceled each other out. The unusual settings and set decorations also were nominated.

With Montgomery Clift

Long Day's Journey into Night

AN EMBASSY PICTURE   1962

CAST

Mary Tyrone   Katharine Hepburn
James Tyrone, Sr.   Ralph Richardson
James Tyrone, Jr.   Jason Robards, Jr.
Edmund Tyrone   Dean Stockwell
Cathleen   Jeanne Barr

CREDITS

Director   Sidney Lumet
Co-Producers   Ely Landau, Jack J. Dreyfus, Jr.
Scenarist   Eugene O'Neill
Based on the Play by   Eugene O'Neill
Photographer   Boris Kaufman
Production Designer   Richard Sylbert
In Charge of Production   George Justin
Editor   Ralph Rosenblum
Musical Score   Andre Previn
Costumer   Motley

SYNOPSIS

This is the story of the Tyrone family, compressed into
a long day and night in the year 1912 in a seaside cottage
in Connecticut, doomed as was the house of Atreus. Young
Edmund Tyrone has a melancholy foreboding that tubercu-

With Jason Robards, Jr.,
and Ralph Richardson

With Dean Stockwell

losis will cut short his not-yet-budding career as a writer. His doting mother has a guilt complex because her father died of consumption, and because when Edmund was born, she suffered an illness which sent her to the escape of drugs.

The actor father is considered a miser by his two sons, who hold him indirectly responsible for their mother's affliction, considering that she had inept medical care. Now the father is ready to condemn his youngest son to a state health farm. His older son, Jamie, finds some solace in drink and willfully leads young Edmund on carouses which make his own sins seem less deep by comparison. Eventually, all the members of the family rail against one another and their fates.

With Jason Robards, Jr., and Dean Stockwell

CRITICS' CIRCLE

"Hepburn, soaring in the tragic and varied role of the drug-addicted mother departing into psychosis, is great, though there may be some viewers who will be stopped short by her remembered mannerisms of voice, laughter and tooth."

—ARCHER WINSTEN
New York Post

"Katharine Hepburn's beautifully boned face mirrors her anguish and needs. She makes the role of the mother breath-taking and intensely moving. There is balance, depth and breadth in her acting."

—*Variety*

"Katharine Hepburn caps her distinguished career in the role of the pitiful, dope-addicted mother, groping back to the past for dimly remembered moments of happiness. Her transformations are extraordinary as, in recollection, she suffuses her tense and aging face with a coquettish youthfulness or, in the larger pattern of the play, changes from a nervous, ailing, but loving mother into a half-demented harridan. Her final scene, which contains some of O'Neill's most beautiful writing, is in every way masterful (including Lumet's daring cut from a long pull-back to a huge close-up). What is most extraordinary about *Long Day's Journey into Night* is the way it builds. Shot in progression, the actors come to the peak of their powers just as the play rises to its climax."

—ARTHUR KNIGHT
The Saturday Review

"In his screen version of Eugene O'Neill's *Long Day's Journey into Night*, Sidney Lumet has given us a superb cinematic translation of the only American play to which the much-abused adjective 'great' can seriously be applied. Katharine Hepburn's face—that terrible smile, those suffering eyes—was especially worth watching. I have never been an addict of Katharine Hepburn; she struck me usually as mannered, to say the least; but here, stimulated by O'Neill and Lumet, she emerges as a superb tragedienne. The tremendous final night scene came out even more strongly than it did on the stage. The device for ending it with the camera slowly withdrawing until the family sitting around the table is seen as tiny figures in a vast darkness—this was an inspiration, and I only wish Lumet had not shattered it by suddenly bringing back Hepburn's face in extreme close-up. But perhaps he will have cut this jarring 'effect' by the time the film is released."

—DWIGHT MACDONALD
Esquire

"Katharine Hepburn is tricky and uneven in the difficult role of the wife and mother in this divided family—probably because she has too much to do. In the moments of deepest

With Ralph Richardson

anguish, she is vibrant with hot and tragic truth, an eloquent representation of a lovely woman brought to feeble, helpless ruin. But she is put to so much repetition in the first hour or so of the film, in hinting at the ultimate revelation that narcotics have her hooked, that she strains her own gifts of airy acting and the patience of workaday folks."

—BOSLEY CROWTHER
The New York Times

"Sidney Lumet's direction is the first delight of (this) exceptional film. He has not made a screenplay out of it; he has simply taken O'Neill's text, and with the minimum of adaptation put it directly on film. . . . Lumet would not have accomplished this act of reconciliation had it not been for his cast. As Tyrone, Ralph Richardson gives the performance of his career. It is Richardson's triumph that he never makes Tyrone unlikeable, even at his harshest. Katharine Hepburn matches this most ample performance with one of the same dimensions. Her nervousness never degenerates into tic. A flutter of the hands, a turn of the head, a sudden *accelerando* in speech or gesture—as when at one moment, unable to control her need of morphine, she wrenches round in the living room and runs upstairs—suffice.

"It is a remarkable tribute to the intelligence of the public—constantly underrated both by film makers and stage producers—that a long film, tragic in content, and quite uncompromising in its devotion to a stage text, should be offered with such evident conviction. It would have been easy to conventionalize it.

"*Long Day's Journey Into Night* shows that it is possible to take a modern stage tragedy and transfer it, with the smallest of changes, directly on to the screen. It may not be Shakespeare, but it belongs unmistakably to the same order of tragedy."

—BYRON BENTLEY
Theatre Arts

"Of all the cast, Katharine Hepburn brings the subtlest artistic intelligence to bear on the play's most difficult part, the mother, but without ultimate success. . . . Some of her acting vocabulary becomes predictable, the smile as transition to all emotions, the quiet tones before an outburst, the designedly ineffectual gesture; so that, although all has been thoughtfully planned, little is deeply affecting.

"Miss Hepburn radiates too clear-eyed and intellectual a quality for the character. She is not a cold actress, but her special emotional note is a high-strung sensibility based on perception and intelligence."

—STANLEY KAUFFMANN
Show Magazine

"Director Lumet calls his shots so skillfully that the spectator soon forgets the film is merely a photographed play, and he works his actors for all they are worth. Robards, as he did on Broadway, makes a luminously likable louse; Richardson lacks the fire and charm of Fredric March, but he plays with wit and penetration; Stockwell, in the weakest of the parts, adds up at least as well as Bradford Dillman did; and Hepburn, though she establishes too vivid a presence for a woman who is largely an absence, nevertheless centers in intensity a drama that Florence Eldridge enveloped in pathos. But the play is stronger than the players. In his anguished sincerity, in his dogged loyalty to his own experience, O'Neill sees deeper perhaps than any other dramatist has ever seen into family life. He sees its animal warmth, its blessed monotony, its healing private humor. And he sees all the terrible things people do to each other in the name of love."

—*Time*

NOTES

Eugene O'Neill began working on "a play of old sorrow, written in tears and blood" in the early summer of 1939, at the age of fifty. He finished it the following year. O'Neill's will stated it wasn't to be produced until at least twenty-five years after his death (1951). However his widow relented. The stunning 1956 Broadway production was played by Fredric March, Florence Eldridge, Jason Robards, Jr., and Bradford Dillman.

Long Day's Journey into Night was filmed by director Sidney Lumet for producers Ely Landau and Jack J. Dreyfus, Jr., in New York City in 37 days—the finished film ran 2 hours, 54 minutes. Hepburn agreed to a mere $25,000 (plus percentages of the take if there was any) when she learned that O'Neill's original would not be tampered with—it was filmed complete.

The cast rehearsed for three weeks before shooting began and Lumet shot it in sequence—a practice seldom adhered to. The interiors were filmed at Production Center Studios on West 26th Street and exteriors at an old house on City Island in the Bronx. The film cost $435,000.

Hepburn may have been too high-bred for the part of Mary Tyrone or her voice may not have been just right for such a woman, but these are minor arguments when one is confronted with her powerful portrayal of the dope-ravaged mother. Her colleagues, equally splendid in their respective parts, were: Ralph Richardson, Jason Robards, Jr. (repeating his original stage role), and young Dean Stockwell who handled a difficult part well. This quartet shared acting honors, with the principals of *A Taste of Honey* at the Cannes Film Festival.

The musical score was composed by Andre Previn, who later contributed the music to Hepburn's Broadway musical *Coco*. She received her ninth Academy Award nomination for her part in this film.

With Dean Stockwell

With Dean Stockwell,
Ralph Richardson
and Jason Robards, Jr.

182

With Jason Robards, Jr.,
Dean Stockwell
and Ralph Richardson

With Jason Robards, Jr., and Ralph Richardson

183

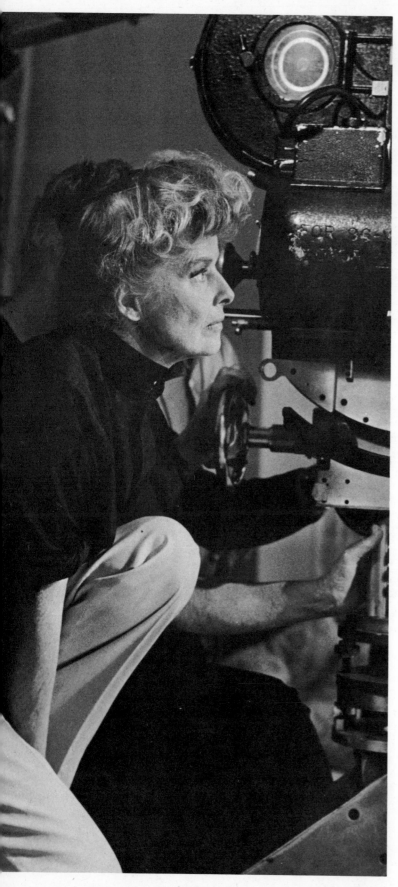

Guess Who's Coming to Dinner

A STANLEY KRAMER PRODUCTION
A COLUMBIA PICTURE IN TECHNICOLOR 1967

CAST

Matt Drayton Spencer Tracy
John Prentice Sidney Poitier
Christina Drayton Katharine Hepburn
Joey Drayton Katharine Houghton
Monsignor Ryan Cecil Kellaway
Mr. Prentice Roy E. Glenn, Sr.
Mrs. Prentice Beah Richards
Tillie Isabell Sanford
Hilary St. George Virginia Christine
Car Hop Alexandra Hay
Dorothy Barbara Randolph
Frankie D'Urville Martin
Peter Tom Heaton
Judith Grace Gaynor
Delivery Boy Skip Martin
Cab Driver John Hudkins

CREDITS

Director Stanley Kramer
Producer Stanley Kramer
Associate Producer George Glass

With Cecil Kellaway

Original Screenplay   William Rose
Production Supervisor   Ivan Volkman
Photographer   Sam Leavitt
Process Photography   Larry Butler
Production Designer   Robert Clatworthy
Set Decorator   Frank Tuttle
Editor   Robert C. Jones
Sound Recorders   Charles J. Rice, Robert Martin
Musical Score   Frank De Vol
Wardrobe Supervisor   Jean Louis
Costumer   Joe King
Special Effects   Geza Gaspar
Assistant Director   Ray Gosnell
Song: "Glory of Love" by   Billy Hill
Sung by   Jacqueline Fontaine

SYNOPSIS

Pretty young Joey Drayton comes home from a ten-day
Hawaiian vacation with the man she loves, John Prentice,
a forty-year-old internationally respected Negro doctor. Joey
is determined not only to marry him immediately, but to
have both sets of parents' blessings. The couple must leave
that night for Geneva and the doctor's post with the World
Health Organization.

Matt and Christina Drayton are extremely likeable, intelligent, wealthy, and hard working. He owns and operates
a crusading newspaper in San Francisco and she runs an
avant-garde art gallery. Now both are faced with a true test
of their liberal beliefs. Further tension is introduced when
the man's parents fly up from Los Angeles for dinner at the
Draytons' and find themselves as shocked and dismayed as
the girl's parents.

With Virginia Christine

185

With Spencer Tracy

With Katharine Houghton

With Spencer Tracy

With Sidney Poitier and Spencer Tracy

186

"Katharine Hepburn, in her ninth appearance with Spencer Tracy, has little to say but she makes her view clear in a few words and gives that magic touch to the role of the girl's mother—and man's wife. In her maturity, Miss Hepburn shines with a beauty that makes some of the big-bosomed glamour girls look cheap."

—WANDA HALE
The New York Daily News

"Both of them (Tracy and Hepburn) are so wholly splendid, both of them are so beautifully matched in *Guess Who's Coming to Dinner* that a lump rises in the throat on the realization that they will never appear together again. Miss Houghton, the young niece of Miss Hepburn, is a fresh, innocent, and lovely girl making her debut on the screen holding high promise for the future, and Mr. Poitier is a dark tower of strength, articulate, civilized, sophisticated, and wholly persuasive."

—LEO MISHKIN
New York Morning-Telegraph

"*Guess Who's Coming to Dinner* is a comedy, though not as flip a one as its title implies. For the producer and director of the picture is Stanley Kramer, a serious man who sometimes clambers up over the timberline of earnestness into the thin-aired high sierras of zeal, and even when he is engaged in making us laugh we can be pretty sure that he is also engaged in championing a good cause.

"The screenplay by William Rose is so ingeniously plotted that one almost forgives it for being, in effect, a drawing-room comedy, better suited to the stage than the screen.

"Mr. Tracy gives a faultless and, under the circumstances, heart-breaking performance. He was ill throughout the shooting of the picture and died just ten days after it was finished, and being aware that it was the last picture he would ever make he turned his role into a stunning compendium of the actor's art. Moreover, the very words that he spoke were written for him deliberately as 'last' words. *Guess Who's Coming to Dinner* is the ninth movie that he and Miss Hepburn made together, over a period of twenty-five years, and when, at its climax, he turns to her and tells her what an old man remembers having loved, it is, for us who are permitted to overhear him, an experience that transcends the theatrical."

—*The New Yorker*

"*Guess Who's Coming to Dinner* gives us another opportunity to flog Stanley Kramer for his naive conception of social significance. If Kramer were not so vulnerable in his sincerity, he would not have made such a tempting target. Unfortunately, Kramer is simply not a very good director. He lacks the intuitive feel for the medium, the instinctively kinetic insight into dramatic materials. He does everything by the numbers, and the lumbering machinery of his technique is always in full view of the audience.

"The casting is wildly uneven. Katharine Hepburn and the late Spencer Tracy are out of sight on the uppermost level. Sidney Poitier stays within reason in the middle level, and the rest is chaos, contrivance, and caricature.

"The character he (Tracy) plays had been accused by a Negro mother of having grown old and having forgotten what love and desire were really like. As Tracy repeats the charge to himself, Kramer shifts deliberately to a profile shot of Tracy on the left foreground of the screen and Hepburn, her eyes brimming with tears, on the right background looking at Tracy, and Tracy says no I have not forgotten, and he says it very slowly, and the two shot is sustained in its ghostly immortality, recording the rapturous rapport between a being now dead and a being still alive, but a moment of life and love passing into the darkness of death everlasting and anyone in the audience remaining dry-eyed through this evocation of gallantry and emotional loyalty has my deepest sympathy."

—*The Village Voice*

"*Guess Who's Coming to Dinner* is an inescapably sentimental occasion. It is the late Spencer Tracy's last movie, and he is coincidentally co-starred in it with his partner of eight previous movies, the glorious Katharine Hepburn. In the course of their long careers they have given us so much delight, so many fond memories, that the simple fact of their presence in the same film for one final curtain call is enough to bring a lump to your throat. They bicker fondly together in their patented manner, and for me, at least, their performances in this movie are beyond the bounds of criticism."

—RICHARD SCHICKEL
Life

"It is this interplay of conflicting emotions—plus the adroit interplay of such seasoned performers as the radiant Miss Hepburn, the graceful Poitier, and the stalwart, irreplaceable Tracy—that provide the film's greatest satisfactions. Despite all its patness, however, and despite a surface slickness that inevitably glosses over the urgency of its theme—it would be wrong to dismiss *Guess Who's Coming to Dinner* as a failure. The very elements that prevent it from coming to dramatic grips with its potentially explosive material are probably also the ones that would commend it to a wide audience—and Kramer's canny enough as a producer to recognize this."

—ARTHUR KNIGHT
The Saturday Review

"William Rose . . . has written what I can honestly only call a load of embarrassing rubbish. In the circumstances there is very little that director Stanley Kramer can do but see that his cameras plod from room to room and make the best of people sitting down and getting up again.

On the set with Spencer Tracy, Katharine Houghton, Sidney Poitier and director Stanley Kramer

"Which brings me, thank goodness, to Tracy and Hepburn, and while either or both are on the screen the most savage criticism is replaced by gratitude. To me, at any rate, that craggy face and burly build, the exploding humour, extraordinary gentleness and toughness of old leather, have always represented the ideal man—and that is real film-fan talk. I found it very moving to see him in this, his last picture, talent, presence and personality all unimpaired. Miss Hepburn, is, of course, unchanged and unchangeable. Anyone who feels as I do about this pair will go and see *Guess Who's Coming to Dinner* regardless of its fallacies and its hokum. It's a pity, though, that the picture is so very unworthy of them."

PENELOPE MORTIMER
The (London) Observer

NOTES

William Rose's so-called "social comedy," in the hands of producer-director Stanley Kramer, became the ninth Tracy-Hepburn picture. Kramer had directed Tracy on three previous occasions and they got along well, despite his continued illness. Hepburn hadn't acted in five years so that she could be with him.

This script's light treatment of a touchy social subject came under the attack of the critics—but millions of moviegoers were far more interested in the cast. Besides the work of the stars, the acting was of a high caliber. Sidney Poitier was splendid in a casually written part and Hepburn's niece,

Katharine Houghton, was charming in a role that required little else of her.

Guess Who's Coming to Dinner won ten Academy Award nominations: Picture, Actor (Tracy), Actress (Hepburn), Director (Kramer), Supporting Actor (Kellaway), Supporting Actress (Richards), Editing, Art Direction, Music and Screenplay.

William Rose won an Oscar on his first nomination and Hepburn won her second Oscar on her tenth. Tracy's nomination was his ninth—a record among actors. Had he been voted Best Actor (his wife was at the ceremony in the event he did), it would have been the first time an acting award was presented posthumously.

With Katharine Houghton and Sidney Poitier

The Lion in Winter

A MARTIN POLL PRODUCTION
AN AVCO EMBASSY FILM
IN PANAVISION AND EASTMAN COLOR   1968

Rehearsing with Peter O'Toole

CAST

Henry II   Peter O'Toole
Eleanor of Aquitaine   Katharine Hepburn
Princess Alais   Jane Merrow
Prince Geoffrey   John Castle
King Philip   Timothy Dalton
Prince Richard, the Lion-Hearted   Anthony Hopkins
William Marshall   Nigel Stock
Prince John   Nigel Terry
and Kenneth Griffith, O. Z. Whitehead

CREDITS

Director   Anthony Harvey
Producer   Martin Poll
Executive Producer   Joseph E. Levine
Associate Producer   Jane C. Nusbaum
Scenarist   James Goldman
Based on the Play by   James Goldman
Photographer   Douglas Slocombe
Art Director   Peter Murton
Set Decorator   Peter James

With Anthony Hopkins,
Nigel Terry and
John Castle

190

With Peter O'Toole

191

Editor   John Bloom
Sound Recorder   Simon Kaye
Musical Score   John Barry
Costumer   Margaret Furse
Production Supervisor   John Quested
Production Manager   Basil Appleby
Assistant Director   Kip Gowans
Makeup Artist   William Lodge
Hair Stylist   A. G. Scott

SYNOPSIS

In 1183, the middle-aged Henry II summons his imprisoned wife, Eleanor of Aquitaine, and sons Richard, Geoffrey, and John to make his selection of his successor. They spend the Christmas holidays squabbling and plotting in an attempt to settle the thorny question of the succession to the throne on Henry's death, a succession which affects the fate of both England and France.

Young Philip Capet, King of France, and his sister Alais, mistress to Henry and promised bride to Henry's successor, join the regal goings-on with the twelfth century royal family. Eleanor and Henry are torn apart by fierce political ambitions, yet are joined by deep repect and affection. This family reunion is roaring, rambunctious, and revealing.

CRITICS' CIRCLE

"Katharine Hepburn, Peter O'Toole, and John Castle, in particular, leaping at one another's throats with crocodile tears of family love in their eyes, make the film quite watchable as a medieval variant on *The Little Foxes*. Above all, Anthony Harvey, with his meticulously controlled, unostentatious direction, proves that *Dutchman* was no mere flash in the pan."

—*The (London) Observer*

"Miss Hepburn's performance is amazing. Whether coldly scheming some political coup, sincerely or insincerely remorseful over a failed marriage, or—at one dramatic highlight—crying out that people, not abstract causes and martial things, are the breeders of war and tumult, she is terrific. Her lightning-bolt flashes of irony show the Queen as a woman totally aware."

—*Variety*

"Miss Hepburn's Eleanor is virtually faultless, with an irrepressible elegance and charm making her thoroughly believable both as a queen and a woman. Here, Miss Hepburn has an advantage in that the part calls for an older woman. At the time of the play, Henry was 50 and Eleanor was 13 years older. This age difference is important to the play, and in Miss Hepburn's capable hands, it brings a poignancy to the story which was not there on the stage."

—THOMAS BRENNAN
The Villager

192

"Arguably, indeed, the performance of her (Hepburn's) career. Playing the relentlessly intelligent, ambitious, cunning, devious, and yet after all, when one least expects it, human and vulnerable Eleanor of Aquitaine she finds possibilities, both in herself and in the text which we would hardly have guessed at. Mr. O'Toole is here transformed: aged to 50, disguised behind a beard, and given an antagonist to his own measure he comes over remarkably well as Henry. The rest of the cast provide, what is required, excellent support. For when we come down to it this film is most importantly a great duet, superbly rendered. Above all, it is Katharine Hepburn's film, and a monument to Katharine Hepburn as a growing, developing, still surprising actress, not merely a monument to a monument."

—JOHN RUSSELL TAYLOR
The (London) Times

"This is Mr. O'Toole's second portrayal of Henry II on film. The contrast between the limp, ineffectual king in *Becket* and the bold dynamism of the crowned head in *The Lion in Winter* emphasizes the range of Mr. O'Toole's talents.

"Miss Hepburn is every bit his equal. With sure control and brilliance she lives up to this description of Eleanor of Aquitaine given by playwright James Goldman: 'She is truly a handsome woman of great temperament, authority, and presence. She has been a queen of international impor-

With Jane Merrow

tance for 46 years and you know it. Finally, she is that most unusual thing: a genuinely feminine woman thoroughly capable of holding her own in a man's world.' In addition to the talents of Mr. O'Toole and Miss Hepburn the film boasts an unusually literate and satisfying script, provided by Mr. Goldman from his own play. Director Anthony Harvey has managed to convey the tragedy and occasional humor of the conflict in cinematic terms."

—JOHN ALLEN
The Christian Science Monitor

"*Lion* is really the supreme consolidation of the traditional techniques of movie making to enhance the spoken word on film. In this sense, *Lion* is one of the best talkies ever made. He (O'Toole) gives the character a boisterous regal depth. Miss Hepburn has to be seen twice to be believed. Her Eleanor is a fractured mirror giving off exquisite images and shadows. Her monologue about a woman scorned, delivered into a vanity table mirror, is just beautiful."

—BRUCE BAHRENBURG
Newark (N.J.) Evening News

"Katharine Hepburn is their mother, and her accent is so peculiarly hers that we just accept it as the way she talks. And it seems proper for a queen to sound like Hepburn.

"As Rosemary Harris played the role on Broadway, Eleanor of Aquitaine was hard and funny—a tough cat who

On the set with director Anthony Harvey

enjoyed scratching and fighting—and it might have been a good role for the brittle high priestess of modernism if she had still held her own. But Hepburn plays Eleanor as a gallant great lady. She's about as tough as Helen Hayes."

—PAULINE KAEL
The New Yorker

"In the performances of O'Toole and Miss Hepburn, there are evoked portraits of massive power and forcefulness, Miss Hepburn alone conveying the character of a strong-willed but anguished queen with glowing luminosity, enduring grace and no little beauty."

—LEO MISHKIN
New York Morning-Telegraph

"A film as intellectually delicious as the stageplay and surpassing it in depth of characterization as well as in atmosphere and setting. The last two are not surprising (centuries and castles usually are better seen on screen than stage); but certainly those of us who found Rosemary Harris and Robert Preston so satisfying in the Broadway production can but marvel at the handiwork of Miss Hepburn and Mr. O'Toole.

"Miss Hepburn certainly crowns her career as Eleanor, triumphant in her creation of a complete and womanly queen, a vulture mother who sees her sons too clearly, an aging beauty who can look her image in the eye, a sophisticate whose shrewdness is matched only by her humor. A pity it is that Miss Hepburn won an Oscar for sentimental reasons for last year's *Guess Who's Coming to Dinner*, when this year it would be hers by right of performance! She is simply stunning. And Mr. O'Toole is her match. (He), somehow, makes this play almost a sequel to *Becket,* for his characterization is an extension of the one he created there, of the dark, vibrant and cunning young king, a man delighting equally in the pleasures of the flesh and the pleasures of power, ruthless in his enjoyment of either, burning with a possessiveness in both. He is superb."

—JUDITH CRIST
New York

NOTES

Director Anthony Harvey, formerly an editor to such directors as Bryan Forbes (*The L-Shaped Room*) and Stanley Kubrick (*Dr. Strangelove*), had only one directorial credit to his name (*Dutchman*) before directing *Lion.* He was given no end of encouragement by stars O'Toole and Hepburn, who responded well to his suggestions and judgment.

Harvey shot his film simply, avoiding the customary approach to grand pageantry. The great stone castles in the south of France echoed their own kind of spectacle—without deterring interest from the personal drama.

Hepburn and O'Toole, joined by the other cast members, rehearsed for nearly two weeks on the stage of London's Haymarket Theatre before proceeding to Dublin for interior shooting. Hepburn's Eleanor was rich and full; O'Toole's Henry vibrant and robust. Together they made sparks fly.

Every member of the cast acted well, bringing *Lion* a total of seven Academy Award nominations: Best Picture, Best Director, Best Actor, Best Actress, Best Screenplay, Best Costumes; and Best Musical Score. John Barry won an Oscar for his score but no one believed Hepburn would win a *third* Academy Award—it seemed just impossible, but she did.

Said director Harvey on Kate: "A passion for life, that is the thing about Katharine Hepburn. She adores every moment. She is always amazed."

Co-star O'Toole later named his daughter after Kate.

With Timothy Dalton, Peter O'Toole, Anthony Hopkins, Nigel Terry, Jane Merrow and John Castle

194

195

The Madwoman of Chaillot

AN ELY LANDAU–BRYAN FORBES PRODUCTION
A COMMONWEALTH UNITED CORPORATION FILM
A WARNER BROS.–SEVEN ARTS PICTURE
IN TECHNICOLOR 1969

CAST

Aurelia, the Madwoman of Chaillot Katharine Hepburn
Broker Charles Boyer
Dr. Jadin Claude Dauphin
Josephine, the Madwoman of La Concorde Edith Evans
Reverend John Gavin
General Paul Henreid
Commissar Oscar Homolka
Constance, the Madwoman of Passy Margaret Leighton
Gabrielle, the Madwoman of Sulpice Giulietta Masina
Irma Nanette Newman
Roderick Richard Chamberlain
Chairman Yul Brynner
Prospector Donald Pleasence
Ragpicker Danny Kaye
Police Sergeant Fernand Gravey
The Folksinger Gordon Heath
Julius Gerald Sim
and Jacques Marin, Joellina Smadja, Henri Virjoleux,
  Giles Segal, Gaston Palmer, Harriett Ariel,
  Catherine Berg

CREDITS

Director Bryan Forbes
Producer Ely Landau
Executive Producer Henry T. Weinstein
Associate Producer Anthony B. Ungar
Scenarist Edward Anhalt
Based on the Play by Jean Giraudoux
As Translated into English by Maurice Valency
Photographers Claude Renoir, Burnett Guffey
Production Designer Ray Simm
Art Director Georges Petitot
Set Decorator Dario Simoni
Editor Roger Dwyre
Sound Recorder Janet Davidson
Sound Mixer Bill Daniels
Musical Score Michael J. Lewis
Orchestrator Wally Scott
Production Manager Henri Jacquillard
Wardrobe Designer Rosine Delamare
Assistant Director Louis-Alain Pitzeie
Titles Robert Ellis Films
Makeup Artist Monique Archambault
Hair Stylist Alex Archambault
Song: "The Lonely Ones" by Michael J. Lewis, Gil King

SYNOPSIS

Aurelia, the Madwoman of Chaillot, an eccentric countess, is stunned to learn that the world is an unhappy place. She immediately hits upon a unique plan for doing away with a group of war-minded capitalists who wish to convert the beautiful city of Paris into a giant oil field. She confides with her closest friends, Josephine, Constance and Gabrielle—madwomen all—and, together with some of her friends from the streets, holds a mock trial in the catacombs of her large house.

Having previously convinced each conspirator that there is oil under her house, Aurelia pits them against one another and, later, leads the entire group to the lower depths for a glimpse of the oil reserve.

CRITICS' CIRCLE

"Slow-paced pic holds slim b.o. potential except for ardent Katharine Hepburn worshippers, who will be disappointed. Producer Ely Landau and director Bryan Forbes deliver a film chockful of fanciful dialog, stylized performances and arty effects. Story of struggle between good and evil becomes audience's struggle against tedium.

"Film doesn't come off. Miss Hepburn, for example, fails to capture the fantasy-spirit of the Countess. Her performance suffers because of indecision. Instead of the madwoman of Chaillot, Miss Hepburn is merely an extroverted eccentric."
—*Variety*

With Giulietta Masina, Edith Evans and Margaret Leighton

With Richard Chamberlain

With Danny Kaye

"There is the spectacle of Katharine Hepburn pretending to be the crazy old countess. At heart, of course, the madwoman is just as authoritative and no-nonsense a personality as Miss Hepburn, but she should mask her sanity behind a facade of dead-panned lunacy. Miss Hepburn's madwoman is as sentimental (and therefore, as redundant) as her mannerism of gently clenching her perfect teeth, looking into the middle distance and weeping through her tears."

—Vincent Canby
The New York Times

"A very beautiful film! Delightful score and fine acting. It is Miss Hepburn's film; she is a perfectionist!"

—Redbook

"Katharine Hepburn plays the title role—a deliciously daffy creature, full of warmth and whimsy."

—New York Daily News

"Mated with fine attention to detail, place, color and costume, as well as person in all these superbly qualified stars. Full of consequential sayings and strong blows struck at sanity, love, values and human beings. The strong blows are all struck against the faceless perpetrators of war, profit and repression. Katharine Hepburn is, of course, tremendous."

—New York Post

"Katharine Hepburn and an all-star cast in an elaborate but flat rendition of Jean Giraudoux's witty French fantasy about a mad Countess who rids the world of its evils. . . . The decision to update the play, contemporizing the evils the dotty Countess Aurelia destroys, has given an earthbound

With Oscar Homolka, Nanette Newman, Donald Pleasence, Charles Boyer, Paul Henreid, John Gavin, Yul Brynner, Danny Kaye, Giulietta Masina, Margaret Leighton, Edith Evans, Claude Dauphin and Richard Chamberlain

heaviness to what was originally an enchanted, whimsical conceit. Katharine Hepburn, in the title role, only adds to the discomforting reality; her characterization is far too sensible a person to be living in the past."

—Lloyd Ibert
Independent Film Journal

NOTES

The Madwoman of Chaillot was a tame follow-up to The Lion in Winter not only in her performance but also as a film.

In 1967, John Huston signed Kate for the part of the mad Countess Aurelia, but had to wait until she completed her role in Lion. By the time Hepburn was ready, Huston had bowed out, because of differences over the script. These differences (over the modernizing of a timeless fantasy) were the prime reason Madwoman failed in its screen adaptation.

During its filming at the Studios de la Victorine in Nice, under the direction of Bryan Forbes, Hepburn said, "I think The Madwoman of Chaillot has more relevance today than it did twenty years ago. The world has gone cuckoo. We're still dominated by greed, and that's what Giraudoux was talking about. The Madwoman represents the possibilities of man, she represents a hope."

With John Gavin, Oscar Homolka, Paul Henreid,
Charles Boyer, Yul Brynner and Donald Pleasence

The cast assembled for *Madwoman* consisted of people known throughout the world of cinema. All of them wanted a part in this film, but only Danny Kaye, strangely enough, gave an outstanding characterization. Hepburn was unusual, but far from mad. There was too much sentiment and too little excitement in her eyes.

The Madwoman of Chaillot was Hepburn's thirty-seventh film in as many years but only her eighth in color.

Biking to the set in the Victorine Studios, Nice, France

On the set with
director Bryan Forbes

A Stage Chronicle

"Miss Hepburn is not an actress easy to describe. She has intelligence, breeding, fire, a voice in its emotional scenes can be satin, a body Zorina might look upon with envy, and a personality of such compulsion that, without meaning to do it, she can make the center of the stage wherever she happens to be. There is grace—a lovely and arresting grace—about her very awkwardness; about the tomboyish attitudes she strikes from time to time; and most especially, about that free-limbed quality of hers which can turn her very crosses into the poetry of motion."

—John Mason Brown

1928

SUMMER STOCK: 1928.

The Edwin H. Knopf Stock Company, Baltimore, Maryland

Hepburn's first professional appearances quickly followed her graduation from Bryn Mawr. In a stock company that boasted such talents as Mary Boland, Alison Skipworth, Dudley Digges, and Violet Heming, Hepburn appeared as a Lady-in-Waiting in *The Czarina* by Melchior Lengyel and Lajos Biro and as a flapper in Russell Medcraft and Norma Mitchell's *The Cradle Snatchers.*

The Big Pond

BY GEORGE MIDDLETON AND A. E. THOMAS.
PRODUCED BY EDWIN H. KNOPF AND WILLIAM P. FARNSWORTH.
STAGED BY MR. KNOPF.

CAST

Francesco   Marius Rogati
Ronny Davis   Reed Brown, Jr.
Mrs. Billings   Marie Curtis
Mrs. Livermore   Doris Rankin
Barbara   Katharine Hepburn[1]
Pierre De Mirande   Kenneth MacKenna
Henry Billings   Harlan Briggs
Sarah   Virginia Russell
Molly Perkins   Penelope Rowland

These Days

BY KATHARINE CLUGSTON. PRODUCED BY ARTHUR HOPKINS. SETTINGS BY ROBERT EDMOND JONES. STAGED BY MR. HOPKINS. CORT THEATRE, NEW YORK, NOVEMBER 12, 1928.

CAST

Rosilla Dow   Mary Hall
Virginia MacRae   Mildred McCoy
Pansy Larue Mott   Gertrude Moran
Veronica Sims   Katharine Hepburn[2]
Miss Guadaloupe Gorham   Gladys Hopeton
"Chippy" Davis   Bruce Evans
Dwight Elbridge   William Johnstone
Stephen MacRae   Edwin Phillips

Frannie MacRae   Elaine Koch
Mrs. MacRae   May Buckley
Mr. MacRae   George MacQuarrie
Miss Dorothea Utterback   Marie Bruce
Stephanie Bliss   Ruth Reed
Miss Signhild Valdemir Van Alstyne   Helen Freeman
Miss Cleo Almeda Young   Ada Potter
Winifred Black   Suzanne Freeman
Miss Wilda Hall   Mary Hubbard
Miss Serena Lash   Nellie Malcolm
Dolly   Marian Lee
Marjory   Ruth Wilton
Richard   Francis Corbin Burke
Guy   Willard S. Robertson
Philip   Henri Lase
Puss   Ruth Wilcox

"Miss Mildred McCoy makes the finished flapper a vigorous and human portrait. . . . Miss Mary Hall as an exuberant sub-deb with a lusty tongue, and a perfect passage of repressed deviltry done gorgeously by Miss Katharine Hepburn."

—JOHN ANDERSON
New York Evening Journal

Holiday

BY PHILIP BARRY. PRODUCED BY ARTHUR HOPKINS. STAGED BY MR. HOPKINS. PLYMOUTH THEATRE, NEW YORK, NOVEMBER 26, 1928.

CAST

Linda Seton   Hope Williams[3]
Johnny Case   Ben Smith
Julia Seton   Dorothy Tree
Ned Seton   Monroe Owsley
Susan Potter   Barbara White
Nick Potter   Donald Ogden Stewart
Edward Seton   Walter Walker
Laura Cram   Rosalie Norman
Seton Cram   Thaddeus Clancy
Henry   Cameron Clemens
Charles   J. Ascher Smith
Delia   Beatrice Ames

[1] Hepburn's inexperience and headstrong attitude were responsible for her being fired after one performance of the pre-Broadway tryout at Great Neck, Long Island, New York. When the show arrived on Broadway in August 1928, Barbara was played by Lucile Nikolas.

[2] Hepburn's Broadway debut closed after eight performances. In 1934 RKO Radio made this play into a film called *Finishing School,* with Frances Dee and Ginger Rogers.

[3] Hepburn understudied Hope Williams for six months but the star never missed a performance. Hepburn began her duties on Broadway in late December 1928. *Holiday* closed in June 1929.

Death Takes a Holiday

BY ALBERTO CASELLA. ADAPTED BY WALTER FERRIS.
PRODUCED BY LEE SHUBERT. STAGED BY LAWRENCE
MARSTON. SETTINGS BY ROLLO WAYNE.

CAST

Cora   Florence Golden
Fedele   Thomas Bate
Duke Lambert   James Dale
Alda   Ann Orr
Stephanie   Olga Birkbeck
Princess of San Luca   Viva Cirkett
Baron Cesarea   Wallace Erskine
Rhoda Fenton   Lorna Lawrence
Eric Fenton   Roland Bottomley
Corrado   Martin Burton
Grazia   Katharine Hepburn[4]
His Serene Highness, Prince Sirki, of Vitalba Alexandri
   Philip Merivale
Major Whitbread   Frank Greene

1930

A Month in the Country

BY IVAN TURGENEV. PRODUCED BY THE THEATRE GUILD,
INC. TRANSLATED BY M. S. MANDELL. ACTING VERSION
AND DIRECTION BY ROUBEN MAMOULIAN. SETTINGS &
COSTUMES BY M. S. DOBUZINSKY. EXECUTED BY RAYMOND
SOVEY. GUILD THEATRE, NEW YORK, MARCH 17, 1930.

CAST

Herr Shaaf   Charles Kraus
Anna Semenova   Minna Phillips
Natalia Petrovna   Alla Nazimova
Mikhail Aleksandrovich Rakitin   Elliot Cabot
Lizaveta Bogdanovna   Eda Heinemann
Kolia   Eddie Wragge
Aleksei Nikolaevich Bieliaev   Alexander Kirkland
Matviei   Louis Veda
Ignati Ilich Spigelski   Dudley Digges
Viera Aleksandrovna   Eunice Stoddard[5]
Arkadi Sergieich Islaev   John T. Doyle
Katia   Hortense Alden[6]
Afanasi Ivanych Bolshintsov   Henry Travers

---

[4] Rose Hobart played Grazia when the play arrived on Broadway on
December 26, 1929. Hepburn, who was billed as Katherine, played the
part for five weeks but after many fights with director Lawrence Marston
was fired during the week of November 25 while at Philadelphia's Adelphi
Theatre.

202

SUMMER STOCK: 1930.

The Berkshire Playhouse, Stockbridge, Massachusetts

In a company that included George Coulouris and Laura
Harding, Hepburn appeared in G. Martinez Sierra's *A
Romantic Young Lady* (which had been adapted into English
by Helen and Harley Granville-Baker) and Sir James M.
Barrie's *The Admirable Crichton*.

Art and Mrs. Bottle or, the Return of the Puritan

BY BENN W. LEVY. PRODUCED BY KENNETH MACGOWAN
AND JOSEPH VERNER REED. STAGED BY CLIFFORD BROOKE.
SETTINGS BY RAYMOND SOVEY. MAXINE ELLIOTT THEATRE,
NEW YORK, NOVEMBER 18, 1930.

CAST

Michael Bottle   G. P. Huntley, Jr.
Judy Bottle   Katharine Hepburn
Sonia Tippet   Joyce Carey
Parlormaid   Elise Breton
George Bottle   Walter Kingsford
Celia Bottle   Jane Cowl
Charles Dawes   Lewis Martin
Max Lightly   Leon Quartermaine

"An uncommonly refreshing performance was given by
Katharine Hepburn as the young daughter."

—ALISON SMITH
New York World

With George Coulouris in a stock production at the Berkshire
Playhouse, 1930

---

[5] Hepburn was Miss Stoddard's understudy.
[6] Hepburn replaced Hortense Alden in the second month of production.
Others to replace cast members included Leonard Mudie, Douglass Dumbrille, and Franchot Tone.

"Katharine Hepburn, in the part of the daughter, is delightful, if a bit high-strung."

—GRETTA PALMER
New York World-Telegram

"It (*Art and Mrs. Bottle*) uncovers a young actress whose performance last night ordinarily would raise her to stardom. The young lady is Katharine Hepburn."

New York American

With Marie Curtis in *The Big Pond*

1931

SUMMER STOCK: 1931.

The Ivoryton Players, Ivoryton, Connecticut

In this season of summer stock, Hepburn joined the Milton Steifel and Julian Anhalt company—along with Henry Hull—to appear in *Just Married* by Adelaide Matthews and Anne Nichols; John Willard's *The Cat and the Canary*, and *The Man Who Came Back* by Jules Eckert Goodman.

The Animal Kingdom

BY PHILIP BARRY. PRODUCED BY GILBERT MILLER AND LESLIE HOWARD. STAGED BY MR. MILLER.

CAST

Owen Arthur   G. Albert Smith
Rufus Collier   Frederick Forrester

Cecelia Henry   Lora Baxter
Richard Regan   William Gargan
Tom Collier   Leslie Howard
Franc Schmidt   Betty Lynne
Joe Fisk   Harvey Stephens
Daisy Sage   Katharine Hepburn[7]
Grace Macomber   Ilka Chase

1932

The Warrior's Husband

BY JULIAN THOMPSON. PRODUCED BY HARRY MOSES. STAGED BY BURK SYMON. COMBATS STAGED BY RANDOLPH LEYMEN. INCIDENTAL MUSIC BY RICHARD MALABY. LIGHTING EFFECTS BY LEO HARTMAN. SETTINGS AND COSTUMES BY WOODMAN THOMPSON. MOROSCO THEATRE, NEW YORK, MARCH 11, 1932.

CAST

First Sergeant   Paula Bauersmith
Buria   Virginia Volland
Second Sergeant   Edna Holland
First Sentry   Frances Newbaker
Second Sentry   Avalon Plummer
Third Sentry   Rita Rheinfrank
Caustica   Bertha Belmore
Heroica   Dorothy Walters
Pomposia   Jane Wheatley
Hippolyta   Irby Marshal
Sapiens   Romney Brent
Sapiens Major   Arthur Bowyer
Antiope   Katharine Hepburn
Captain of Archers   Helene Fontaine
Theseus   Colin Keith-Johnston
Homer   Don Beddoe
Runner   Thelma Hardwick
Hercules   Al Ochs
Gaganius, the Herald   Porter Hall
Achilles   Alan Campbell
Ajax   Randolph Leymen
Amazon Sentries and Guards: Eleanor Goodrich, Nina Romano, Agnes George, Eve Bailey, Clara Waring, Dorothy Gillam, and Rose Dresser
Amazon Huntresses: Theodosia Dusanne, Mary Stuart, Miriam Schiller, and Barbara Dugan
Greek Warriors: Thaddeus Clancy, Walter Levin, Arthur Brady, and Jerry Feigan

[7]Hepburn was fired after the Pittsburgh opening and was replaced by Frances Fuller. Reports have stated that she was (a) too good; (b) too tall; (c) too troublesome.

With Colin Keith-Johnston in *The Warrior's Husband*

With Jane Cowl and G. P. Huntley, Jr. in *Art and Mrs. Bottle*

With Romney Brent in *The Warrior's Husband*

"As Antiope, the Amazon who knows when she is beaten by love, Katharine Hepburn gives an excellent performance."

—BROOKS ATKINSON
The New York Times

" . . . Miss Katharine Hepburn, as the young Amazon, Antiope, who finally deserts her band for love of the dashing Theseus—a boyish, steel-spring-like figure, woman in spite of herself, who suggests a somewhat tougher and more dynamic version of Maude Adams's Peter Pan."

—ARTHUR RUHL
New York Herald Tribune

"Miss Katharine Hepburn comes into her own as Antiope the royal Amazon Theseus falls in love with. Ever since she

204

supported Miss Jane Cowl in *Art and Mrs. Bottle*, I've been waiting for Miss Hepburn to fall heir to a role worthy of her talent and her beauty. Antiope is that role and Miss Hepburn makes the most of it, bringing out its tenderness, its humor, its bite. It's been many a night since so glowing a performance has brightened the Broadway scene."

—RICHARD GARLAND
New York World-Telegram

SUMMER STOCK: 1932.

Before going to Hollywood in the Summer of 1932, Hepburn fulfilled a stock engagement as Psyche Marbury in Will Cotton's *The Bride the Sun Shines On* for a stock company at Ossining, New York.

1933

The Lake

BY DOROTHY MASSINGHAM AND MURRAY MACDONALD. PRODUCED BY JED HARRIS. SETTINGS BY JO MIELZINER. STAGED BY MR. HARRIS, ASSISTED BY GEOFFREY KERR. MARTIN BECK THEATRE, NEW YORK, DECEMBER 26, 1933

As Stella Surrege in *The Lake*

With Blanche Bates in *The Lake*

CAST

Mildred Surrege Frances Starr
Williams J. P. Wilson
Lena Surrege Blanche Bates
Henry Surrege Lionel Pape
Marjorie Hervey Roberta Beatty
Stella Surrege Katharine Hepburn
Ethel Esther Mitchell
Cecil Hervey Geoffrey Wardwell
John Clayne Colin Clive
Maude Mary Heberden
Stoker Edward Broadley
Stephen Braite Philip Tonge
Dotty Braite Wendy Atkin
Jean Templeton Audrey Ridgwell
Anna George Vera Fuller-Mellish
Mrs. George Rosalind Ivan

Miss Kurn Florence Britton
Mrs. Hemingway Eva Leonard-Boyne
Dennis Gourlay O. Z. Whitehead
Lady Stanway Reginald Carrington
Captain Hamilton James Grainger
Miss White Lucy Beaumont
Lady Kerton Elliott Mason

"There is no point in pursuing Miss Hepburn with her limitations as a dramatic actress. The simple fact is that as a result of her sensational achievements on the screen she has been projected into a stage part that requires more versatility than she has had time to develop. She still needs considerable training, especially for a voice that has unpleasant timbre."

—BROOKS ATKINSON
The New York Times

"Not a great actress, by any manner of means, but one with a certain distinction which, with training, might possibly take the place of great acting in an emergency."

—ROBERT BENCHLEY
The New Yorker

"Too young and too shy, in the presence of an audience, to seem as commanding a personality on the stage as on the screen, she gave a talented, clever performance marred only by a trick of keying her voice to a high, flat monotone to indicate emotional intensity." *—Time*

1934

SUMMER STOCK: 1934.

The Ivoryton Players, Ivoryton, Connecticut (cancelled)

Hepburn had agreed to return to the Ivoryton Playhouse, under the management of Milton Steifel and Julian Anhalt, as Judith Treherne in George Brewer's tragedy *Dark Victory*. This was to be its first production. Her co-star, Stanley Ridges, however, withdrew because of a family illness shortly before the opening and this pre-Broadway tryout was canceled. The role later was played on Broadway by Tallulah Bankhead and Bette Davis did the celebrated movie version in 1939.

1937

Jane Eyre

BY CHARLOTTE BRONTË. DRAMATIZED BY HELEN JEROME. PRODUCED BY THE THEATRE GUILD, INC. STAGED BY WORTHINGTON MINER. SETTINGS AND COSTUMES DESIGNED BY LEE SIMONSON. PRODUCTION SUPERVISED BY THERESA HELBURN AND LAWRENCE LANGNER. ON TOUR FROM DECEMBER 1936 TO APRIL 1937.

In the title role in the Theatre Guild's production
of *Jane Eyre*

CAST

Mrs. Fairfax   Viola Roache
Leah   Phyllis Connard
Jane Eyre   Katharine Hepburn
Mr. Rochester   Denis Hoey
Adele Varens   Patricia Peardon
Mason   Irving Morrow
Grace Poole   Teresa Dale
Blanche Ingram   Sandra Ellsworth
The Maniac   Teresa Guerini
Lady Ingram   Katharine Stewart
Lord Ingram   Reginald Carrington
Briggs   Wilfred Seagram
Rev. Wood   Reginald Malcolm
Diana Rivers   Barbara O'Neil
Hannah   Marga Ann Deighton
St. John Rivers   Stephen Ker Appleby

"*Jane Eyre* suits her better than *The Lake* and she is more of an actress now than she was then. Her part in the current piece is prim and quaint, particularly on the surface, and she keeps it fragile, dainty and immaculate all through the evening. . . . She plays Jane with exquisite grace of movement."

—Brooks Atkinson reviewing the
Chicago production for
The New York Times

1939

The Philadelphia Story

By Philip Barry. Produced by the Theatre Guild, Inc. Staged by Robert B. Sinclair. Scenery and Lighting by Robert Edmond Jones. Supervised by Theresa Helburn and Lawrence Langner. Shubert Theatre, New York, March 28, 1939.

CAST

Dinah Lord   Lenore Lonergan
Margaret Lord   Vera Allen
Tracy Lord   Katharine Hepburn
Alexander Lord   Dan Tobin
Thomas   Owen Coll
William Tracy   Forrest Orr
Elizabeth Imbrie   Shirley Booth
Macaulay Connor   Van Heflin
George Kittredge   Frank Fenton
C. K. Dexter Haven   Joseph Cotten
Edward   Philip Foster

As Tracy Lord in Philip Barry's *The Philadelphia Story*

Seth Lord   Nicholas Joy
May   Myrtle Tannahill
Elsie   Lorraine Bate
Mac   Hayden Rorke

"A strange, tense little lady with austere beauty and metallic voice, she has consistently found it difficult to project a part in the theatre. But now she has surrendered to the central part in Mr. Barry's play and she acts it like a woman who has at last found the joy she has always been seeking in the theatre. For Miss Hepburn skips through the evening in any number of light moods, responding to the scenes quickly, inflecting the lines and developing a part from the beginning to its logical conclusion. There are no ambiguous corners in this character portrayal. Dainty in style, it is free and alive in its darting expression of feeling."

—Brooks Atkinson
The New York Times

"Mr. Barry's play at its best is no more than a nice red carpet he has unrolled for her (Hepburn). . . . She is no impassive beauty. Her finely chiseled face is a volatile mask. If it is difficult to take one's eyes off of her, it is because she is also blessed with an extraordinary personality. Slim and lovely as she is, Miss Hepburn likewise possesses a voice which in her emotional scenes can be sheer velvet."

—JOHN MASON BROWN, *New York Post*

With Nicholas Joy and Vera Allen in *The Philadelphia Story*

With Dan Tobin, Joseph Cotten, Van Heflin and Shirley Booth in *The Philadelphia Story*

1942

Without Love

BY PHILIP BARRY. PRODUCED BY THE THEATRE GUILD, INC.
STAGED BY ROBERT B. SINCLAIR. SCENERY AND LIGHTING
BY ROBERT EDMOND JONES. SUPERVISED BY THERESA
HELBURN AND LAWRENCE LANGNER. MISS HEPBURN'S
CLOTHES BY VALENTINA. ST. JAMES THEATRE, NEW YORK,
NOVEMBER 10, 1942.

CAST

Patrick Jamieson Elliott Nugent
Quentin Ladd Tony Bickley
Anna Emily Massey
Martha Ladd Ellen Morgan
Jamie Coe Rowan Katharine Hepburn
Kitty Trimble Audrey Christie
Peter Baillie Robert Shayne
Paul Carrel Sherling Oliver
Richard Hood Robert Chisholm
Robert Emmet Riordan Neil Fitzgerald
Grant Vincent Royal Beal

"As the unloved wife Miss Hepburn is giving a mechanical
performance that is not without considerable gaucherie in
the early scenes. In both the writing and the acting, *Without
Love* is theatre on the surface of a vacuum."
—BROOKS ATKINSON
The New York Times

1950

As You Like It

BY WILLIAM SHAKESPEARE. PRODUCED BY THE THEATRE
GUILD, INC. STAGED BY MICHAEL BENTHALL. SCENERY AND
COSTUMES BY JAMES BAILEY. INCIDENTAL MUSIC WRITTEN
AND ARRANGED BY ROBERT IRVING. TECHNICAL ASSISTANT:
EMELINE ROCHE. SUPERVISED BY LAWRENCE LANGNER AND
THERESA HELBURN. CORT THEATRE, NEW YORK, JANUARY
26, 1950 AND ON TOUR.

CAST

Orlando William Prince
Adam Burton Mallory
Oliver Ernest Graves
Dennis Robert Foster
Charles Michael Everett
Celia Cloris Leachman

With Elliott Nugent in Philip Barry's *Without Love*

Rosalind Katharine Hepburn
Touchstone Bill Owen
Le Beau Jay Robinson
Frederick Dayton Lummis
Lady in Waiting Jan Sherwood
Duke Aubrey Mather
Amiens Frank Rogier
Lord Everett Gamnon
Corin Whitford Kane
Silvius Robert Quarry
Phebe Judy Parrish
Jaques Ernest Thesiger
Audrey Patricia Englund
Sir Oliver Martext Jay Robinson
William Robert Foster
Rowland Craig Timberlake
Ladies in Waiting & Shepherdesses: Jan Sherwood,
   Marilyn Nowell, Margaret Wright
Lords, Attendants & Shepherds: Kenneth Cantril,
   Charles Herndon, William Sutherland, Richard Hepburn,
   Robert Wark, John Weaver, Craig Timberlake

With William Prince in *As You Like It*

1952

The Millionairess

BY GEORGE BERNARD SHAW. STAGED BY MICHAEL BENTHALL.
SETTINGS BY JAMES BAILEY. MISS HEPBURN'S DRESSES BY
PIERRE BALMAIN. NEW THEATRE, LONDON; SHUBERT THEATRE,
NEW YORK, 1952.

CAST

Julius Sagamore Campbell Cotts
Epifania, the Lady Katharine Hepburn
Alastair Fitzfassenden Peter Dyneley
Patricia Smith Genine Graham
Adrain Blenderbland Cyril Ritchard
The Doctor Robert Helpmann
The Man Bertram Shuttleworth
The Woman Nora Nicholson
The Manager Vernon Greeves

"Miss Hepburn shouts, screams, yells, tumbles, fights, sprints
and otherwise carries on, as the spoiled woman who has
only money in Bernard Shaw's comedy. Of course Miss
Hepburn overacts! Of course, as you have undoubtedly
heard, *The Millionairess* is second-rate Shaw. But second-
rate Shaw and a dynamic actress, assisted by good direction
and cast, give a most provocative and interesting theatrical
evening."

—*Cue*

1955

SUMMER TOUR:

Hepburn joined Robert Helpmann and the Old Vic
Company in a highly successful tour in Australia of three
Shakespearean plays: *The Taming of the Shrew, Measure for
Measure,* and *The Merchant of Venice.*

1957

The Merchant of Venice

BY WILLIAM SHAKESPEARE. PRODUCED AT THE AMERICAN
SHAKESPEARE FESTIVAL THEATRE, STRATFORD,
CONNECTICUT. STAGED BY JACK LANDAU. SCENERY BY
ROUBEN TER-ARUTUNIAN. COSTUMES BY MOTLEY.
PRODUCTION AND LIGHTING BY JEAN ROSENTHAL. MUSIC BY
VIRGIL THOMSON. OPENED JULY 10, 1957.

CAST

Antonio Richard Waring
Salerio John Frid
Solanio Kendall Clark
Bassanio Donald Harron
Lorenzo Richard Lupino
Gratiano John Colicos
Portia Katharine Hepburn
Nerissa Lois Nettleton
Balthazar Michael Kennedy

Rosalind in Shakespeare's *As You Like It*

With Robert Helpmann in *The Millionairess*

Shylock Morris Carnovsky
Lancelot Gobbo Richard Easton
Old Gobbo William Cottrell
Prince of Morocco Earle Hyman
Jessica Dina Doronne
Prince of Arragon Stanley Bell
Tubal Jack Bittner
Stephano Russell Oberlin
Duke of Venice Larry Gates
Attendants, Citizens, Dignitaries: Conrad Bromberg,
James Cahill, Richard Cavett, Harley Clements, Tamara
Daniel, Michael Kasdan, Simm Landres, Michele La
Bombarda, Michael Lindsay-Hogg, Susan Lloyd, William
Long, Jr., Michael Miller, David Milton, Vivian
Paszamont, Ira Rubin, D. J. Sullivan, Peter Trytler,
Gail Warner

"There was extraordinary interest, of course, in the appearance of Katharine Hepburn as Portia, and it must be reported at the outset that this dauntless lady swept through
Shakespeare like a cool, refreshing breeze. Her Portia is no
mere lovely picture; she is a girl of intelligence, humor and
iron determination—which is almost type-casting. She lifts
the lighter parts of the play to a fine level of high comedy."
—JOHN CHAPMAN
New York Daily News

212

Much Ado About Nothing

BY WILLIAM SHAKESPEARE. PRODUCED AT THE AMERICAN
SHAKESPEARE FESTIVAL THEATRE, STRATFORD,
CONNECTICUT. STAGED BY JOHN HOUSEMAN AND JACK
LANDAU. SCENERY AND COSTUMES BY ROUBEN
TER-ARUTUNIAN. PRODUCTION SUPERVISED BY JEAN
ROSENTHAL. LIGHTING BY THARON MUSSER. DANCES
ARRANGED BY JOHN BUTLER. MUSIC BY VIRGIL THOMSON.
OPENED AUGUST 3, 1957.

CAST

Borachio Jack Bittner
Antonio Morris Carnovsky
Balthazer Russell Oberlin
Margaret Sada Thompson
Ursula Jacqueline Brookes
Dogberry Larry Gates
Verges Donald Harron
First Watchman Richard Lupino
Second Watchman William Cottrell
Friar Francis Kendall Clark
Sexton John Frid
Leonato John Colicos
Messenger Donald Harron
Beatrice Katharine Hepburn
Hero Lois Nettleton
Don Pedro Stanley Bell
Benedick Alfred Drake
Claudio Richard Easton
Don John Richard Waring
Conrade Mitchell Agruss
Soldiers & Servants: Michael Borden, Benita Deutsch,
Michael Kasdan, Michael Miller, David Milton, Joe
Myers, Dino Narizzano, Ira Rubin, Judith Steffan,
Peter Trytler, Jack Waltzer, William Woodman

With Cyril Ritchard in *The Millionairess*

"The lines Shakespeare gave Beatrice are eminently suited to Miss Hepburn and she reads them with a lean suggestion of hysteria that makes them scratch arrogantly at her Benedick, whom she feuds with as a prelude to love."

—PAUL V. BECKLEY
New York Herald Tribune

1960

Twelfth Night

BY WILLIAM SHAKESPEARE. PRODUCED AT THE AMERICAN SHAKESPEARE FESTIVAL THEATRE, STRATFORD, CONNECTICUT. STAGED BY JACK LANDAU. PRODUCTION DESIGNED BY ROUBEN TER-ARUTUNIAN. LIGHTING BY THARON MUSSER. MUSIC AND SONGS BY HERMAN CHESSID. OPENED JUNE 3, 1960.

CAST

Orsino, Duke of Illyria   Donald Davis
Curio   Stephen Strimpell
Valentine   John Harkins
Viola   Katharine Hepburn
A Sea Captain   Will Geer
Sir Toby Belch   Loring Smith
Maria   Sada Thompson
Sir Andrew Aguecheek   O. Z. Whitehead
Feste   Morris Carnovsky
Olivia   Margaret Phillips
Malvolio   Richard Waring
A Boy   David Gress
Fabian   William Hickey
Antonio   Clifton James
Sebastian   Clayton Corzatte
A Guardsman   Claude Woolman
Priest   Patrick Hines
Sailors, Fishermen, Guardsmen and Ladies: Constance Bollinger, Lorna Gilbert, Donald Hatch, Charles Herrick, Alfred Lavorato, George Parrish, Donald Pomes, Howard Poyrow, Robert Reilly, Lou Robb, Sandra Saget, George Sampson, Wisner Washam, Beverly Whitcomb

"Miss Hepburn has always been one of the most fetching creatures to have been bestowed upon our time, and fetching isn't the half of it as the lady takes a stubborn, or a petulant, or a slightly fearful stance in her white ducks, brass-buttoned jacket, and sleek black boater."

—WALTER KERR
New York Herald Tribune

As Portia in *The Merchant of Venice*

With Rae Allen, Earle Hyman, and Robert
Ryan in *Antony and Cleopatra*

With Alfred Drake in *Much Ado About Nothing*

With O. Z. Whitehead and Loring Smith in *Twelfth Night*

214

Antony and Cleopatra

BY WILLIAM SHAKESPEARE. PRODUCED AT THE AMERICAN
SHAKESPEARE FESTIVAL THEATRE, STRATFORD,
CONNECTICUT. STAGED BY JACK LANDAU. PRODUCTION
DESIGNED BY ROUBEN TER-ARUTUNIAN. LIGHTING BY
THARON MUSSER. MUSIC BY NORMAN DELLO JOIO. OPENED
JULY 22, 1960.

CAST

Antony   Robert Ryan
Cleopatra   Katharine Hepburn
Canidius   Douglas Watson
Scarus   John Harkins
Enobarbus   Donald Davis
Mardian   Patrick Hines
Alexas   Earle Hyman
Charmian   Rae Allen
Iras   Anne Fielding
Octavius Caesar   John Ragin
Lepidus   Morris Carnovsky
Agrippa   Will Geer
Thidius   John Myhers
Dolabella   Stephen Strimpell
Pompey   Clifton James
Menas   Claude Woolman
Octavia   Sada Thompson
A Soothsayer   Richard Waring
Egyptian Messenger   Ted Van Griethuysen
Eros   Clayton Corzatte
Officers, Soldiers, Attendants: John Abbey, Stephen
   Carnovsky, David Clayborne, Jack Gardner, David Groh,
   Donald Hatch, Charles Herrick, Lloyd Hezekiah, Joseph
   Kleinowski, Alfred Lavorato, Christopher Lloyd, Robert
   Packer, Christian Parker, George Parrish, Don Pomes,
   Howard Poyrow, Robert Reilly, Lou Robb, George
   Sampson, Frank Spencer, Richard Thayer, Herman Tucker,
   Wisner Washam

"The production of *Antony and Cleopatra* here is sprinkled
with intelligence and assorted glimpses of Katharine
Hepburn as Cleopatra. In the early scenes Miss Hepburn
is surprisingly and happily unevasive, a half-naked woman
with a genuine capacity for enjoying the wanton, sporting
pleasures of the bed. In attempting to give the part infinite
variety, Miss Hepburn has thrown away the opportunity
of letting the events of the play lift her to any large emotional
peaks, or of revealing a vulnerability that might engage our
sympathies."

—*The Saturday Review*

"Miss Hepburn offers a highly versatile performance as
Cleopatra, changing from kittenish comedy to tigerish passion, occasionally seeming to be playing Beatrice, once or
twice going in for her famous mannerisms and always being
fascinating to watch."

—RICHARD WATTS, JR.
New York Post

1969

Coco

BOOK AND LYRICS BY ALAN JAY LERNER AND MUSIC BY
ANDRE PREVIN. PRODUCED BY FREDERICK BRISSON. SETS AND
COSTUMES BY CECIL BEATON. LIGHTING BY THOMAS SKELTON.
ORCHESTRATIONS BY HERSHY KAY. DANCE MUSIC
CONTINUITY BY HAROLD WHEELER. MUSIC DIRECTION BY
ROBERT EMMETT DOLAN. MUSICAL NUMBERS AND FASHION
SEQUENCES STAGED BY MICHAEL BENNETT. STAGED BY
MICHAEL BENTHALL. MARK HELLINGER THEATRE, NEW
YORK, DECEMBER 18, 1969.

In *Coco*

215

(OVERLEAF) As Gabrielle "Coco" Chanel in *Coco*

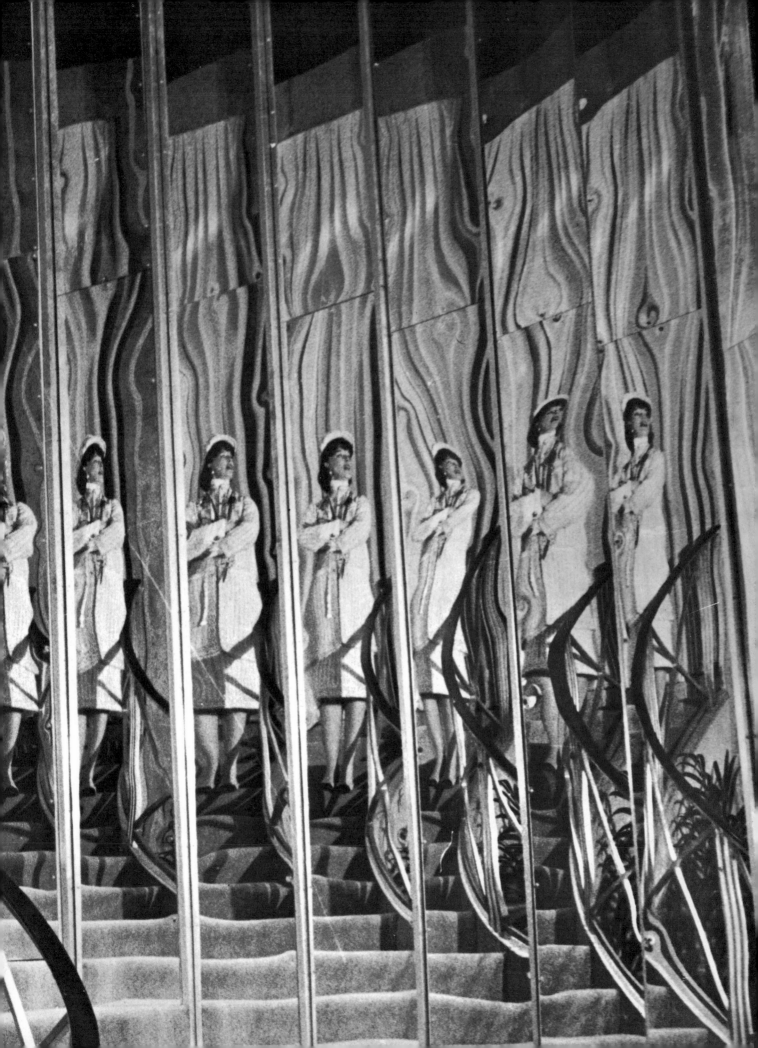

CAST

Helene Maggie Task
Pignol Jeanne Arnold
Armand Al DeSio
A Seamstress Nancy Killmer
Albert Jack Beaber
A Lawyer Richard Marr
Louis Greff George Rose
Docaton Eve March
Coco Katharine Hepburn
Georges David Holliday
Loublaye Gene Varrone
Varne Shirley Potter
Marie Lynn Winn
Jeanine Rita O'Connor
Claire Graciela Daniele
Juliette Margot Travers
Madelaine Carolyn Kirsch
Lucille Diane Phillips
Simone Charlene Ryan
Solange Suzanne Rogers
Noelle Gale Dixon
Sebastain Baye Rene Auberjonois
Dr. Petitjean Richard Woods
Claude David Thomas
Dwight Berkwit Will B. Able

Eugene Bernstone Robert Fitch
Ronny Ginsborn Chad Block
Phil Rosenberry Dan Siretta
Lapidus Gene Varrone
Nadine Leslie Daniel
Grand Duke Jack Dabdoub
Charles Michael Allinson
Julian Lesage Paul Dumont
Papa Jon Cypher

"Miss Hepburn generates an amazing lot of steam as she dominates a lavish and visually beautiful show. She talks her songs with crisp assurance and makes every dramatic point in the libretto right on the button."

—JOHN CHAPMAN
New York Daily News

"The show has become a showcase, a form of endearment, a gesture of assent, an open palm of respect, Miss Hepburn will never be old enough or tired enough to undergo one of those official evenings of tribute at which everyone gathers to summarize and reminisce. And so it's been arranged right now, with her doing all the work. If Coco is anything, it is Miss Hepburn's gala Benefit Performance, for our benefit."

—WALTER KERR
The New York Times

With Rene Auberjonois in Coco

Hepburn Heroines— A Gallery

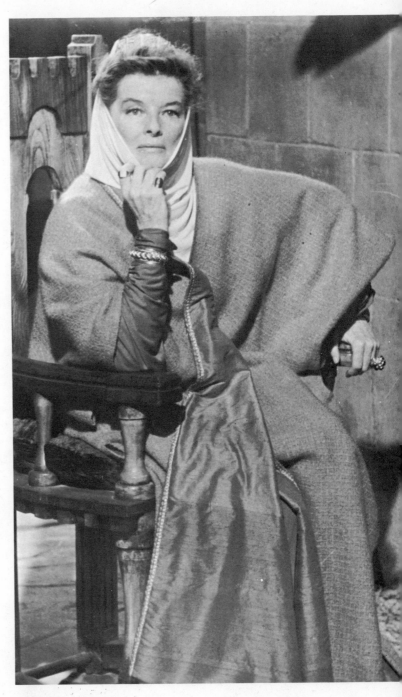

Eleanor of Aquitaine

Eva Lovelace

Rose Sayer

Christine Forrest

Jane Hudson

220

Mary Matthews

Vinka Kovelenko

Lady Cynthia Darrington

Jade

Terry Randall

Susan Vance

Lizzie Curry

223

Constance Dane

Sydney Fairfield

Clara Wieck Schumann

Countess Aurelia

Alice Adams

Mary Stuart

Phoebe Throssel

Lady Babbie

Pat Pemberton

230

Mary Tyron

Sylvia Scarlett

Ann Hamilton

Lutie Cameron

Linda Seton

Jamie Rowan

Jo March

234

Mrs. Violet Venable

Bunny Watson

Trigger Hicks

Pamela Thistlewaite

237

Christina Drayton

Amanda Bonner

Tracy Lord

ss *Harding*

239

1968   The Lion in Winter

Kate—
The Oscar Champion

WINNER: BEST ACTRESS OF THE YEAR

1   1932/33   MORNING GLORY

2   1967   GUESS WHO'S COMING TO DINNER

3   1968   THE LION IN WINTER

RECORD OF NOMINATIONS (asterisk [*] denotes winner)

1932/33   * KATHARINE HEPBURN (MORNING GLORY)

MAY ROBSON (LADY FOR A DAY)

DIANA WYNYARD (CAVALCADE)

1935   ELISABETH BERGNER (ESCAPE ME NEVER)

CLAUDETTE COLBERT (PRIVATE WORLDS)

* BETTE DAVIS (DANGEROUS)

KATHARINE HEPBURN (ALICE ADAMS)

MIRIAM HOPKINS (BECKY SHARP)

MERLE OBERON (THE DARK ANGEL)

1940   BETTE DAVIS (THE LETTER)

JOAN FONTAINE (REBECCA)

KATHARINE HEPBURN (THE PHILADELPHIA STORY)

* GINGER ROGERS (KITTY FOYLE)

MARTHA SCOTT (OUR TOWN)

1942   BETTE DAVIS (NOW, VOYAGER)

* GREER GARSON (MRS. MINIVER)

KATHARINE HEPBURN (WOMAN OF THE YEAR)

ROSALIND RUSSELL (MY SISTER EILEEN)

TERESA WRIGHT (THE PRIDE OF THE YANKEES)

1951   KATHARINE HEPBURN (THE AFRICAN QUEEN)

* VIVIEN LEIGH (A STREETCAR NAMED DESIRE)

ELEANOR PARKER (DETECTIVE STORY)

SHELLEY WINTERS (A PLACE IN THE SUN)

JANE WYMAN (THE BLUE VEIL)

1955   SUSAN HAYWARD (I'LL CRY TOMORROW)

KATHARINE HEPBURN (SUMMERTIME)

JENNIFER JONES (LOVE IS A MANY-SPLENDORED THING)

* ANNA MAGNANI (THE ROSE TATTOO)

ELEANOR PARKER (INTERRUPTED MELODY)

1956   CARROLL BAKER (BABY DOLL)

* INGRID BERGMAN (ANASTASIA)

KATHARINE HEPBURN (THE RAINMAKER)

NANCY KELLY (THE BAD SEED)

DEBORAH KERR (THE KING AND I)

1959   DORIS DAY (PILLOW TALK)

AUDREY HEPBURN (THE NUN'S STORY)

KATHARINE HEPBURN (SUDDENLY, LAST SUMMER)

* SIMONE SIGNORET (ROOM AT THE TOP)

ELIZABETH TAYLOR (SUDDENLY, LAST SUMMER)

1962   * ANNE BANCROFT (THE MIRACLE WORKER)

BETTE DAVIS (WHAT EVER HAPPENED TO BABY JANE?)

KATHARINE HEPBURN (LONG DAY'S JOURNEY INTO
    NIGHT)

GERALDINE PAGE (SWEET BIRD OF YOUTH)

LEE REMICK (DAYS OF WINE AND ROSES)

1967   ANNE BANCROFT (THE GRADUATE)

FAYE DUNAWAY (BONNIE AND CLYDE)

DAME EDITH EVANS (THE WHISPERERS)

AUDREY HEPBURN (WAIT UNTIL DARK)

* KATHARINE HEPBURN (GUESS WHO'S COMING TO
    DINNER)

1968   * KATHARINE HEPBURN (THE LION IN WINTER)

PATRICIA NEAL (THE SUBJECT WAS ROSES)

VANESSA REDGRAVE (ISADORA)

* BARBRA STREISAND (FUNNY GIRL)

JOANNE WOODWARD (RACHEL, RACHEL)

1932–33 Morning Glory

242

As this book goes to press, Katharine Hepburn is on location in Spain, filming *The Trojan Women* by Euripides, in which she plays Hecuba. At the right she is seen with Michael Cacoyannis (scenarist and director), Alberto Sanz (Astyanax), and Vanessa Redgrave (Andromache). The cast also includes Genevieve Bujold (Cassandra), Irene Papas (Helen of Troy), Patrick Magee (Menelaus), and Brian Blessed (Talthybius). Asked why she had chosen Greek tragedy for her thirty-eighth film role, Hepburn replied, "My time is running out, and one wants to have done everything."

Photos by Miss Alix Jeffry